Stories of
Strength

By the writers of AbsoluteWrite.com

*Dedicated to the survivors of Hurricane Katrina
and all those who are helping them.*

Published using
Lulu.com
3131 RDU Center, Suite 210
Morrisville, NC 27560

ISBN 1-4116-5503-6

Printed and bound in the United States of America.

ACKNOWLEDGMENTS

If you get me started, the acknowledgments could run the length of the book itself. It took a village to rear this baby.

Thank you, first, to MacAllister Stone, one of the kindest people I've ever met, who read every submission and made the difficult first decisions. She also worked with numerous writers on revisions, and is certainly the "MVP" of this team.

The editors who pushed other work aside to shape this book and work one-on-one with the writers became the angels on our shoulders. Thank you to Janet Paszkowski; Julia Rosien; Amy Rea; Lisa Waterman Gray; Frank Baron; Denise DiFulco; B. J. Robinson, Ph.D; Sue Poremba; Gwen Moran; Jacqueline H. Kessler; and Jim Zola.

My message board's co-administrator, Charlie Stuart, took on countless leadership roles, and enlisted the help of his company's desktop publishing expert, Sharlene Giesbrecht, for advertising help. Charlie gets extra thanks for making me smile every day and always being a person I can count on.

Lisa Abbate (www.wordmountain.com), our copy editor, was a terrific asset who worked quickly and meticulously.

Danny Mehl (www.dannymehldesign.com), our talented cover designer, was a pleasure to work with.

Katie MacKay and Aviva Rifka Bhandari get big "thank yous" for the proof-reading help.

Thank you to Lulu (www.lulu.com), the printing company, for the tremendous support and enthusiasm for our project. They treated us like VIPs, and are generously donating their proceeds from this book to the cause, as well. Go, Lulu!

Thank you tons to the bloggers, editors, writers, and website owners who announced our call for submissions and are helping us to get the word out about this book to readers. Submissions often came with notes attached that said, "I read about this on Paperback Writer's blog," or "I found out on IMDB." I'm proud to be part of such a supportive writing community.

It's amazing how many people wrote to offer help. Numerous writers offered to proofread, send press releases, write reviews, find sponsors . . . my inbox was full of "I'm ready to help—tell me what to do" letters. What a gift.

Thank you to the hundreds of writers who sent submissions for this anthology. I wish we could have included all of you. It means a lot to me that you believed in this project and used your talents for a good cause, and I hope you're as proud as I am of the result.

CONTENTS

INTRODUCTION

The world seems like a callous place sometimes, with strangers cutting each other off in traffic, neighbors arguing about fence lines, and people fighting about everything from favorite sports teams to political views. But things change in times of crisis. Almost instantly, we forget our pettiness and remember we all belong to the human race and are, in some way, brothers and sisters. And we long to help even when we don't have much to give.

This book was born on the AbsoluteWrite.com message boards, where many writers gathered during the days after Hurricane Katrina and agonized over how helpless we felt. Those who had money to give did so, but it didn't feel like enough. Those who didn't have money donated blood, or sold things on eBay to raise money, or gathered items to send to evacuees. But we kept watching those images on television, and the problem didn't go away. It became clear that it wasn't going to go away soon, and we wanted to find a way to help long-term.

I suggested this anthology project. If we could get enough compelling stories to fill a book, I figured, that book's sales could go on for years to come and keep donations rolling in to charities to help with disaster relief. My simple suggestion was met with amazing enthusiasm and we got to work immediately. This project belonged to all of us, and we were going to make something beautiful happen.

What you're about to read comes from writers the world over. Some are long-time professional authors whose names you may recognize. For others, this is their first publication ever. I asked writers to submit essays, poems, and short stories about strength, and within a week, we had more submissions than we could ever fit in this book.

But the generosity didn't end there. No one just submitted a piece and disappeared. Instead, people stuck around and offered help in other areas. A graphic artist offered to do our cover art. Numerous editors wrote to offer to share the duty of editing the work on a quick deadline. Writers spoke to their colleagues and friends to ask for help with formatting, advertising, publicity, corporate sponsorship, and bookstore distribution.

The book matters to us because people matter to us. This is one way for us to use our love for writing to help others, and we are so thankful that you've become part of that effort. Visit www.storiesofstrength.com to follow our progress.

May you always find the strength you need, with enough left over to lend to others. I hope the stories you read here will inspire you and remind you just how little it can take for strength to blossom in unlikely places.

~Jenna Glatzer

Let No Hands Be Idle Here

Prayerfully ♩ = 60-66

1. Let no hands be id - le here. Let no heart be filled with fear.
2. Leave no brok - en heart a - lone. Leave no lone - ly soul un - known.
3. Give the beg - gar what he asks. Give the will - ing work - er tasks.
4. Like a riv - er life can seem: Dip a cup in - to the stream,

Let no child un - cared for be. Where the need is, O let me!
Lead all wan - der - ers to Thee. Where the need is, O let me!
Give to all un - stint - ing - ly. Where the need is, O let me!
Drink, and share it o - pen - ly: Love of God, so sweet to me!

after last verse only:

Love of God, so sweet to me!

Text: Orson Scott Card
Music: Mark Mitchell

Copyright © 2004 by Mark Mitchell and Orson Scott Card
Please contact the authors at www.hatrack.com
to request permission to perform this hymn in public.

STRENGTH OF SPIRIT

"Nor stony tower, nor walls of beaten brass,
Nor airless dungeon, nor strong links of iron,
Can be retentive to the strength of spirit."

~ William Shakespeare (*Julius Caesar*)

THE SHRINE

By Matthew James

My mom was always fanatical about the refrigerator. It had to be clean, spotlessly clean, and if a wayward milk dribble made its way down the jug and onto the shelf long enough to settle and dry, she would spend an hour removing everything from the inside and scrubbing, scrubbing, scrubbing it clean. The outside of the fridge was the same. Nary a mark, scuff, thumbprint, banana sticker was allowed to tarnish the shiny, off-white Kenmore for more than a mere second. And God forbid someone even suggest the use of a magnet. That fridge was her temple, my dad would say. Her special quirk.

Which is why I knew something was terribly wrong the day I came home to find the Post-It note stuck right to the middle of the freezer door.

Stay Strong, it said.

Seeing that note was like a punch to the stomach. I knew she'd had an important doctor's visit earlier. I knew about the lump she had found in her breast. I knew my father was worried, but still, that note . . . I was 17 years old, and at that moment I knew life would never be the same.

She had cancer, and it was bad. Stage three, the doctor said. I didn't know what that meant at the time, but I knew the odds were less than even.

She cried a lot, especially right after the surgery and during the chemo. I was helpless. My father was strong, a decorated military officer, but even he crumbled under the pressure of seeing my mother, his wife, in that state. His hair turned gray and thinned noticeably, all in a matter of months.

I began to do terribly in school. I would just sit in class, staring out the window, surprised when the bell would ring. Sometimes I wouldn't want to go home after school or work, and I felt ashamed. I would look at my mother, and I could see her slipping.

A few weeks into her treatment a magnet appeared, about six inches below the Post-it. It was a pink ribbon. Then an American Cancer Society magnet a week after that. She began to trade postcards with other cancer patients, and those all made their way onto the Kenmore. Soon the refrigerator became a temple of another sort. A shrine more than anything. A beacon of strength.

And I don't know why, but with every new addition to the refrigerator, my mother would get better. It was as if she suddenly woke up one morning and decided that she was going to live, and that she was going to pull herself out of it, bit by bit. Every ounce of strength she used to put into cleaning that thing now went into healing herself. And all the little tangible things she used to help herself were put there on that shrine.

This was my cue. My father and I both began to find things and put them on the fridge also. We never talked about it, but we had both found a way to help her, and we did. I found magnets at the mall with silly jokes about shopping. My dad would take the junk-mail magnets advertising pizza delivery and insurance companies and snap them on. Calendars appeared, a bumper sticker that read "I (heart) my Chihuahua" was slapped onto the side, and we didn't even have a dog. The shrine grew and grew, and when we ran out of room, we began to cover the older with the new.

And my mother lived.

It's been more than ten years now, and they have since purchased a new refrigerator. It's a fancy silver one with the side-by-side doors and one of those ice and water things right there. The inside is still pretty clean, but the exterior is another story. Old postcards, magnets for businesses that have closed down years ago, bumper stickers she had collected while she was sick, they all remain, along with every single possible refrigerator accessory known to man. It doesn't even look like a refrigerator anymore. It's a shaggy beast, standing there in the kitchen, completely out of place with the rest of the house.

And underneath it all, it's still there. I know it's there even though I can't see it, because I can feel it. I can feel it when I look into my mother's eyes, when I walk into her house and just breathe the air, when I see her put her head on my father's shoulder. By God, I can feel it.

Stay Strong.

Matthew James lives in Tucson, Arizona with his wife and family. He may be contacted at bizarizona@gmail.com.

THE ORGAN MAN

By Janet Ross-Pilla

His perfect Windsor knot and tailored suit make him a misfit in this world of sterile blue gowns and paper hairnets. Dark hair emphasizes a gleam of excitement in his deep sable eyes. I etch every feature of his incited face into my mind as I wait and cry. I am invisible to him. To me, he is a distortion through teardrops pooling on the ledge of my lids.

Wide pupils dart back and forth in front of the computer screen as if he is underlining data—data that translates into human beings in need of organs—hearts, kidneys, livers, lungs, eyes. Does it matter if the eyes are sparkling blue? I don't think so.

I stand outside the hospital room in ICU and watch elation grow and form the facial features of this young, pristine man. Behind me, methodical pumping of a respirator keeps alive the body of my best friend's son. It seems that with every other hiss of the pump the object of my amazement stops and focuses; his eyes open wide as if they are portals for the transfer of information. The light of the screen focuses back and bathes his face in a Frankenstein, monster-green glow. I am mesmerized. Through swollen lids, I lock on to the small lifts at the corners of his mouth. It's as if the computer is talking to him, telling him stories with happy endings—but not for everyone.

His elation serves as contrast to the heartbreaking pain emanating through a thin cotton barrier. My eyes hold fast while my ears tune into low mournful cries of, "No, not my baby." My heart cracks in empathy.

I shout, "Damn you, look up from that screen and wipe that smile off your face. He is more than data running through organ banks. He is a special child, more than you will ever know." The organ man might have heard me if my lips had opened beyond a quiver.

An innocuous white bag appears as if dinner has been ordered, another callous reason to hate him. Organ man nods to the bearer, then strides by me down the hallway to a balding courier who paces impatiently. Organ man's impeccable dark blue suit screams perfection and control. "Get this to the University," he tells the courier. I am surprised at the edge of command in a voice I think of as being barely beyond the squeak of change to adulthood. I hear him say the name of the beautiful boy lying behind the curtain, the victim of youth and the speed of a fast car. *Brain dead*, they told my friend an hour earlier, *say your goodbyes*. How can a parent ever say goodbye to a child? A vibrant 28-year-old child named Chad.

I watch the balding man hurry away and wonder what information a nondescript paper bag can hold. If it is any reflection of the love Chad's mother feels for him, it should be mindfully cradled away in a gilded box covered in precious jewels and lined in velvet. Organ man whisks past me with a bead on the computer as if it is calling his name. He still does not acknowledge the sounds of impending death that are so close he could reach out and wipe away the tears surrounding it.

He's so young, I think. His baby face says he is younger than the boy behind me being held by his mother for as long as they will leave her to grieve. How can the organ man do this for a living? What drives a person to choose a career of matching organs from accidental death victims?

Two weeks later an answer comes, if an answer is ever possible. I am busy with my life—laundry the priority of the day—when I hear the television say, "Thanks to the courage of a donor's family this 12-year-old girl has a new heart." I backtrack to the voice. Could it be Chad's heart? I listen for a clue but it doesn't seem to matter to the girl's family. They are filled with joy that their baby girl has another chance—a purpose in life to fulfill. The mother and father praise the donor family's strength in the face of their own pain and sorrow.

I decide it doesn't matter if I never find out if it is Chad's heart. I pick up the phone and dial the number of my friend, the number of a courageous mother whose son filled her purpose in life for 28 short years.

Janet Ross-Pilla is a writer of fiction, including screenwriting. Awards for her writings include: finalist in 2005 Moondance Competition, Storyteller Award from the Hollywood Black Film Festival. Published stories appear in Summit Avenue Review and Ariston.

TRUST IN THIS DARK NIGHT

By Aviva Rifka Bhandari

Now that I am faced with this trial of the moment, let me pause.
Reflect on previous trials.

The race forward is not about the hurdles already jumped,
It is about the confidence and skill at jumping acquired.

Now that I am faced with this impossibly high wall, let me think.
Remember previous walls.

The difficulty of scaling any height or distance can be shrunk;
It is ever as simple as deciding where to place the next step.

Now that I am faced with this sorrow of the moment, let me stop.
Consider previous sorrows.

Didn't I learn that joy always resurfaces?
Give joy a space and it will place itself there unaided.

Let me trust.

Even as I am faced with this darkness
Don't I already know that the sun is rising?

Aviva Rifka Bhandari has donated this poetic meditation to the 'Stories of Strength' anthology in the hope that it might be a help to all those waiting for the sun to rise.

THE WONDERFUL TRANSFORMATION
OF THE LIBRARY TROLL

By Amy Mullis

Sometimes the lessons we learn in childhood are the ones we remember when the chips are down and the "o" is all that's left of our gusto. When I face challenges, which seem to occur with increasing ferocity as I get older, I think back to a little girl who climbed her own Matterhorn and came out on top. This is her story.

The town where I grew up was big enough to support one elementary school, one post office, and one Library Troll. The public library was approximately the size of a rattlesnake's cage and the way the wicked librarian, Miss Wentz, presided over it you'd have thought she was Queen Venom. She was about 800 years old and my big brother, with the wisdom of a boy who has assailed to the heights of second grade, told me she wore her wiry gray hair in those little tight curls because the pain of her hairdo helped her stay tough. Her desk was like a tollbooth, and she sat there like a dragon on a treasure chest, presiding over lost books and past-due fines. You'd have thought she was St. Peter taking roll at the gates of heaven the way she looked over her half-moon glasses to see if you were worthy of a book.

In the children's section, we whispered rumors of how she hated children so much she couldn't even eat them for dinner like in the storybooks because she'd get a rash and stomach cramps and have to swallow one of the antidote pills she kept in her pocketbook. She would give us stern looks from her gallows and sharpen her pencils meaningfully to a terrifyingly sharp point, admiring the weapons gleefully under the fluorescent lights.

I had a habit of checking out stacks of books at a time. Not only did I figure that would keep me from having to go back to the library so often, but if one book turned out to be unable to deliver a story as enchanting as the cover art suggested, I could toss that book aside and move on to the next one in the pile. Of course an occasional misguided book, separated by fate, would end up in a corner, or wedged in the cushions of an easy chair, or stuffed under the seat of the car. This book relocation habit resulted in overdue fines payable in blood. (Rumor had it that Miss Wentz was partial to O positive.) In these circumstances, I would throw myself on the mercy of my older brother or sisters or my parents, who were strong and brave enough to bear the brunt of Miss Wentz's wrath. I sure didn't have a death wish of my own.

One day, tunneling under my bed in search of a lost treasure, I came upon a forgotten library book. I brushed off the dust bunnies, opened the cover, and peeked at the card. It was months overdue. I was doomed. Miss Wentz was probably on her way to my house that very second, dragging her scythe of death behind her. There was only one thing to do. I begged my dad, who had never before displayed traitorous tendencies, to return the book for me.

Parents pick the worst times to teach life lessons. I don't know why he didn't pick a time when the consequences were less dire, but apparently my life, short as my time on Earth had been, was worth sacrificing to the Child-Hating Library Troll. He drove me to the library. On the way I decided he probably got a commission for every fresh body he delivered. Unfortunately we found a parking spot near the building, and I trudged down the sidewalk until I reached the steps.

There's a mountain in Switzerland known as the Matterhorn, a mountain so craggy and dangerous that only the strongest and bravest dare attempt to climb even its most accessible face. It resembles nothing more than the sore tooth of a giant, and the ghosts of men who have died trying to defeat this landmark litter the surrounding area like fruit flies on a rotten orange. Compared to the library steps that day, the Matterhorn was a freckle on the face of the earth.

I stood at the bottom of those steps on shaky 6-year-old legs, craned my neck to see the peak, and started my ascent. Talk about a bittersweet victory. I scaled the Matterhorn and still had to face the Ice Monster. I hoped the library would be closed, I hoped Miss Wentz would be away from her desk (even though anybody that knew anything about trolls and dragons knew they never deserted their posts), I hoped Jesus had the good sense to pick this moment to return to Earth and would sweep me away in triumph on his white horses to a place where libraries didn't exist. I checked the sky, but didn't notice any indication of help from above. The air was thick and still in the Southern summer heat. I pushed open the heavy door and went inside to face certain death. True to my rotten luck, the Library Troll was working in her laboratory, probably poisoning library paste, as I trudged up to her desk and laid the wretched volume on the corner.

"This is overdue," I whispered, not wanting to add prohibited library volume to my list of offenses, and also because I was too afraid to speak any louder.

She reached out and grasped the book in her talons, opened the cover and looked down at me over her glasses in order to better hex me. She opened her mouth and I closed my eyes and ducked to miss the noxious gasses that I heard she used to paralyze little children.

"Thank you for returning this book."

I peeked through one eye. "What?"

"Thank you for returning this book. I was afraid it was lost. I won't charge you this time, but please be more careful from now on."

She was letting me go. I tried to say thank you, stuttered, tripped on my words and raced out of the building, sailing down the small steps two at a time. All the way home, I wondered at the strange turnaround in the librarian's behavior. After that, whenever I visited the library, Miss Wentz and I exchanged a secret smile, and she would often hold out special books that she thought I might like. Sometimes I would say hello to her when I came in and she would say hello right back. And she never once put a hex on me.

Amy Mullis lives in a small town in South Carolina that has almost as many inhabitants as off-brand noodle soup has chicken bits. She has published humor in The Christian Science Monitor, on ParenttoParent.com and in the Just for Fun section of AbsoluteWrite.

WILLOW

By Kimberly Ripley

By June the willow had grown full. Its branches hung like lace in long delicate strands touching the ground. The strands fell close together, intertwining. Seeing through them was difficult. I liked being inside the strands. I could hide within the shade of that old tree for hours and no one could find me, except for one special friend.

It wasn't even my tree. It belonged to the next-door neighbors. They had a son my age. Danny was a grade behind me in school. We used to spend hours just talking. I would sit in my bedroom window, and he would perch on the fence that separated our two houses. The willow sat just over the fence on his side. One night after we'd talked for almost an hour I asked him what it was like inside his enormous tree.

"It's like a different world inside the willow," he told me.

"Can you see the stars from in there?" I asked.

"You can see starlight, but not each and every star."

That night I did something I'd never dared to do before. I pulled the chair from my desk over to the window. Hoisting myself up onto the window ledge, I climbed over and out the window. Jumping the seven or eight feet to the ground, I landed with a loud thud.

"What will your mother say?" Danny asked in amazement.

"She'll never know. She likes me to stay in my room after seven o'clock. I guess she talks on the phone or something, and she doesn't want to be interrupted," I said.

Danny looked a little puzzled, shrugged his shoulders, and motioned for me to join him under the tree.

Pulling the long vines aside, he held them open for me like a door. I bent low to the ground, walked under his arm, and entered Danny's world inside the willow. It was a magical sight. The soft glow from the stars and the moon through the willow's vines made woven patterns of light all over the ground. Covered with the tiny smooth leaves from the tree, the ground was cushioned.

"It's a fortress!" I exclaimed.

"It's more like a secret hideaway," Danny said. "I like to come here and think. I don't like anyone to know I'm in here."

Danny seemed older than the other boys his age. The other boys still liked to play with guns and knives and draw stupid pictures of soldiers in combat. Danny talked more about people. He wondered what happened to people who died, and whether or not their souls made it to heaven. He asked me if I knew what grief felt like. I didn't. He talked about animals having hearts and souls. After all, God made them, too.

I loved those conversations. At times they were all that connected me to the world outside my room. Inside the willow, I felt a bond developing. Danny and I shared secrets. It made me feel loved to have him for my friend.

It was under the willow that I fantasized about the Beatles. Paul was my favorite, with those puppy dog eyes and boyish smile. Ringo was my second favorite. I loved how he shook his head back and forth while banging on his drum set. I loved the long thick hair that fell into his face. We pored over fan magazines and tore out the pictures we liked best. These we pinned to our bulletin boards or the backs of our bedroom doors.

Danny had a drum set in his cellar. He was the only person I knew who had a real, not toy, set of drums. Some of the other kids in the neighborhood would bring their guitars and tambourines and join him in his cellar, attempting to form a rock and roll band. I much preferred sitting under the willow and pondering the world's uncertainties. American boys not much older than Danny were fighting in a war on the other side of the world. They were dying and arriving home in body bags or not at all. Chris Nelligan's boyfriend died there. She told me he looked so still and gray in his casket that she really didn't believe it was him at all. Some of those boys were blown to bits, their mangled body parts scattered all over Vietnam. Daily reports on the evening news left me with an uneasy feeling in my stomach that never seemed to go away.

Here at home, young people were fighting, too. They protested and started fights and said they were doing it all in the name of peace and love. It made no sense to me. Danny and I discussed this at great length. We both attended St. Joseph's on Sundays and Catechism on Saturday mornings, and a lot of what Father Harvey was teaching us made no sense. Was it a sin to doubt our faith? Why would a powerful and loving God let those American boys die? We never did figure that one out. And besides, could we even believe what Father Harvey told us? Didn't we see him at the basketball games climbing high up into the bleachers with his brown paper bag, obviously drunk?

When summer turned to fall that year and the willow's lush strands grew thin and straggly, Danny and I started to drift our separate ways. I went to a new school while he remained a grade behind. School friends and ball games took the place of our evening chats. We crossed paths at Catechism, but it just didn't feel the same.

The magic seemed to die with the willow's leaves that year. When the wiry wisps that remained were pummeled with autumn's strong winds and heavy rains, the safe haven inside was left open, exposed. I felt like that, too. Afraid that I had maybe divulged more than I should have to a boy I no longer spent time with, I wondered if he was sharing our secrets with others. Did he talk to someone else about my love for Paul and Ringo? Did he tell them that I cried when Bobby Kennedy died?

The following spring my mother sold our home and moved us to a new community. I had to start from scratch, new school, new friends, new home. It was traumatic. It took a long time to adjust. I'm not sure I ever did.

I never saw Danny again. It's been more than 30 years since we shared our thoughts inside the willow, but I can see his face like it was yesterday. His jet black curly hair, his crooked front teeth, the intensity with which he played his drums; the pictures dwell in my mind like cherished keepsakes from another life.

A girl from the neighborhood, a woman now like me, said she heard a few years back that Danny got married and has some kids. I'll bet they live a good life. I'll bet he turned out to be a good man.

I live not far from middle age; some of my children are growing up and leaving home. My husband is a good man, too, kind and gentle, generous and sweet.

Two years ago I visited the old neighborhood. No one from my childhood lives there now. My old house looks the same. So does Danny's. The willow is gone. It's somehow fitting, though. Life as it was then is gone, too. Days of pondering, trying to make perfect sense in an imperfect senseless age; it had to end.

I watch my two youngest children playing in our backyard. My husband is helping them build a tree fort. The tree is oak; its branches reach far into the sky and spread wide apart. It's not our willow, but my senses tell me lots of learning and growing will take place under the stars and the moon in that tree.

I won't interfere, but I'll linger nearby. And if they ask for my help I'll open my arms wide like the willow's great strong ropes. Appearing to be weeping, the willow is instead a pillar of strength and shelter, for its arms are strong, its refuge safe. That was my lesson learned on a moonlit starry night so many, many years ago. And like the gift of childhood friends, my lesson will one day be shared.

Kimberly Ripley is a freelancer and author of six books. She lives in New Hampshire with her husband, family, and very faithful dog. Visit Kim's website at www.kimberlyripley.writergazette.com.

L O O K B E Y O N D

By Moira Richards

when a wall of stone blocks the road
refusing any passage by
look to the aloe
that seeks a tiny crevice
and makes its anchor of the rock

when mighty seas pummel the beach
answering to none save the moon
look to the dolphins
that ride over under waves
and tease them to delight and play

when fire rages through the veld
destroying all that flee before
look to the fynbos
that lays claim to the ashes
and draws the salts to their new growth

when a wind blows its dominion
whipping sands to blast its ire
look to the sun's rays
that slant towards close of day
and transmute the dust to splendor

when spirit wavers on its path
feeling that it can no further
may nature lend her skills
to glean blessing where she be
and light new stars of strength and hope

Moira lounges around the staff rooms of absolutewrite.com, womenwriters.net, and moondance.org—usually sipping tea, sometimes Jack Daniels. Off-line, she teaches accounting-related subjects at the Nelson Mandela Metropolitan University in South Africa.

THE ART OF FORGIVING

By Sarah Crabtree

It was on a day like this that you told me you were leaving. The sun shone so brightly on the forsythia that every time I passed by the frosted glass of the hallway window, I swore it was a big yellow removal van come to take away all your possessions.

But then, had I looked more closely, I'd have seen that all your things were disappearing of their own accord: like the diminishing supply of clean handkerchiefs in the drawer next to the bed. I caught myself counting them, but denying the truth. For I couldn't picture an amorous young mistress boil-washing on your behalf. They say the wife is always the last to know. But not this time.

Somehow I was waiting for you to leave me. Yet there were moments when I'd panic and say: *This can't be happening to me. I thought he loved me. I thought he said he'd never leave me.* I'm not a mawkish person. So I won't dwell on the sentimental things: the missed anniversaries, the meals for one, and the empty pillow next to mine.

Instead, for a moment, I'll remind you of the practical problems I faced in having to bring up a daughter—our daughter—alone. I know plenty of children are brought up by a single parent or by grandparents or another member of an extended family. You would be quick to remind me that your own father lost his life in the Second World War, leaving a widow to raise a son and daughter.

You made your choice, and so I made mine. I moved Sacha to another area when she was ready to change to secondary school. I was tired of being judged by a community too small to lose oneself in, and too large to forget what we'd shared. Instead we lived in Ibiza, where I ran a small gift shop during the summer months, and in the winter we returned to England, where she was tutored privately, had her teeth straightened, and went skiing with her school, thanks to the money you kept insisting upon sending me.

Sacha is mature beyond her years. Somebody, I can't remember who, told me that children of divorced parents often do grow up more quickly. She seems to accept things better than I did at her age. And when years later, after Sacha had happily married, you asked me if you could come and stay, I so wanted to tell you to stay away. That I had survived all the hungry years without you—and although part of me had never healed—I like to think it was the very part that had prevented me from becoming one of those dreadfully smug women who are fortunate enough to have more control in their marriage. But I let you come and stay.

The main reason you returned was to see your first grandchild. Our first grandchild. Alicia was a joy from the second I saw her.

Already the cracks had formed in your second marriage. Again, a part of me basked in this. You chose this woman over me, so you should suffer her, too. But a more compassionate part felt pleased that you wanted me back. It was a small victory, yet a victory all the same.

And when you finally flew back to Nice, I felt secure in that I'd refused to allow you in my bed once more for old time's sake. When the letter arrived this morning, it was like a huge blow to the stomach. I keeled over the kitchen table and wept as I read your second wife's—Jenna's—words. ". . . We'd hoped the first course of treatment would remove any sign of malignancy, and therefore made the joint decision not to inform you. But things have progressed for the worse. Quickly. We can pay for you to come and visit, if you choose. However, you probably won't recognize him . . ."

I don't know what it was I wept for. All I knew was that I needed to get in my car and drive away from this terribly domestic scene at the kitchen table. Sacha was busy with Alicia, who was having problems with some of the children at school. Mainly, I needed time to think things through. I felt too proud to accept your offers of financial help. But the practical side of me thought of Sacha. Maybe she would want to see her father for the final time.

I drove the three-mile trip to the coast. It cleared my head when I shut the car door and stepped out onto the shingle. It was warm for March, and thankfully empty of holidaymakers with their irritating need for ice cream and ball games.

As I walked along the beach, I looked up towards the sky and watched the cloud shapes sweeping across the horizon. If I closed my eyes a little, I could imagine the days of long ago when we would take Sacha to the beach with her little flip-flops and her red bucket and yellow spade. The world seemed younger then. We all seemed more free-spirited. My only explanation is that we were close enough to remember the relief of a country no longer involved in a World War. And we were never going to take anything for granted ever again. I felt the tears coursing down my cheeks. The warm wind brushed them away.

After I walked the length of the beach to the headland and back again, I returned to my car and drove to Sacha's house. Somehow I think she and Alicia were expecting me. They say that blood is thicker than water.

Sleep well now, darling. Remember Alicia. She has your eyes. And your smile. Even though we can't be with you at the end, we are with you in our dreams, and I forgive you everything.

Sarah Crabtree is the author of Terror From Beyond Middle England, published by ENC Press (www.encpress.com) and nominated for a British Fantasy Award in 2005.

MIRROR OF TIME

By David Lee Summers

My daughter smiles at me even
after losing a board game and I
remember myself at that age,
happy, proud, and loving.

My mother tells me about giving
my uncle morphine to ease his
last day alive and I see myself
growing lonely, yet still loving.

Like telescopes, the generations
hold mirrors, reflecting the past.
Also like telescopes, they are
windows to the future.

*First published in
SpinDrifter Magazine,
Volume 1, Number 4,
Winter 2004/5*

URANUS

Limpid green and quite serene,
Jupiter's grandfather watches me
with nary a twinkle as I pan the sky
for stars, confirming his identity.
I am content to sit in my backyard,
the elusive planet captured only in
the eyepiece of my telescope.

Daughter Myranda bursts through
the back door—a tempest wanting
to see the moon that shares her name.
I tell her it's too close to the "star" in
the telescope to see. Nodding sagely,
she tells me she'll go there one day
and see for herself.

*First published in
SpinDrifter Magazine,
Volume 1, Number 4,
Winter 2004/5*

*David Lee Summers is an author, editor, and astronomer living somewhere between the
Western and final frontiers in Southern New Mexico. His most recent novel is Vampires
of the Scarlet Order.*

MY MOTHER'S TABLE

By Noreen Braman

The house is silent, so silent . . . not at all as it was on that day 40 years ago when the Schwartz Furniture Company delivered my mother's dining room set. All morning she paced the house, swatting the already-immaculate room with a dust rag, picking invisible lint out of the soft, dark carpeting. The chandelier she had brought with her from Poland as a young bride was polished and shining brightly. Now, after so many years, a table would reflect its sparkling glow.

I was 12, and old enough to sense my mother's excitement. For years we had heard the stories of her family's magnificent dining table, and the way her parents and sisters and aunts and uncles and cousins had sat around it time after time, laughing in joy or crying in sorrow. My mother talked wistfully about the delicately-embroidered linens that her own grandmother had done in her youth, and how the openwork lace allowed the shiny surface of the tabletop to show through. It seemed, from my mother's stories, that everything of importance was discussed at that table, and that if it could speak, it would relate the history of at least four generations of her family.

She grieved for it, I knew that, even though she rarely spoke of the night it was lost. Surely, in light of the horrendous events that followed, the loss of one table was hardly important. The screams, the terror, the sound of heavy boots and glass breaking—these were what the family remembered, and tried to forget.

Perhaps because my mother was young and unable to fully comprehend the destruction of her family's way of life—the long dark train ride, the foreign soldiers who shouted at her and pushed her along, the lingering death of each of her brothers and sisters—this may have been why the memories of her family's table were the only ones she could speak of happily.

Secretly, I worried. After so many stories and the passage of so many years, could our table ever live up to the ghost-inhabited one turned to ash so long ago?

And now, here I was, pacing that same floor, that same room, my hands gently gliding over the well-polished surface of the table. If I closed my eyes slightly, I could still see the image of my father sitting at the head of the table, my mother to his left and me to his right. In the fourth chair was sometimes a dinner guest, often a man their age, who had lived what they had lived, seen what they had seen, and had survived despite it all. In our little enclave in Central New Jersey were many such survivors, often the only living remnant of a once-thriving family. There were no grandparents, no aunts and uncles, no cousins to gather with us. Only other sad survivors, grateful to share a meal at my mother's table.

Even in her old age, long after my father had passed on, my mother continued her tradition. It was hard for me to visit often; my life had taken me far away, and I had my own family to care for. So my mother filled her table with others like herself: women who had lived through the worst of times, widowed women who had kissed their children on the front porch and watched them drive off to the world. Their voices, heavily accented, rose and fell at the table, often speaking rapidly in the language of their childhood. There was history imprinted on my mother's table, maybe not the four-generation chronicle that had been absorbed by the table in Poland, but a history nonetheless.

I wanted the table, and yet could not bear to take it. The crystal chandelier, the delicate plates and glasses—all had been carefully packed up and shipped to my home. Yet the glossy table, its chairs, and the matching china closet remained standing as silent sentinels in my mother's empty house. To look at it was to look at a ghost—a sad, wailing ghost who, having lived a tortured life, could not rest in the afterlife. I was not sure that I could live with it in the small apartment that now constituted my home. After my children grew and started their own lives, after my husband had left me, I had moved into a small retirement community. Unlike my mother's neighborhood enclave, the place was inhabited by dozens of solitary residents who kept to themselves and left their stories untold. The table, in my home, would starve for words.

And so I was passing it on. Not to my sons, whose wives declared it ugly and unfashionable, and not to my daughter, who might auction it off on eBay to classic furniture collectors. Instead, I was giving the table to a former student, one whose work was full of the richness and vibrancy alive in family history. Each item in her home had a story, from the heavy glass vase that was a wedding gift to her grandmother, to the row of handkerchief vases on her living room shelf. One once belonged to the great aunt of a neighbor, another to a local spinster whose house was a treasure trove of period furnishings, yet another from a garage sale of a family down on its luck. I knew, in her care, the table would hear its fill of stories; absorb laughter, tears, and baby formula.

I heard a truck in the driveway and my heart quickened, just as my mother's had on that day 40 years ago when the table had been delivered. Now, the table would make another journey, to another 40 years of serving as the heart of a home. I wiped a tear that had fallen to its shiny surface, then went to open the front door. The sun broke through the clouds, slanting through the mature elm trees on the front lawn. It was a good day to move furniture. A good day to transplant history.

First published in the 2004 Summer Fiction Issue of the US1 Newspaper and reprinted in Plum Biscuit e-zine.

Noreen Braman is a writer from Jamesburg, New Jersey. Links to some of her online writing can be found at www.noreensdigitaldreams.com.

GONE FISHING

By Diane Stilwell

Fish.

That's what I was thinking as my soul left my body. I had gone from wondering why the room was getting fuzzy to thinking the wall would hold me up as I leaned against it and followed it down to the floor. I heard my mother's calm voice while she spoke to my aunt on the phone asking what you should do when someone passes out and you can't wake them up. And I slowly sunk deeper within myself until eventually all I could think of was one thing.

Fish.

It felt good, not feeling my body anymore. Not to have that weight pulling me down. I could fly and I did. High above myself, I soared, enjoying the freedom my body had just given my soul. *Wow*, I thought. *This is it. I'm dying.* And it was wonderful.

Fish.

There was no coming back now. I knew that as I reminded myself of all I hadn't accomplished in my life. I thought of all that I was doing that would go unfinished. And all that I had wanted to do that would never be done. But I didn't care. It was too beautiful, this feeling that now embraced my soul and filled it with a peace that words could never describe. I was only 21. It was a shame to die so young, I thought. But oh, well.

Fish.

The paramedics came. I could hear them from the distance asking my mother if I had been depressed lately. Had I recently broken up with a boyfriend? Did I have any pills I could have overdosed on? Her voice was even further as she answered "I don't know" to all the questions. I could hear a siren and a male voice announce "possible teenage suicide." I knew if I were back in my body I wouldn't appreciate that. I wasn't a teenager. And this wasn't suicide.

And that's when I decided I knew what it was. What it had to be. I had a headache earlier and I'd taken some aspirin. Recently there had been stories in the news of a well-known headache medicine that was laced with cyanide. People had died from it. And now, I thought, I would face the same fate. So there it was. I had solved my own case. But I was too far away to tell anyone. And the doctors around me were too sure I had tried to kill myself to look for any other symptoms.

Instead, they yelled at me, demanding that I acknowledge them. That I speak to them. That I come back from my peaceful oasis to validate their existence. It made sense, their anger. After all, they were all about saving lives and I appeared to be taking one, albeit my own. But still, I thought, if I really had tried to kill myself, shouldn't they have been a little nicer to me?

Besides, I wasn't having any of it. I liked where I was. Why would I want to come back? I had stopped thinking about fish now. All I could think of was something else.

Peace.

I was put in a room with my mother and sister. Their voices were distant as they contemplated what had put me in this sudden comatose state. And as the concern in their voices rose, I couldn't help but wonder what would happen if one of them were to get a headache. And take the aspirin.

That's when I knew I had to come back, if only just long enough to warn them. I gathered all the strength I could find to pull my soul back into my body. It wasn't as easy to come back as it was to leave. But I had a purpose. There were lives that had to be saved. And these were the people who were nearest and dearest to me.

The light was the first thing that hit me, piercing my eyes and reaching into my head like a knife. My hands covered my face to block the pain. I mustered up all my strength and spit out what I thought might be my last word.

"Cyanide," I whispered.

"What?" my mother asked. It wasn't enough. They needed more. I took a deep breath.

"Cyanide in the aspirin," I explained.

I had done it. My mission was accomplished. My family was now safe. I felt a wave of relief come over me, until my mother responded.

"She's joking? I can't believe she's joking at a time like this!"

It was a heroic act on my part, even if no one recognized it. And even if I had been wrong—which we quickly found out I was, after a doctor decided to look at my stomach and discovered a rash.

It wasn't suicide. It wasn't cyanide. It was meningitis. That was one mystery solved. But I still had another one. Why had I been thinking about fish all that time? My mother was the one who got to the bottom of that. After I had passed out, my mother had called my aunt, mainly because my uncle drove an ambulance for the local fire department. My uncle had come racing over, and as it happened, he had just been fishing.

It was about 15 years later that my uncle died peacefully in his sleep. We all mourned the loss of a man who loved his family, who loved to fish, and who would run to anyone's side whenever they were in need. But having cast my soul out and reeled it back in many years earlier, I knew this great man had gone to a wonderful place.

Diane Stilwell is a freelance writer, living and working in New York City.

A REAL, SUPER, HUMAN

By Jill Miller Zimon

He's been called a motard—a combination of moron and retard.

He's had a bathroom door shoved open while he's inside.

In gym class, he's the last one chosen for every team.

And, with a poker face, my oldest child tells me to accept that he's a geek.

But every morning, from September through June, he wakes up at 6:30 with few groans, albeit with his pillow clasped around his head to shut out the alarm clock.

When I knock, then open his door, he's upright on the bed, clutching a squishy pillow (not intended for sleeping, but rather for squashing) to his waist, crushing it down into his lap with the weight of his elbows.

He doesn't pretend he's sick. He doesn't beg to stay home. He doesn't hide under his comforter. At nearly 12 years old, he's too big for that anyway.

"Just checking," I say. "Be down in ten minutes, okay?"

"Okay, Mom."

The drum-pounding sound of his footsteps tells me that he's on his way down the stairs. He sleepwalks to the kitchen table, the sun still below the horizon.

"I made fresh corn muffins." My voice upticks as though I'm asking a question, rather than introducing a warm breakfast with the flair of a game show model revealing prizes.

"Yeah, okay." He doesn't express desire the way 1950s-era sons in plaid, pressed shirts and loafers might, but that he's here at all seems to be enough.

In my mind, I'm working to prop him up. But the truth is, his fortitude fuels me.

My son spoke before he was one, dialogued in full sentences by 15 months and, at his 2-year-old check-up, the pediatrician asked us, "Do you have any idea how unusual he is?"

We didn't.

But over the years, the anecdotal evidence grew to support everyone's suspicion that this child was beyond bright. Then, in 2003, we learned that he is in the upper end of the profoundly gifted spectrum. The psychologist who tested my son told me that kids like ours were one in 250,000.

"When do you think he'll find kids he can relate to?" I asked.

"When he goes to MIT." My son had just turned ten.

Some parents might see stars, straight As, and Stanford after hearing this response. But my eyes glazed over as I clasped an open hand to my mouth in a classic It's-All-Clear-To-Me-Now posture.

More than explain his intellect, this blessing-slash-curse confirmed my belief that my son speaks a different language and sees the world through different lenses than same-aged peers.

In third grade, he came home in tears after his gym class teammates blamed him for their loss in a game of crab walking. He'd stopped in the middle of the contest because the black pavement was hot. He decided to walk back to his team, after which the teacher disqualified them.

"Mom, the pavement was, like, over 100 degrees. That's just not fair to us." Unfortunately, he let his not-so-wrong logic prevail at a time when everyone else wanted to win.

In fourth grade, classmates verbally abused him for knowing nothing about sports. Yet when the teacher and I spoke with the children to better understand what was going on, they described a curious envy for the very one they were victimizing. "Do you know that I'll *never* be able to read like him? My parents would die if I could read like that."

During one winter break when he was nine, he broke down on the carpet near my desk, inconsolable about his lack of friends at school.

"Why do you think you don't have friends in school?" I asked this because he's maintained several friendships outside of school.

"Because I'm fat and I like books." Envision a child slouched and soaking in his sobs.

"Well, what do you think you'd have to do to get those kids to be your friends?"

"Stop reading, play sports, and be mean to girls." Imagine arms and hands flapping up and down from exasperation.

"Do you really want to do any of those things? Or give up what you like? Do you want to be friends with kids who don't like what you like?"

"No!" he said. And then, through the short breaths caused by crying so hard, complete with arms still slapping, he said, "I *love* reading. I *love* books. But I *hate* not having any friends."

Sigh. Big, motherly sigh.

But, despite his refusal to conform—and thereby invite teasing, he likewise clings to certain beliefs about right and wrong. In third grade, with nothing more than words, he forced a recalcitrant bully to stop verbally abusing a class-mate during a field trip to a play.

And in fifth grade, after being terrorized for an entire semester during which the school's methods to curb the perpetrators' behavior failed repeatedly, he convinced four administrators—an assistant principal, the school psychologist, the school guidance counselor and the district coordinator for gifted services—to let him confront the boys directly.

On the day of the intervention, the assistant principal accompanied the boys to the office and overheard the following exchange, which she loves to describe to others.

"It's your fault that we have to do this," said the main bully, as he strutted through the hall.

"No. It's *your* behavior," my son said, equally sure of himself.

These days, it seems to be in style to complain about the superhuman nature needed to be a mom, particularly to a child like my son. But every morning, when I see him clutch that tension pillow to his chest and rise without complaint for another school day, I know I'm watching a *real*, super, human.

Jill Miller Zimon writes regularly for Cleveland Family. Her op-eds, essays and features have been published in The Plain Dealer, The Writer, Writer's Digest, Connecticut Parent and other print and online markets. You may contact her through www.jillmillerzimon.com.

WHAT IS STRENGTH?

By Debbie Burton-Peddle

Strength is a test—and it's not whether we pass or fail the test,
but that we complete it.

Strength is elusive—it can often hide from us,
but when found, remains very close by.

Strength is not measured by quantity, weight, or force,
but by human spirit.

Strength is individual—yet it is the individual
who determines his or her own strength.

Strength helps us through life's journeys, yet
it is in these journeys that we gain our strength.

Strength is something we can call upon in time of need,
not only for ourselves, but for others.

Strength is not loud, arrogant, or a seeker of attention.
Rather it is quiet, humble and a seeker of peace.

Strength is something special we receive . . .
and even more special when it's something we share.

Debbie Burton-Peddle is a Registered Nurse, married with two daughters and a son. She enjoys writing poetry and inspirational prose, having numerous publications with Blue Mountain Arts/SPS Studios. She lives in St. John's, Newfoundland, Canada.

The Truths about Rains and Floods

By Raymond K. Wong

September 2004, Friday, 4:30 p.m. Just a few layers of clouds. The repair shop called and said my laptop was ready for pickup. As I blissfully drove with the top down on I-279 toward Bridgeville, I felt rain on my hands. I pulled over and put the top up just in time before a heavy downpour hit. Now, rainstorms were not uncommon in western Pennsylvania during the summer, but this one came fast and hard. Within minutes, visibility reduced to only a few yards ahead. I took the exit, but two state trooper cars were blocking the on-ramp to I-79 South. Right then, I knew something crazy had happened. *What is it? A fire? A landslide?*

I took the other on-ramp and got on I-79 North, heading back home. As I slowly got off at my exit, my car skidded, making a half-doughnut onto the open road. Fortunately, I quickly regained control and the cars behind me were at a safe distance. My nerves were shot, though. As I drove down Rt. 65, which ran along the Ohio River, I realized the severity of the situation: water everywhere, rising to one or two feet at certain points. Within 15 minutes of the first raindrops, the Ohio bank had flooded.

A quick errand turned into a nightmare. All the exits toward my house were closed, police cars everywhere. Following a long line of cars that had nowhere to turn, I reluctantly took the detour, without knowing exactly how to get home. I stopped near an intersection where an officer directed traffic. I rolled down the window and waved.

"I need to get to the North Hills," I said, fierce rain splashing my face.

"Can't go this way, sir," the officer said, his face soaked under the hood of his raincoat. "All the roads are blocked up that way. They're all flooded."

"Where should I go? I'm not familiar with this neighborhood."

"I'm sorry, I don't know. You'll have to follow the detour."

So I did. As the convoy of cars curved around Rt. 65 around Bellevue, we drove through at least a foot of water. My tiny car must have looked like a bathtub toy, sloshing its way through the turbid ripples. I tried a shortcut. What a mistake. Turn after turn, all the access roads to the highway were blocked, cars stranded like ants on a burning hill. The rain didn't stop.

After being stuck in traffic for more than 20 minutes, I turned into an alley, away from the main streets . . . into a dead end. I made more turns, meeting more dead ends, some of them in at least two or three feet of water. I had to go uphill. My instinct eventually guided me up a small road, twisting and turning about rows of houses and swaying trees that the heavy rain continued to bludgeon. I was hopelessly lost. But I also realized truth #1: *If you keep going uphill, eventually you will come down.*

I was right, and soon, I came out on Perry Highway, a familiar sight. I thought, "Finally." I was now heading straight home.

Alas, truth #2: *The shortest path is not always a straight line.* Unfortunately, as I drove toward my destination, I had a rude awakening: All roads leading to my house winded downhill. Our exodus came straight from a Hollywood movie about the Apocalypse: cars strewn for miles, wrapping around and around, going somewhere but nowhere. We were all trapped, aimless, and no one could help us. But here came truth #3: *No matter how dire the situation is, people won't give up.* The long lines of cars kept moving, inching toward our destinations, as the rain continued to badger. Physically and emotionally.

An hour later, just blocks away from my house at last, I noticed a long line of cars coming back in my direction. A blue Honda CRX stopped next to my car, and the petite blonde driver rolled down her window and shouted.

"Turn around. It's all flooded down there. The entire thing, from Evergreen all the way to Millvale. There was about three feet of water at the bottom and cars were stalling. Your car is even smaller than mine. You'll never make it. Just turn around."

She gave me a thumbs-up and waved; then she was gone, back up the hill. I pondered for a few seconds, and realized truth #4: *Sometimes you simply must trust a total stranger, who has no ulterior motives other than to help you.* I turned around.

For the next 40 minutes, I felt like I was in an episode of the Twilight Zone, stuck on "replay." I kept driving around, going up and down the hills, being turned around again and again, roads blocked or flooded. Then I heard a beep. The orange light came on—my car was on empty. No gas station in sight. All the restaurants were closed as well. Hungry, tired, and stressed out, I decided to drive all the way to Troy Hill and take a break. I didn't have enough gas to keep driving around. I stopped at the only place open, a mini-mart. I got the only food and drinks I could find: a package of bologna, a bag of hotdog buns, and two bottles of Coke. I actually chuckled as I paid for the items, all the while wondering how the heck I ended up there. The long-haired, stubbled guy next to me at the counter, in a Black Sabbath T-shirt, grinned at me and shrugged.

"Crazy, isn't it?" I said.

"Yeah. I came all the way here to deliver my last pizza, and now I'm stuck."

"Too bad. We could have loved the pizza."

We laughed. And that was that. A sudden realization: *Life doesn't have to suck.* When the rain pours, grab a lemon and make lemonade.

As I sat in my car in the parking lot, drinking my Coke and shoving slice after slice of bologna in my mouth, I was thankful. I was thankful that my car didn't get sucked into a vortex. I was thankful that I had food and water. I was thankful that however long it took, I would find home.

And I did. The rain stopped and the floods receded in many areas. As I slowly cruised my way back through roads that had been reopened, the sun setting behind me, I thought of this eternal truth:

Through rains and storms, the sun will always rise.

Always.

Raymond K. Wong is the author of the novel The Pacific Between. *Ray has written and edited at Scholastic in New York, and his work has been published in the* Pittsburgh Post Gazette, Asian-American Anthology, Cincinnati.com, *and* Writers Post Journal. *He also writes a column for* Actors Ink. *When Ray isn't writing, he is a film and television actor. Visit: www.raymondwong.com.*

TAKING BACK MY HEART

By Deborah Rose

A year ago, my heart was broken. I just found out the offending party has gotten married. Of course he has. Isn't that always the way it goes? However, there is a big difference between last year and this year, and that difference is *me*.

You see, I have a large hole in my heart. Not a literal hole, but a figurative one, left there by the deaths of my parents when I was a child. This hole normally sits quietly and doesn't bother anyone, but when a man comes into the picture, the hole becomes like an awakened volcano.

When my parents died, I stopped receiving nurturing, affection, and unconditional love. A child who doesn't have these basic human needs filled gets stuck emotionally. Even as an adult, there always remains a needy child inside, one who is vulnerable to any opportunity for love. For many who were victims of abuse or neglect as children, this leads to poor judgment with the opposite sex, although they may be sound of mind in other areas of their lives.

Because I was neglected emotionally as a child, and endured years of psychological and sexual abuse, I believed I was unworthy and easily fell prey to people who play mind games. My uncle controlled everything I did. He always watched me and went through my belongings. When he made me go somewhere alone with him and assaulted me, I felt helpless. I don't want to be a helpless victim now that I'm an adult and have control over my life.

When I met Brian, the sparks flew immediately. If there had been a scientist nearby, he could have made something spectacular out of all the chemistry that was exploding through the room. Thus began a three-month emotional rollercoaster.

One minute, Brian was sweet and disarming, flirting and drawing me in. The next minute, he was rude. The pendulum swung with abandon and left me in a constant state of disequilibria. It seemed Brian wanted to keep me off-kilter. All the better to control me. There was never a commitment made, but there were endless glances and constant observation to make sure my focus was always squarely on him.

When Brian knew he'd pushed me too far, he was suddenly cute and solicitous. He flattered me ("You have beautiful hair!") and gazed longingly into my eyes, acting like a giddy schoolboy when I responded favorably.

Brian loved to impress me with his music and carpentry skills, and he made a point to be very kind and attentive to my son. Once I was thoroughly roped back in, the emotional abuse could begin anew. He became distant and aloof for no apparent reason, even ignoring me. He made subtle criticism of things I did.

He was very adept at using body language, such as turning his back to me or dramatically looking away when I approached him.

And that's not even the disturbing part. The disturbing part was observing the seething cauldron of neediness I turned into when Brian was around. I was a woman obsessed. I could barely think of anything else. I analyzed everything he said and did; every look, every word he spoke to me. I tried to reassure myself that I wasn't imagining what was going on.

When Brian and I were with friends, I was so focused on him that I ignored everything and everyone around me. I went from being an independent, strong woman to being a little puppy following him around, seeking his approval.

I saw the problem in myself. I saw it in the eyes of my baffled and frustrated friends as they struggled to knock me back to reality. Yet I seemed helpless to control it. It devoured me whole and left me feeling completely lost without Brian. I thought I could not go on if I didn't have that adrenaline rush I got when things were good with us, if I couldn't feel his touch and, worse, if he ended up with someone else and I had to watch it happen.

I overlooked red flags and behavior I never would have under ordinary circumstances. I don't normally tolerate rude behavior, and I am usually repulsed at the thought of an abusive or controlling man.

I caught Brian in a few lies—another thing I don't normally accept. The rational part of me knew he wasn't good for me, but my broken heart, which longs to be loved and protected, could not let go of the hope that being with him had ignited.

I acted in goofy ways that were out of character, playing the dumb blonde, acting helpless, things that I am not. I began to sacrifice who I was and what I needed to appease Brian and keep the flow of endorphins from his adoration coming.

I settled for a man who treated me with a lack of respect and consideration, who didn't seem to care about my well-being. Brian was, in many ways, the opposite of what I wanted and needed, but I let the "chemistry" we had control my judgment.

In time, mutual friends made comments to him after observing us together and noting "the way you two look at each other." Thus came *The Phone Call* in which Brian informed me he wasn't ready for a relationship, and he was sorry if he had given me the impression he was. I was stunned.

More than that, I was angry that Brian tried to make it appear I had imagined everything. At the same time, he wanted to keep me close, and became quite angry that I wouldn't continue to play the Game. He didn't want a commitment, but he wanted me to continue to spend a lot of time with him. Brian wanted the attention, the flirting, the longing looks . . . he wanted me to go on feeding his ego, without any fear of being hemmed in. I had been his little puppet, and he enjoyed pulling my strings.

In spite of my pain and the Neediness Monster, good sense prevailed some-how, and self-preservation motivated me to avoid Brian for a while. Though ex-quisitely painful for a time, the wound eventually started to heal. It was months before I truly gave up hope of things beginning again with Brian, but once I did, I didn't look back.

I wrote my autobiography last fall, detailing the deaths of my parents and the abuse I endured from various caregivers. Everyone asks me if it was "cathartic." I do know that it gave me a new outlook on myself.

For someone who has always struggled with self-esteem and self-worth, writ-ing the book allowed me to see myself in a different light. Instead of victim, I see strength. Instead of inadequacy, I see someone who has overcome great odds. Instead of someone who doesn't deserve better, I see myself as someone who deserves nothing less than genuine love and respect.

A year later, I can look back on The Brian Experience with insight and ap-preciate what I learned. It made me face some unfinished business with regard to loving myself. I needed to understand what I need in a relationship and, more importantly, what I deserve.

The experience helped me see that I'm stronger than I thought I was. The course of comfort and least resistance would have been to continue to play the game as Brian wanted it, and to hope that things would change.

It hurt so much to give up that hope, but I knew it was the wise choice. For that, I'm proud of myself—proud that I was strong enough, and able to get past my immediate needs and look to what was best in the long run.

The support from my family and friends at that time—and observing how much they hurt for me—made me realize that I am loved and worthy of more than I got from Brian. I am still alone, but I'm at peace.

Deborah Rose is the author of Ellie. She resides in Northern California, where she has been a foster parent for 16 years.

I WAS IN MY ROSE GARDEN

By Janet Paszkowski

keen shears wielding
when terror struck

Now I no longer ache
for glossy green foliage
a garden grown to look at

I bow to the revealing grace
in a garden grown to live in
to learn from, to commemorate—

evanescent souls
with everlasting blooms
of virtue and thorns

bearing honey-scented petals
to be withered and strung
like prayer beads

I gather my teardrops to yield
buds on flowering wood
burgeoning upward

Janet Paszkowski is a fiction writer, poet, and visual artist. She lives in Georgia with her husband and three children. Her work has received numerous regional and national awards, and she's been published in several literary journals and mainstream venues.

BEACHSIDE REVELATIONS

By Shelly Wiseman Webb

"I don't like the idea of your going," my husband said to me. "You two are just like Thelma and Louise."

"What? Do you think we're going to drive off a cliff, like in that movie? We just want to go to the beach."

"Well, I've seen your map-reading skills." A smile flitted across his face. "Maybe I should go with you. Why this sudden need to leave, anyway?"

My husband Larry had reason to worry about me. I had been struggling for several months with a serious depression that had robbed me of my sense of humor, my energy, my ability to hold a job, and—at times—even my will to live. The storm of self-hatred that raged in my head was so painful, so debilitating, that I had tried to kill myself more than once. My sudden desire to spend a few days away from home was the first spark of interest I had shown in anything in a long time, so Larry wanted to foster whatever might help me despite his reservations about my going. As it was, I could barely handle a trip to the grocery store, let alone a 600-mile drive away from home. And what was more, I couldn't explain to him fully why I felt compelled to go—only that once the idea took shape in my mind, it was too powerful to resist.

My best friend Luanne and I had been talking the previous day about how wonderful it would be to get away for a few days. "Why don't we go to the beach?" I said. "Larry's uncle lives in South Carolina, and I'm certain he would let us crash at his place. We'd need money only for gas and food."

"We could take a cooler and pack the food we would need," Luanne replied. She was already hooked on the idea.

Against the advice and wishes of our family, we set out three days later. We stopped at Uncle Dick's long enough to stop in and say "hello," drop our things into his guestroom, and change into our beach clothes. Now that we were so close, we could not ignore our longing to be at the ocean's edge. We had already called our homes to let everyone know that we had arrived safely, and that anyone who needed to reach us should leave a message on the cell phone. We'd get back to them. Whenever.

We spread our blankets on the sand and slathered ourselves in sunscreen. As I took in our surroundings—the crash and energy of the waves bounding onto the sand, the briny breeze—I started to understand why I felt the need to be right where we were. Time is suspended at the ocean's edge. The smell, the feel, the sound, the sight of it all washed over me like a baptism, carrying away everything that was negative inside of me. There was nothing left but the present, and it filled me until it spilled over. I felt reborn. For the first time in my life I sensed the promise of what was possible within me, unburdened by the regrets of what might have been. There was only now, and now was filled with the sand and salt, and the delighted squeals of children discovering the push-pull of the waves and the bitter taste of the ocean for the first time. I began the glorious extravagance of living in the moment for three days.

The beach transformed us. We turned tan, and our skin was polished baby-smooth by the sand. We swam in the warm water. We jumped into the waves and let them take us wherever they wanted us to go. I built a Great Pyramid, and we planted our beach umbrella in it. We fed grapes to the seagulls and laughed whenever a bird caught one in its mouth. We read and slept and walked, all at our leisure—no rules but our own.

On our last day by the shore, we stayed almost until sundown. We packed the car full of our things and the sand that had worked its way into everything, and we walked back over the dune bridge for one last goodbye.

I stood on the beach—sorry that our trip had come to an end, and yet so very grateful for the opportunity to be there at all. I needed to do something about it. Luanne had already turned to go to the car. "Come back for a moment," I shouted. She stood next to me as I knelt down and traced the word "THANKS" with my index finger in the sand at the water's edge.

We started back to our waiting car. I turned around at the top of the bridge and looked back at the water. Though the ocean was receding as low tide neared, I noticed that she had accepted our offering of gratitude.

"Well, did the trip to the beach make you happy?" my husband asked me when we returned at dawn the next morning.

"I think I got out of it what I needed," I replied after a moment.

I no longer recall quite so distinctly the sound the waves made when they hit the shore. I have washed the salty smell of the beach from my clothing. My tan is fading. But the seed of possibilities planted in me when I was at the water's edge continues to grow.

Shelly Wiseman Webb lives in southeastern Ohio, a country mile from her hometown of Parkersburg, West Virginia. She is currently working on a collection of humorous essays about her family. She can be reached by email at swebb@wscc.edu.

OF BUILDINGS AND BABIES

By Linley B. Marcum

In the years since September 11, 2001, a lot has changed in my life and in the life of my country.

I had always viewed the very familiar and comforting skyline in New York City, from my home in the mountains of West Virginia, as a constant. I had lived my entire life with it like that, and believed any children I might have would live their entire lives seeing it, too. It's funny what something as trivial as a building or a pretty view can do to one's psyche, but as with most things, we usually don't realize what we have until it's gone.

I don't think I will forget September 11, 2001, as long as I draw breath. I can tell you what clothes I was wearing when I found out (pajamas—I worked night shift at the time, and my husband woke me up from a dead sleep); the first words said to me ("Honey, you need to get up. You need to see this"); the first thought that ran through my mind (*Oh, just another movie star we like is in trouble*); and what chair I sat in (the old green upholstered rocker with the broken leg).

I think my feelings were probably close to what people must have experienced when they found out that Kennedy was dead, that the stock market had crashed in 1929, and many other tragedies that happened before my time.

I also remember that, even living in West Virginia, I was too scared to go to work that day. I spent most of the afternoon alone in my rented townhouse crying and praying, and hoping that if something happened in Charleston my husband would get home from work in time to be with me when the effects got as far as our little community located an hour away. Fear overwhelmed me that day as I helplessly watched one of the greatest tragedies of American history unfold before me on the television screen.

In the months to come, I became more and more brokenhearted as the stories of those who had died began to surface. I couldn't tear myself away from the news coverage, no matter how many tears I shed or how many times I saw a different name or picture of someone lost on the screen. I think it was the thought that they had been simply erased for all time that really bothered me. Seeing all the pictures of the dead and missing was the hardest part and realizing the loss of whole lives, full of families, friends, and memories.

Shortly after that day I found that, following nearly two years of trying, my husband and I were finally going to have a baby. I was thrilled. It felt like God was saying to us, *Yes, children, I'm still here*. I took all the precautions and did everything I was supposed to do, which in my case included two shots of insulin a day for gestational diabetes.

After studying the charts and figuring the dates, I came to a stunning realization. My baby had been conceived on September 11.

Nine months passed quickly. It seems like you're just finding out you're pregnant when it's time for you to deliver. On May 28, 2002, I gave birth to a baby boy who was relatively healthy considering my condition during my pregnancy. He had a heart murmur and some problems with his breathing and sugar level when he was born, but these issues have resolved themselves and he is a happy and healthy little boy.

As I lay in labor on Monday, May 27, I watched quite a bit of television. All the news channels could talk about on this Memorial Day was the fact that on the next day the last column still standing from the World Trade Center would be torn down and removed from the site, and the clean-up would be complete. My child was born at 12:50 a.m., May 28, the day the clean-up ended.

In the days that followed our baby's birth, I contemplated the turn of events since September 11, and the irony of it all. On such a day of tragedy, God saw fit to give me the beginnings of a child, and he chose an important day in the history of our country, the day the last of the Towers came down, to bring him into this world.

The baby and the towers are quite similar. There's nothing at the Twin Towers site now, just a pit and a new canvas upon which to paint a new picture.

It's kind of like a new child. My husband and I have a new person to mold and teach and eventually send out into the world. Our hope is that when he finally does go out and forge his own path we will have taught him well. We hope he will be able to not just function in a society where the future is very unsure right now, but shine as a beacon in his compassion, beauty of soul, and capacity for tolerance and love.

This, too, is my hope for the site of the 9/11 tragedy. It is our responsibility, as Americans, to mold what is placed there. We should treat this site like a newborn child, and make the most of the tools we all have to fashion it into something the entire world can see as a beacon of compassion, beauty, honesty, love, peace, and above all, memory.

Linley B. Marcum is a stay-at-home mother and full-time writer. She and her husband Chris, son Connor, and stepson Christopher live on a large plot of forested, mountainous land in Southwestern West Virginia.

JUST BELIEVE

By Kim Gogo-Melvin

When what lies ahead seems too much to bear
And you look for help but nobody's there

When you've lost hope, don't know where to start
Don't give up too early, my friend, take heart

No matter the mess you find yourself in
You have the solution, just look within

The fear that you have when you feel alone
Escape its grip from within, on your own

So many fail because they don't even try
Letting all chances for success go by

You have all you need to figure it out
Just believe in you, that's what life's about

When at the start, just believe and begin
Give it all you have, my friend, and you'll win

Kim Gogo-Melvin (gogo@magma.ca) writes children's stories, poetry, fiction and nonfiction in Ottawa, Canada. Her strength comes from her children, Cody and Kaley, her husband, Matt, her family, and from her faith.

THE BEAUTY WITHIN

By Erin D. Zapletal

When I was a kid, I just wanted to be beautiful.

But genetics weren't good to me in the looks department—most specifically my buck teeth, bad eyesight, and, as I found out later, jaw bones out of whack. I loved my long, waist length, naturally curly hair. It was my only pride.

I'd been made fun of more times and by more people than I count. Sometimes, even now, something will thrust me back into time: darkened hallways, a cacophony of laughter, and me with tears in my eyes, my world collapsed inside itself. For every insult and joke, another piece of my soul crumbled to the ground.

I'd never said or done anything to them, but for some reason, kids picked on me endlessly. In one class, I didn't have a single friend. The teacher looked the other way as they stole things from me, nearly set my hair on fire, passed around nasty notes, and spread lies about me. I often ended up in the counselor's office and frequently came home in tears. To say it was a rough year would not touch it. It's something I still can't think about without feeling a profound sense of loss. No one would listen to me. No one seemed to care. And I couldn't stop it.

Depression haunted me on those lonely nights, and many times I thought to end my own life, but held on to hope that things would get better. *I* would get better.

I prayed to God to end my pain—silence the laughter, let me be a kid—a normal, happy kid. Make me beautiful. God answered my prayers, but not in the manner I'd thought. That lonely kid who thought she was ugly never would have believed that she would become the woman I am today.

One fateful day when I was 12, my orthodontist gave us the grim news: that after eight years of endless braces, retainers (five), and a lot of pain, we weren't through yet. I'd need to have my jaw bones broken and realigned. If I didn't, I'd lose all my teeth by the age of 20.

TMJ, they called it. My father's side of the family had serious jaw problems. My dad never underwent any surgery for his jaws, but he lives on pain pills, sometimes working through severe headaches. Once, his jaw locked in place. When he eats, you can hear a faint clicking noise. And by golly, I didn't want that, nor did I want to be fitted for dentures as my first foray into adulthood.

The X-rays at age 15 were sobering—my joints had literally worn away. Doctors had wanted to wait for me to finish growing, and by then I'd stopped, so the surgery was scheduled. But first, I had to make preparations: I had my wisdom teeth taken out to make a hole where I could feed myself (and to prevent future issues with the teeth themselves), special braces, and gave my own blood because I'd probably need a transfusion. I've got a cast-iron stomach, but it was still a real trip.

And *oh yeah*—I'd be wired shut for up to eight weeks. That sure sounded like fun, blending all my food up into a puree to eat.

Because I love steak, and would miss it (and all solid food, actually), that's what my mom cooked as my last solid meal. I was too excited and nervous to sleep. I had to be up at the ungodly hour of 3:45 a.m. for surgery.

The hospital was beautiful, with marble tiles and pretty colors. I remember being wheeled into the OR. After that, I remember nothing. I woke up at 2:00 a.m. throwing up my own blood. My stomach being pumped was a blast, too. But, heck, I felt no pain whatsoever.

Until I got a look at my new self.

I was so swollen my head looked about two times as big. I had ice packs attached to my cheeks. Look Mom, I'm a chipmunk! I had a fabric thing stuck to my chin—apparently so everything would stay together. My mom told me later that they'd put an X in the middle of my forehead so the doctor could realign my nose. I had both jaws realigned and my chin brought forward. And, as I discovered later, I was given nice cheekbones, a real chin (I never had one, medically speaking), and a new nose. I swear, it wasn't a nose job.

After three difficult days filled with messy liquids and labored breathing, I happily went home to my own bed. Everything was still too swollen to speak, so I resorted to note-writing. Mom became my nurse, using a syringe to feed me during the first few weeks. She was terrified to choke me, so she fed me super slowly.

My family was too afraid to eat in front of me. I felt pretty depressed my first week, knowing that I had to subsist on Ensure and Lipton's Cup a Soup. Occasionally milkshakes, too. But still. Food just wasn't possible—and grinding it up is nasty. I tried, it grossed me out, I won't do it again.

So they used to sneak downstairs to eat stuff—cake, miscellaneous goodies. Over time, I stopped caring—the thought of solid food just didn't grab me anymore. I guess I was truly in the rhythm of non-solid life and embraced it. But God bless them, they were wonderful to me. My first words ever after the surgery were "I love you." Spoken to my Mom, of course.

I went back to school in September and many people didn't recognize me. My French teacher wanted me to attempt French while wired. She walked up to me after class and said I was brave for doing this. Bravery didn't hit my radar at the time: I was just doing what I needed to do. But bravery? Looking back on it, I realize now how brave it was. I had to eat (drink) in between classes, and for a while it was weird, coming in late to class, talking to the office people, garnering strange looks from some people. I graduated to lunch like a normal person and cheerfully sipped my Ensure like it was nothing. But it was something.

I met a girl who I now credit with saving my life. The constant torment and humiliation for years left me with fragile self-esteem. I was too afraid of reaching out, getting hurt again. All I could see was their accusing eyes. Their laughter still rang inside my head. It paralyzed me. Until I met Jenny, I didn't believe I was worthy of anything—friends, happiness, a normal life. The wounds cut deep, and it took a long time to heal them and end my self-imposed isolation.

It was Jenny who looked beyond the superficial and saw me as I was, not some label thrust upon me by my tormentors. She stood by me when no one else did, and I finally learned the value of true friendship.

Jenny introduced me to Job's Daughters, a youth group for girls who have Masonic ties. The weekend of my first dance, I stayed at her cousin's house with about 15 other people, and made shakes, soup, and drank Ensure. No one thought it odd, but they were amazed by my story. My first dance was such fun—I even got to dance with a guy I'd had a crush on forever. That's also where I met my first boyfriend (something I believed impossible).

It was around that same time that I began writing poetry. I found beauty and wonder in the mundane; I opened people's eyes; I journeyed to faraway places on gossamer wings. In those exhilarating moments, I stepped outside my shell and experienced the beauty of life, and the beauty of my own words.

I was somebody. My words meant something; they mattered. And that gave me hope.

I got my jaw unwired at the eight-week mark, but I still couldn't eat solids. At my sister's birthday party, I ate ice cream gingerly and frosting off a slice of cake. But I was happy to have been given the precious gift of normalcy.

The most painful part of the experience was breaking those pesky adhesions that had basically locked my mouth in the same position for two months. I remember gripping my mother's hand, knuckles white, crying, and nearly breaking her fingers. The exercises I had to do were torture. But for me to be able to eat again, it had to be done, so I gritted my teeth and worked on it. My first real meal was a McDonald's Fish Fillet and a chocolate chip cookie. It was strange returning to the world of solid foods. It was almost like being born again; I experienced everything as if for the first time. And it felt good.

My face, however, was something entirely new. I looked . . . beautiful. Not model pretty, but my face had the right contours and nothing seemed out of place. I remember crying, thanking God for answering my prayers.

Thirteen years later, my battle wasn't quite over. The titanium hardware the surgeon had used to fuse everything together became infected and had to be removed. Twice. The removal was more painful than the surgery itself, but I will never regret having the surgery. Not just because I get to keep my teeth and have a nice face, but the experience taught me a lesson in strength: After pain comes the joy of something worth it when it's over.

And I learned something about myself that was—and still is—invaluable: I am beautiful. I really am, inside and out.

In college, I discovered fine art photography and found a whole new world to explore. I mainly do self-portraiture as a way to explore who I am. I found beauty in my own image, but not because of the surgery. My husband once told me that I had a beautiful soul. And that's what I finally found, staring back at me in the images I captured and in my own words.

I now teach photography at our local college, and I tell my students that they are all unique, and they need to embrace who they are and what they do. I've seen some powerful photographs come from people who never dreamt it possible. There is beauty in everything: the moonlight as it caresses a lover's face, a garden filled with a rainbow of flowers, tears in a father's eyes as he hands his daughter off to her groom, a mother as she smiles at her baby for the first time. And yes, there is beauty within you, whether you believe that or not. You just have to find it, hold onto it tightly, and never, ever let go.

I am beautiful now. But I was beautiful then, too. It took me a long time to realize that. I carry with me that same bravery I had back then, the will to keep going, and faith to believe that anything is possible—even changing a life forever. The whispers of my tormentors slowly fade away with each passing day, and I am finally at peace.

Erin D. Zapletal is a writer and photographer living in Michigan. She is the office manager for a marketing firm, and teaches photography classes at Macomb Community College. She loves writing, and has several novels-in-progress.

FINDING PEACE
IN TIMES OF CHAOS

By Sheryl McCarty

I decided I couldn't handle any more. Tension and stress built over the last several weeks, leaving me speechless and shaking. Watching hours of hurricane Katrina coverage left me unable to think of anything else. I had survived a direct hit from hurricane Hugo, which left me with post-traumatic stress disorder, and in some sick twist, riveted to the current tragedy. I was a pot ready to boil over. I needed to find some peace if that meant I had to hunt it down, whack it over the head, and drag it home.

My husband and daughter were out of town, so I decided to take advantage of my alone time. I went riding. Riding has always been a way for me to relax, rebuild, and rethink. I loaded my horse onto the trailer and drove the thirty minutes to a favorite local state park. As the trailer got closer to the park, I began to feel better. The pot still bubbled, but was not threatening to spill.

Few riders took advantage of the isolated park on this day. I took off at a nice slow walk—unusual for me. Normally, I like to ride hard and fast for hours. I knew the trails well and soon we were deep into the woods. Closing my eyes, I thought about peace and how much I needed to find it.

I began the deep breathing exercises I used to scoff at, saying "peace" each time I exhaled. I felt better. Muscles I didn't realize were tight began to relax against my mantra for peace. Riding calmly through the woods, I noticed the light playing off the river, a Red Tail's wings brushing against the trees, and the chipmunks darting right and left to avoid horse's hooves. All the times I had dashed down these trails in the name of relaxation, I had missed this.

After two hours, my horse and I headed home. I felt lighter. All I could think about was how good it felt to let go of the torment of daily life.

You don't need a horse to find peace in times of chaos. You may not know where to begin looking, but you must believe it is out there. Breathe slowly and evenly, and say the word "peace" as you exhale, either aloud or in your mind. Say it over and over until you feel your body relax. Look around your environment to find something of beauty. It doesn't matter if you are cooped in your house on a stormy day or standing on a flooded street surrounded by total devastation. It can come from anywhere. Notice the way raindrops cause greens to be deeper or the pink streak across a darkening sky. It can even be found inside you if you look through the beautiful places in your mind. Focus on that beauty as you think about peace.

The next time you find yourself bubbling over, try closing your eyes and searching for peace. You might be surprised that you find it.

Sheryl is a Registered Nurse and novelist living on a small farm in Westminster, Maryland with her family.

JUST SOME OLD MAN?

By Michele Ivy Davis

"He's just some old man," the plump waitress says
As he shuffles, head down, through the door.
My hot mug suspended, I watch him proceed,
Through the chairs on the coffee bar floor.

The young woman with him—his granddaughter? nurse?—
Gently braces his stooped-over form.
They stop and sit down at a table nearby;
Exertion has made them both warm.

But soon they move on to the front corner stage,
The single step almost too high.
They make it together, the man and the girl,
And he sits on the bench with a sigh.

At the keyboard he squints and he studies its keys,
Then he slowly commences to play.
Oh, the music that comes from those delicate hands!
All the old songs not heard much today.

And his spirit stands tall; it laughs and it leaps,
As his white hair falls into his eyes.
"He's just some old man," the waitress had said,
But a young man I see with surprise.

Too soon his bent fingers the final notes strike,
And his shoulders droop once more with age.
He leans on the girl, she holds most of his weight;
As he slowly steps down from the stage.

Yet his eyes are now glowing, he wears a sly grin,
As he makes his way back to the car,
I see an old man—with a young man inside—
Departing the hushed coffee bar.

Michele Ivy Davis has had her writing published in a variety of magazines and newspapers, as well as Chicken Soup for the Sister's Soul. She is the author of the novel Evangeline Brown and the Cadillac Motel. www.MicheleIvyDavis.com

PHYSICAL STRENGTH

"Marathon swimming is the most difficult physical, intellectual and emotional battleground I have encountered, and each time I win, each time I touch the other shore, I feel worthy of any other challenge life has to offer."

~ Diana Nyad (*Other Shores*)

JUST KEEP GOING

By Wil Wheaton

In January 2004, one of my wife Anne's best friends was diagnosed with cancer. It was a complete shock to both of us.

Anne wrote on my blog, "A year and a half ago, Wil and I participated in the Avon 3 day breast cancer walk. We didn't know anyone with breast cancer. We just wanted to help raise money for research and be part of the walk-a-thon. It was by far the most incredible experience of our lives. Between the two of us, we raised over $17,000. We always knew we'd do something like this again.

"What I didn't realize was that I would be doing something like this because one of my very close friends, Kris, would be diagnosed with acute myelogenous leukemia. My 45-year- old friend, a wife, a mother of two, an active, loved member of the community, was just diagnosed with a life threatening disease."

Kris was admitted to the City of Hope Cancer Hospital in Duarte, near Los Angeles. She went through several different treatments, including one hundred days of chemotherapy, radiation, and a stem cell transplant. It was so hard to watch our friend struggle mightily against a seemingly unstoppable and cruel disease, and feel powerless to truly help her.

Until Anne came home one afternoon with a flyer for the 2004 San Diego Rock-n-Roll Marathon. We could walk it or run it, the flyer said, and we could raise money for the Leukemia and Lymphoma society in the process.

"Will you do this with me?" Anne said, "For Kris?"

I didn't have to think about it at all. "Of course."

We trained for months, and documented the entire experience on my blog. Hundreds of people left thousands of comments for Kris, which Anne printed out and delivered to her. Kris hand-wrote several replies, which Anne posted on my blog. People who had never met our friend were sending their thoughts, prayers, and support to her, and her doctors told us privately that it helped Kris maintain a positive attitude throughout her entire ordeal.

WIL WHEATON dot NET readers ended up contributing over $27,000 to the Leukemia and Lymphoma Society, which was wonderful . . . but there was a much more immediate benefit that neither Anne nor I expected: Kris fought her cancer with the strength of a thousand women. One day, in the middle of Kris' treatment, when she felt weak and tired, and her mouth was covered with painful sores from radiation treatments, Anne told Kris, "Please don't give up."

Kris smiled and said, "I have to meet you at the finish line in June." She pointed at a stack of comments and e-mails. "And I'm not going to let all these people down."

She didn't.

This story is about part of the marathon. It was originally published on my blog on June 29, 2004.

* * *

At the pre-race dinner, John Bingham said, "At some point tomorrow, you'll know that you're going to finish. It may come at mile 5, it may come at mile 26 . . . but you'll know. You will also have some miles that are great, some miles that are not so great, and some miles that are just awful . . ."

At mile 9, I knew I was going to finish: The weather was great, I felt great, and we'd just finished the only tough part of the course. Mile 16 was the first "just awful" mile for me: my quads ached, and my arms felt like they were made of stone. A wind had picked up, and it was blowing smoke and ash from a fire in Mexico right into our faces. By the time we crossed mile 17, I started to get scared that I might not finish. Maybe I'd spoken too soon at mile 9.

"It may help to have a mantra," John Bingham had said, "to get you through those awful miles."

I recalled my mantra from the Avon 3*Day: The pain is temporary. The memories last forever.

It didn't work. The pain may have been temporary, but it was climbing up my legs and spreading across my lower back.

You can do it, Wil. You can do it.

No luck with that. I didn't know if I could do it. I called my own bluff and folded that idea.

Just keep going.

Wait a minute . . . that may work.

Just keep going. Just keep going.

Yeah! That works. Nothing to really think about, nothing to trick myself into believing. It's just a simple but effective motivation in three short words.

Just keep going. Just keep going. Just keep going. Just keep going.

I looked up at the horizon, relaxed my neck and shoulders, and just kept going. I filled my conscious mind with my new mantra, and let my subconscious mind find a way to let my body continue moving forward. After a few minutes (I think) I put myself into a sort of trance.

Just keep going. Just keep go—

" . . . doing?" Anne said, from down a long, metallic tunnel. I barely heard her over the thumping of my feet on the ground, and my heart and breath throbbing in my ears.

"How are you doing?"

Just keep going. Just keep going. Just keep going. Just keep going.

"I'm fine," I said.

"Are you sure?"

No.

"Yeah. Let's just keep going." Just keep going. Just keep going. Just keep going.

Mile 17 wound around the North side of Mission Bay, and through a residential neighborhood. Several families were out on their lawns, cheering us on. Children ran into the street and offered high-fives.

Just keep going. Just keep going. Just keep going. Just keep going.

After a few more minutes, the road passed between two tall apartment houses, and I discovered that I'd been staring at one of those blue reflectors in the middle of the street—the ones that we always drove over in high school (a stupid-but-incredibly-entertaining practice we called "Smurfing"). Next to the reflector was a small laminated piece of paper with a paper clip at the top. I immediately recognized it: I'd seen several of my fellow participants wearing tags like this on their shorts, with the names of people they were running or walking for.

I stopped at the reflector, much to the consternation of the woman who almost ran into me.

I crouched down, and picked it up. My legs were so tired and sore, I felt like one of those dreams where no matter how hard you try, you can't move more than a few inches. I looked at the tag:

IN HONOR OF
Shelia H.
Bob M.
Bob S.
Doug S.
In Memory Of Dennis T.
Jan. 04, 2004

The pain is temporary. The memories last forever . . .

If Kris can take 100 days of chemo and radiation, I can take a few more tough miles . . .

In Memory of Dennis T . . .

Just keep going . . .

Just. Keep. Going!

I stood up.

"What are you doing?" Anne said.

I showed her the tag I'd picked up.

"Someone was walking or running for these people, and it didn't seem right to leave them here on the ground. I'm going to take them with me."

"Okay," she said.

"How are you doing?" I asked.

"Okay. Let's just keep going," she said. I hear that women have been trying to find ways into their husband's heads for centuries . . . maybe she'd done it!

I stood up, and clipped the tag onto my shorts.

"Yeah. Let's just keep going," I said. Was she really in my head?

You're one hot mamma! I glanced at her, but she was focused on the horizon.

Hey, baby . . . huh huh huh.

"What?" She said.

"What?!" I said.

"Why are you staring at me?"

"Uh . . . I don't know."

Whew.

When we passed mile 18, I looked at the clock, and realized that mile 17 had taken us almost 18 minutes—our longest mile, yet.

"Let's see if we can take some time off this mile," I said. Maybe having an extra five sets of feet with me helped, or maybe it was some natural athletic rhythm that I didn't know about . . . but I began to feel better. My spirits lifted, and my legs started to feel better.

"I can't think about taking time off," she said. "I just need to keep going."

"That's what I've been telling myself," I said. "Just keep going. Just keep going. Just keep going. Just keep going."

"I've been telling myself that if Kris can do 100 days of treatment, we can do a few hours of walking," she said.

"I'm going to talk about the areas of my body that feel great," I said.

I mentally scanned my body, starting at the top of my head.

"The breeze on my face feels awesome," I said, "and my right forearm is nice and relaxed."

I reached out, and took Anne's hand.

"Now, my hand feels great," I said, as we neared a water station. A volunteer handed me a cup or water, and a cup of Gatorade.

"Thanks for being here," I said, as I took one cup in each hand.

"I am the Walrus, and the grasshopper hops to the East!" he said with a waggle of his gigantic, elephant ears, and a spin of his propeller cap. I was a little delirious, so maybe he said something different, like, "You're welcome," and tipped his baseball cap . . . I can't say for sure.

When we finally crossed the finish line, Kris was waiting there for us. Anne wrote, We walked through the archway and down the path to the finish line. I kept saying, "I can't believe we did it! I can't believe we did it!" to Wil. Even now as I'm typing this, over a month later, I have tears in my eyes. We did it and so did Kris. She was there at the finish line, jumping and waving and yelling for us. It was by far, the most incredible moment of our lives.

Wil Wheaton is the author of Just A Geek, Dancing Barefoot, and Do You Want Kids With That? His classic gaming column "The Games of our Lives" is published weekly in The Onion AV Club. He is also an actor, best-known for work in Stand By Me and Star Trek: The Next Generation. His award-winning blog is at www.wilwheaton.net.

A FATHER'S CONSOLATION

By B. J. Bourg

"Kick, Brandon! Kick!" I glanced anxiously at the scorecard. Four to five—
Brandon was down by one point. He squared off with his opponent, who had a
white sash hanging from the back of his karate belt. When the referee gave the
signal, he rushed in and tried to land that overhead back-fist again. His opponent blocked and shot a quick sidekick to the midsection. My heart sank. The
referee screamed, "Break!"

All judges pointed to Brandon's opponent. The referee turned to the score-
keeper. "One point, White!" He turned back to the fighters, but the little red
beanbag that signaled "time over" went sliding across the linoleum floor. The
referee picked up the beanbag, had the fighters bow to each other, then declared
Brandon's opponent the winner.

I sank to my seat and watched a disheartened Brandon take his place on the
floor amongst the other 10-year-old fighters. He peeled his headgear off and sat
staring at the floor. This was his fourth year in the karate tournament circuit,
but he had yet to place in one.

After the awards ceremony, Brandon sulked to where his mother and I sat. I
grabbed his bag and ruffled his straight, brown hair. "Good job, Buddy!"

"I lost! How is that a good job?"

"It's not about winning," Cathy said. "You fought well and that's all that matters."

I knelt in front of Brandon and pushed his chin up with my index knuckle.
"Look son, winning isn't everything. It's okay to lose, as long as— "

"Well, Mom said you never lost a fight, that you took first place every time
you fought in a tournament. I want to do that, too!"

"Brandon, you can't compare yourself to me. I was 24 before I entered my
first tournament."

"So, you still never lost a fight."

"Well, check this out—by the time you turn 24, you'll be a much better
fighter than I was at that age. I started at 16 and you started at five."

Brandon just nodded and walked away, his head hung low.

The drive home was a familiar one—Cathy and I trying to lighten Brandon's
mood and Brandon staring out the window at nothing.

Two weeks after Brandon's tournament, I received a call from my boxing
promoter. "Hey, Billy, you ready for your first fight?"

"I guess."

"How's your weight?"

"I'm at 177."

"You need to be at 170, or the guy won't fight you."

"But the fight's in three days. I'll never get my weight down to that."

"Dry yourself out."

That night I passed on supper. I didn't eat or drink anything the next day at work. When I got home, Cathy asked what I wanted for supper. "I can't eat anything. I have to get down to 170 by tomorrow night for the weigh-in."

"Are you crazy?" Her voice was incredulous. "You're gonna make yourself weak. You can't do this."

"But the guy won't fight me unless I weigh 170."

"Then don't fight!"

"That's not an option."

The next night couldn't come fast enough. At the weigh-in, I was weak and my head felt like someone had driven a Monster truck right through the middle of it. I sat idly on the edge of the ring. After a long wait, my promoter called my name.

I stepped up to the black and white scale, where the paunchy boxing commissioner was waiting with a clipboard. I stripped to my shorts and stepped gingerly onto the platform and held my breath.

The boxing commissioner glanced over his eyeglasses at the numbers on the scale and adjusted the weight. He paused, then turned back to his clipboard. "170 pounds!"

My promoter slapped my back. "I knew you could do it! Now, eat good tonight and you'll be ready tomorrow."

I stood alone in the crowded dressing room. Fighters warmed up. Coaches gave last minute instructions. Family members and friends offered words of encouragement. I didn't hear any of it. I was alone inside my head with the demons. Look what you've gone and done! You're in trouble, now! That's it, you'd better go out there and knock him out, or you're gonna get knocked out! I slapped the side of my head with my gloved hand—something I'd done plenty of times. This time was different. This time it made me dizzy. If my own slap made me dizzy, what would my opponent's power punches do?

I entered the ring to the screaming of the crowd. I danced around and surveyed the auditorium. It didn't take me long to find them. They were on their feet and they screamed the loudest. I lifted my gloved hand and my wife and son cheered even louder. For a split second my demons were silenced . . . my fears forgotten. It was just them and me in this arena.

"Fighters, to the center of the ring!"

I complied with the referee's order. After his instructions, I retreated to my corner. When the bell rang, I rushed out. It didn't take long for me to get hit. Each punch made me dizzier than the last. Somehow, I survived the first round.

As I dropped to the bench in the corner, my coach threw water in my face. "How you feeling?"

"Good," I lied, trying to clear my vision. The one-minute break seemed like ten seconds.

I rushed out to round two. I knew I had to knock this guy out, or I'd be going to bed early. We met at the center of the ring for a few exchanges and I even got him on the ropes for a few seconds, but he slipped away. As he backed away from me, I lunged forward, anxious to drop him, and ran right into a hard right hand. I fell hard to my knees. When I looked up, the referee was crouched in front of me. He said, "Four! Five!"

Hey! What happened to one, two, three? I thought. I shook my head to clear it. *Dude, you need to get up!* I stood to my feet. The referee asked if I was okay and I nodded. He motioned for the fight to continue and I turned to face my opponents—there were three of them. I'd always heard that if you're seeing triple, go for the guy in the middle. I did, but the guy on the right hit me with a barrage of punches that dropped me for the second time, and he urged the referee to stop the fight.

Minutes later, I sat truly alone in the dressing room. I stared dishearteningly at the floor. I cursed myself for resorting to dehydration and starvation to make the weight. As I beat myself up inside, I detected movement by the door. I looked up. My vision was still a little blurry, but there was no mistaking the concern in Brandon's eyes. "Dad, are you okay? I was worried about you."

My heart swelled with emotion. I decided to use my own defeat as a way to uplift my son. "You see, Brandon, now I've lost a fight, too. It's not that big a deal."

"But Dad," Brandon said in a matter-of-fact tone, "*I* never got knocked out."

B. J. Bourg is the Chief Investigator for a District Attorney's Office in Southeastern Louisiana. He applauds the efforts of all those who have come together to assist the survivors of Hurricane Katrina.

THE WELD MAKER

By Jan P. Myskowski

(For David Lawson)

After each of those endless days riding
Bulldozers or loaders across the plains
Of construction sites, every one the same,
Pushing and pulling levers, pushing dirt
Into piles, lifting it onto the backs
Of trucks, before the days of heated cabs,

His relief was to crack a beer in the
Garage, throw the switch on the arc welder
And make a hitch or trailer frame for some
Friend he'd made himself indebted to just
For the excuse to lay those luminous
Beads, and make blue light flash rectangular

In the conifer trees that lined the drive.
Day after day he gave his body up
To the unforgiving sun, gunmetal
Cold, and long endured atrophy's triumph.
So many days he walked stooped to his truck,
Lunchbox in hand, squinting all the way home.

But see him there now, large in his spark-proof
Jacket, long-cuffed gloves, the omnipotent,
Stoic mask, watching through the tinted glass
The firmament, formed as electrons jump
The arc to make steel know his intentions,
With flux smoke rising like greasy incense.

Jan P. Myskowski is a trust and estate attorney in Manchester, New Hampshire. David Lawson is Jan's stepfather, whose work provided inspiration by example.

MERRY CHRISTMAS. PANAMA, 1989.

By Mark Pettus

Mud.

Deep, green-brown mud. In every crease, and under every fingernail. I can't get rid of it. No water to wash with, only enough to drink. In Texas, this stuff would be black, and in weather this hot, it would be dry. Within an hour you could just beat it off of you. Not here. The humidity is so high, everything is wet. Rain is unnoticed. Doesn't cool things off. As soon as it stops, the steam from the ground raises what water didn't get you from above up to get you from below.

Green mud. Stuff grows in mud here; it's always green. It stinks. Breakfast is a pouch of ham and peanut butter crackers. They taste like green mud. The gauze was green to begin with, but now it has a different shade, and smells even worse than the mud. I feel hot. Is it the heat or is it the humidity? It's a fever. I know the difference. I'm a little dizzy, but the adrenaline keeps me alert.

I creep through the trees. As high as my waist, which is as high as I am willing to let my head get, there is green mud. Splattered on the roots, splattered on the leaves. The rain should wash it off, but it splashes more green mud up off the saturated ground and onto the trees. I take two more aspirin. They help fight off the pain. Pain from the places where the belt bites my hip. Pain from the nasty gash in my finger that might heal just fine when I finally let it dry out, but right now looks like wet noodles on top of pink meat, with a side order of . . . green mud.

The pain from that smelly, scary hole under the gauze is not the kind of pain that aspirin will help. It isn't sharp, it isn't an ache, it is just pain, low and constant. The aspirin is to fight the fever, mostly, and because it is something I can do. I can't do anything about that smelly green mud that I know has been soaking through the gauze for too long.

The perimeter is clear, and my squat-walk through the trees with a bunch of mud-covered kids, is over. I have to be strong for these boys; America's mothers' sons, far from home. We scatter to the corners of an opening in the trees. We pray that we have made our last long, slow, smelly walk through those trees, at least for this day. For two days, we have been alone in those trees. The flyboys took care of our last visitor, just after he gave me the one thing I hadn't asked for, the present I had to wrap with green gauze, and smell growing worse and worse in the green smelly mud.

We sit just inside the tree line and open our sealed dinners. Mine is chicken a la king. Not bad hot, edible cold, but disgusting at room temperature, when room temperature is somewhere near body temperature, and when it smells like green mud. But, just the same, it is a special meal, so I eat it all, and am thankful that I am able to eat.

The food, the heat, the fever, the smell. Man, I'm tired. I want to sleep. I lean back into the soft leaves and softer mud. I think of my wife, my kids. Just a few miles away, but in another world, in another life. Mimosas with eggs goldenrod. Brunch after opening presents. I hope they are happy and safe. Thinking of them gives me strength. Maybe this will all be over soon. I hope so. I want to go home. I close my eyes and sleep, and dream of ribbons and bows. Covered in mud.

Merry Christmas. Panama, 1989.

Writer and former soldier Mark Pettus lives in Orange Park, Florida with his wife and two youngest sons. Mark is the author of the novel Transit Gloria, and works full time for Journal Community Publications. You can reach Mark through his website, www.MarkPettus.com.

THE HURDLE JUMPER

By Christine M. Krannich

I watched from a few feet away as the girls from my fifth grade class played jump-rope on the playground. The recess monitor came by and reminded the girls holding the ends of the rope to let everyone have a chance in the middle. I started to walk away, my head down. Even worse than being picked and screwing up was being picked only because the grownups said they had to pick me. I hated recess.

One of them called my name. "Caroline!"

One of the other girls grabbed my arm and pushed me back to the cleared area. "Hurry *up*, fatso. Do it while the monitor's watching so we can get back to having fun."

I didn't know how to get into the center with the rope already turning. I couldn't ask, either, or they'd laugh for sure. I ran toward the rope, eyes closed, hoping I'd get through without tangling it. The pavement rose quickly. My hands flew out, but not in time to stop my face from hitting the ground. My nose hurt.

When I stood up, blood spurted all over. I cried when I saw my new blue shirt, the one Grandma just got for me, soaked with the evidence of my failure. My wails brought the monitor back over. As she walked with me to the nurse's office, I heard the girls re-starting their game. The new chant they picked echoed in my ears: "Care-oh-line, she's so bad, falls on her face and cries so sad."

A few days later, I noticed all the fifth graders crowded around a sign on the wall of the school gymnasium. "Cool," I heard one of the boys say, "Angela's a sure thing for the long jump!" Another insisted, "Carl will outrace everyone in the fifty-yard dash." I waited for the crowd to clear and then read the poster: "Earn a medal for your school! Enter the All-District Track and Field Competition and show everyone how good you really are!" School-level trial heats were in mid-May for the competition a week later.

I looked down at my large body and grimaced. I couldn't even hope to represent the school, much less win a prize. Every year, I tried to jump the hurdles. Flying in the air for a moment, weightless, was such a strong goal that it always overrode my fear of failure and humiliation. And every year, I always stumbled over that first hurdle and never made it any farther.

Remembering what happened at recess a few days before, I decided that this year, I was going to jump all the hurdles. I had five weeks to practice. I didn't want to jump them fast—I just wanted to complete the tryout without falling. I could do that. I knew I could. And I'd surprise everyone.

I started practicing that night after school. I used my father's sawhorses, and balanced a broom across them so it would fall down quickly. Every time I could get over one level five times in a row, I would get new boards to put the broom on and raise it up a bit higher. I had no idea at the time just how high I was jumping.

A week went by. During recess, I would sit on top of the monkey bars, giggling to myself while I watched the rest of the kids prepare for the trials. Some of them made fun of me for just watching. They started a new chant: "Caroline, she's so fat, if she runs she just goes SPLAT!" I ignored them. I was practicing, too; they just didn't know it.

The last day of signups, I waited until everyone else had filled in the paper and walked away from the sign. At the bottom of the list for the hurdles, I wrote my name in very small letters. My spine tingled when I read it. I was going to jump the hurdles, and I would make it this time! Even if I wanted to change my mind now, I couldn't. Scratching my name off the list would be even worse than falling in front of everyone—the other kids would tease me more if I chickened out. I was determined to clear every one of the six hurdles. This year, the kids wouldn't say that I was as big as a Mack truck, only good for pushing things out of the way. This year, no one would laugh at me.

Later, I saw the gym teacher, Mrs. Jamison, looking at the poster. She squinted as she looked at the bottom of the list, then shook her head. She'd probably seen my name there. I knew she liked me; she always said how impressed she was that I always tried, no matter what. But she was probably worried about the other kids teasing me.

On the day of the trials, teachers were at all the different events, doing preliminary timings so the final heats could be run later in the day. My heart sank when I saw that Mrs. Flary was assigned to the hurdles. She was mean to everyone, but she seemed to hate me in particular. I guessed it was because I read better than the sixth graders in her English class. Trying not to worry, I stood on the sidelines to wait my turn. I cheered for the winners and stayed quiet when the others booed the losers.

Finally, it was my turn to jump the hurdles. Mrs. Flary said, "Caroline Zepperty? Is this right? Caroline, did you really sign up to run the hurdles?"

"Yes, Mrs. Flary, I did, Ma'am." I stood at the starting line and waited. The seconds felt like a lifetime, and I got nervous. What if she didn't even let me try out? "I'm ready any time, Ma'am."

"All right, Caroline," she said. "One, two, three—GO!"

I ran as fast as I could toward the first hurdle. I looked at it, closed my eyes, pictured the broom I'd been jumping for weeks . . . and cleared the hurdle. *One.* I opened my eyes, a little surprised, and then there was the second hurdle. I cleared it easily. *Two.* I ran for the third. If anyone cheered or booed, I couldn't hear it—I was concentrating too hard. *Three.* Halfway done! I faltered one step and regained control just in time for the fourth hurdle to loom right in front of me. I forced myself to picture the broom again, and the fourth hurdle was history.

Now I did hear cries in the sidelines. One of the kids hollered, "Caroline's running the hurdles and she didn't fall yet!"

When I sailed over the fifth hurdle, my stomach was in knots and my legs were mushy. *Five.* Only one more to go. I'd never run so hard before. I focused on the sixth hurdle, again seeing the broom, and as I jumped over it, I felt an adrenaline rush for the first time in my life. I landed and ran the rest of the way to the finish line. *SIX! I DID IT!* I had cleared them all! Finally, I had done something right! Some of the kids clapped for me, and I felt on top of the world.

Then Mrs. Flary's voice rang across the field. "Caroline Zepperty, that was the most *terrible* time of the day! You took 13.8 seconds to run those hurdles. There's no way you're going to represent this school in the competition. Why did you even bother entering? You can't do this!"

I swallowed hard, trying to fight back the tears. Why was she so mean? Didn't she see how hard it was for me to even try? I screamed at her, "I don't care about any old stupid competition!" I ran away from her, into the school building, ignoring the pain in my legs. I went into my homeroom class and cried with my head on my desk.

A gentle voice said, "Caroline?"

I looked up and saw the principal and Mrs. Jamison standing by my desk. "Yes, Mr. Brownberg?" I hiccupped, unable to control my voice, or how my body shook.

Mrs. Jamison spoke before the principal said anything else. "Caroline, I have never seen anyone clear the hurdles with such height before! That was just wonderful. How did you do that?"

"I practiced at home," I said. "Ever since I saw the poster, I wanted to be able to jump over all the hurdles. So I used a broom and some sawhorses from my dad's workshop, and I jumped over the broom every night." My body still trembled, but now my voice was steady. "I just wanted to see if I could do it. And I *did!* I did all six of them. But Mrs. Flary only cared about the time. She told me I shouldn't have bothered."

Mr. Brownberg said, "Caroline, Mrs. Flary was wrong. You most definitely should have bothered, and you did. I'm very proud of you."

I smiled, feeling relief wash over me. "You are?"

Then, from outside, we all heard a sound that wasn't like the earlier cheers. Mrs. Jamison went to the window and looked out. "Caroline, please come to the window."

I got up quietly with Mr. Brownberg's hand at my elbow. He walked me to the window. Standing outside, in a half-circle, were a few of my classmates. They had their hands raised and were chanting, "Car-o-line. Car-o-line. Car-o-line."

Shocked, I looked up at Mr. Brownberg and Mrs. Jamison . . . and I was surprised to see tears streaming down their faces.

As I grew older, whenever I faced a new challenge, I remembered the sound of my name on people's lips . . . and the sight of two adults moved to tears over my accomplishment. If an overweight 11-year-old girl could jump all six of those hurdles, then the grownup Caroline could do anything she set her mind to do.

Christine M. Krannich has been writing short stories, narratives, and essays for years. She owes the submittal of this particular piece to her best friend, J, for his continued and loving support.

THE BRACELET

By Sarah Chauncey

"Are you *insane?*" I heard my friend Tom, his voice rising at the end of the sentence, his ever-so-slightly sibilant "s" dragging out 'insane.' I could see his eyebrows raised above those tortoiseshell coke-bottle glasses, that familiar look of incredulity. "I mean, it's very sweet of you, but... are you *insane?*"

Thing is, Tom died in January 1991. This was April 2003.

I was standing on a circular patch of grass outside the Finch subway station, the sole wearer of sweats and sneakers amongst a few dozen lithe bodies in Sugoi cycling shorts and Shimano toe-clip shoes. This was my first training ride for the 2003 Friends for Life Bike Rally, a six-day, 660-kilometer trek from Toronto to Montreal that would raise nearly half a million dollars for the Toronto People with AIDS Coalition.

A blond, tanned man gathered everyone round. "This is just a warmup," he said. "Thirty-five k. Shouldn't take more than an hour."

What the hell am I doing here?

Golden Boy was already out of sight, an acid-trip trail of brightly-colored jerseys on expensive bikes behind him. By the time I picked up my Kona hybrid and made it out of the parking lot, I was exhausted.

I thought of all the reasons I couldn't do the ride:

- I'm out of shape.
- The heat will give me migraines.
- I refuse to wear Spandex.
- I never finish anything.
- I suck.

I pictured Tom rolling his eyes. "You're *crazy.*" I took that as a dare. I had to do it.

Between 1989 and 1991, my three best friends died from AIDS. Before Tom, there was Ray, a swaggering, sexy man who survived a year longer than his doctors predicted. In between was Michael, Ray's partner, a slight man who was justifiably pessimistic. They were 35, 32, and 29, respectively, and their deaths shattered my heart.

After Ray died, I inherited the braided copper bracelet he always wore, the one Michael bought him during Carnivale in Rio one year. Before the first training ride, I wrapped the bracelet tightly around the handlebars for visual and visceral motivation.

When I arrived back at the subway, nearly three hours after I'd left, I could barely walk. *Maybe I should find another way to contribute.*

No.

The next week's training ride was 43k. Well-meaning veterans gave me advice:

"Gear down when you're going up hills."

"Gear up when you're going down hills."

"You really should get toe clips."

"Stand up."

"Sit down."

It never became easy. The first 20k were always hell. I began to accept that and force myself through it anyway. I tried not to care about being so slow that everyone else was finished before I hit the halfway mark.

I ripped out an Adidas ad from a running magazine. It read:

> The Seven Stages of Marathon
> 1. Ritual
> 2. Shock
> 3. Denial
> 4. Isolation
> 5. Despair
> 6. Affirmation
> 7. Renewal

When I was in stages four and five, I looked at the bracelet and thought of Ray, Tom and Michael. I remembered sitting with them one night at a local greasy spoon.

"Some day, there will be a million people with AIDS and the government will have to do something about it," Tom said.

Michael, the Eeyore of the group, turned to me. "Some day, Sarah, you'll think back on this night, and we'll all be dead."

The distances increased every weekend—50k, 75, 100. I wasn't the slowest anymore, but I still cherished my time alone. As I rode through the countryside, I talked to horses, cows, sheep and goats—and, of course, to the boys.

One Saturday, I took off by myself for what had become a familiar, easy ride to Oakville, 30k along the edge of the lake. I felt good, so I kept going to Burlington, another 35k—all downhill. By then it was well over 90 degrees; my swollen feet were bursting out of my shoes, and I realized I still faced roughly 60k of uphill riding. I focused on what I'd learned about hills: Don't look up, and just keep pedaling. One rotation at a time.

By the time I hit the Toronto city line, my feet were burning and blistered. I stopped at a corner store and bought two bags of ice. I hobbled over to the streetcar stop, hoisted my bike up, along with the bags of ice, and slumped into a double seat. I placed one bag of ice across each foot. Cold had never felt so good. The ice melted and trickled down the grooves of the streetcar floor. I began crying—uncontrollable sobs of exhaustion and defeat.

A month before we left for Montreal, I went for an early-evening spin in Sunnybrook Park. With trees on one side and the river on the other, I felt blissful, invincible.

Suddenly I was sliding down the stony riverbank on my left hip, knees twisted and bike in the air—still attached to my feet. A racer had run me off the path, coming around a blind curve. My cycling shorts were shredded. My arm was gashed. I dusted myself off, a little dazed, and calculated: I was still 15k from home. Walking wasn't an option. I got up and kept going.

Five minutes later, I veered to avoid a young boy on a tricycle, and again I went flying. Again I landed full-force on my left leg.

This time, it was harder to get back on the bike, but I didn't have a choice. After washing out my wounds with water from my Camelbak, I cycled very, very slowly. Everything seemed surreal and a bit out of sync.

Every day, I decided not to go through with the ride, and every day, I looked at the bracelet and committed to it again. Even as I was packing my camping gear into the two small Rubbermaid bins I'd been assigned, gathering maps for the routes and signing medical releases, I quit—again and again. Once I realized that my stuff was going to Montreal, I figured I might as well give it a shot.

On the second day of the ride, an hour from the lunch point, a searing poker bore into the side of my knee. For the first time, I understood the phrase *blinding pain*: I couldn't see. I stopped. I stretched. I gulped down Advil and Tylenol, but nothing helped, so I pedaled the next 20k using only my right leg. I had to ride in a van the rest of the way to the campground. I bawled—exhausted, anguished, and feeling like a failure.

Through massage and ice, my knee held up until the fifth day, when I was soaring through the Thousand Islands, keeping up with the middle of the pack. It was heaven. Until the pain returned with a suddenness that made me shriek.

I pulled over and lifted my left leg onto a park bench. I began screaming at my knee like some kind of overzealous coach. "Come on! You can't bail now! You have to start working! Get it together!"

Then I tried cajoling, "You've come so far, you've helped me so much. Just a few more kilometers, just one more day. You can do it. I know you can. Please?"

"Sarah," I heard Tom say, "Do you realize you're talking to your *knee*?"

At the next check-in point, the team doctor pulled me from the ride, explaining that I'd probably been injured back in Sunnybrook Park. Medically speaking, I shouldn't have been on the ride at all. I was to stay off my bike for the next three to six months.

So I didn't make it the full way. That was disappointing. But I made it 500k on a torn meniscus. I learned that I'm capable of far more than I ever imagined. I can do anything, as long as I approach my goals in small increments and don't think about the hill ahead. There may be forces outside my control that shape the outcome, but as long as I don't quit, I won't fail.

As for how I managed the 500 klicks? The bracelet. And the boys.

Sarah Chauncey is grateful to be a part of this project. A full-time writer and editor, she lives in Vancouver, British Columbia.

THE PRIZE IS THE JOURNEY

By Kesi Augustine

Snapshots from
a hike cradled by
the Adirondack Mountains:

A sign,
yellow arrow leaning
toward the trail ahead
thin and worm-like
burrowing sharply around shrubs and trees

Sun light visible in patches
along the forest floor
soft and delicate to the touch
even through a sneaker's sole

Unsteady footsteps
on the ground below
tight, hollow
like a drum's wide belly

Leaves crunch like popcorn underfoot
dominated by clouds of bugs
that hum melodies in ear tunnels

Steep hills, branches poking out
as banisters for support

Membrane-thin endurance
each moment calf-tightening
sweat stimulating
until time seems to be an illusion

And finally,
heaving a sigh when
nearing the top

The mountaintop's liberation
(or, what seemed to be a mountain)
was not the breathtaking view ahead,
but behind—
astonishment of exactly every
trip, fall, scrape, bruise,
bite, rock, climb,
and sweat drop
I somehow survived

For every moment drenched by
misplaced hope
a pot of gold was found
not behind the finish line
but using hidden strength
to overcome the barriers

Kesi Augustine is currently 15 years old and living in New York City. She attends Bard High School Early College and hopes to have one of her novels published in the future. Contact her at thisbrownskin@netscape.net.

RUNNING WITH THE WOLF PACK

By Roberta Beach Jacobson

I didn't get a chance to voice my opinion about running when I joined the Women's Army Corps. When Aunt Sam yelled, "Double-time, march!" off we went in a cloud of dust—no matter if our feet were blistered and our lungs felt ready to pop. Basic training is serious stuff. We'd run at 5 a.m. or at dusk—whenever they said, where ever they said.

I'd never run in my life, save for a few laps around my high school gym. I was a true *tenderfoot*. The first couple of days, our platoon practiced on an oval track, but soon we were running over steep hills, across sandy beaches, along winding forest paths. We would have run into the ocean had the drill sergeant pointed us in that direction, but (luckily) she never happened to think of it.

Did we actually want to run? No. At the outset, most of us would have voted not to run at the crack of dawn, but opted to stay in our bunks for a little more shut-eye. We complained, we winced, we cussed. It wasn't as though we ever did anything when we got to our destination. We'd simply loop around and run back to where we'd started from.

By the third week of training, we found our rhythm. We got in step and stayed in step, singing and clapping. The adventure of running as a team some-how seemed easier. Whereas at the outset, a mile seemed a sheer impossibility, soon we were chalking up three or more miles in a single stretch and hardly complaining. Our attitude had changed drastically.

No matter how exhausted we became, one thing for sure, we never gave up. As distances increased, we became a crazed pack of wild wolves, 50 females strong, charging along together, pushing ourselves to limits we'd never even imagined. There was another, somewhat hidden, motivation to keep us on our feet. When we weren't running, we were stuck in the barracks either scrubbing (a floor, a toilet, a hallway) or polishing (shoes, boots, anything metal), so run-ning had certain distinct advantages.

We never ran indoors. No matter if we would encounter sheets of rain, blinding sandstorms or even late snow flurries, we'd be outside in the fresh air, left, right, left, so many hundreds of thousands of steps you couldn't keep count. Running in our pack had become our way of life.

As all things do, our eight weeks of basic training drew to a close and it was time for 50 fast friends to part ways. Some would be shipped off to Korea, oth-ers to bases around the U.S., many of us to Europe.

The night before our graduation from basic training, we sat in a circle, our feet soaking in buckets of hot water. We laughed about how inept we'd been those first few days, how slow, how clumsy. It seemed a lifetime ago. At our graduation ceremony, we marched around the parade field at a normal walking pace. In our hearts we knew we were a wolf pack of strong women warriors— ready to run, run, run up against anything that dared to get in our way.

Roberta Beach Jacobson writes for True Confessions and True Experience. She makes her home in Greece. Contact her at www.travelwriters.com/Roberta.

STOP, THIEF!

By Charmian Christie

I've always been disgusted by news stories that report witnesses did nothing to help when a crime was committed. Normal people would step in, wouldn't they? My friends beg to differ. The argument goes like this:

Me: Once, I stood up to a large man who was bothering my sister at a bar.

Friends: That doesn't count. It was your sister.

Me: But I've helped at car accidents.

Friends: Accidents aren't crimes.

Me: If someone called for help, I'd help. How could you not?

Friend: Watching news from the safety of your living room and being there in person are different things. You can't judge unless you've been there.

Well, today I went there.

I was shopping at the mall with a friend when a middle-aged woman ran out of the jewelry store screaming, "Hold him!" I looked up to see a young man in a muscle shirt and backwards baseball cap running toward me at top speed. It took a few seconds to realize what was happening, but the clues fell into place like coins in a slot machine. Hysterical woman, high heels, navy blue skirt suit, bronze name badge flapping against her chest as she ran. Young man, furtive looks behind him, arms pushing people out of the way. Robbery in progress. And the thief was heading right for me.

People stopped and watched him run by, as if hypnotized by their confusion. But no one moved. Me? I got mad. Really mad. Someone had to do something.

And from the looks of things, that someone was me.

The next thing I knew, I was running after a pair of baggy jeans and a white muscle shirt and yelling with all the authority I could muster, "Grab him! Don't let him get away!"

Just turned 40, in heels and clutching my fancy Italian bag under my left arm, I ran after him as if I were the one who'd been robbed. *Not in my mall. Not in my community.* And he was heading right for an elderly man with a cane. At that moment, it hit me that someone could get hurt. I bellowed louder, louder than I've ever shouted before. My voice filled the mall. I kept repeating the same words over and over. "Grab him. Grab that man!" squeezing my bag to my ribs and pointing with my free hand. Couldn't they see him? He was running, running so hard he ran right out of his shoes. The abandoned shoes lay on the floor, looking no more threatening than if their owner had casually kicked them off to watch TV. Even his sneakers couldn't be trusted.

I was vaguely aware of people turning to watch. Some of them moved out of my way, others craned their necks to see what was happening. Parents pulled small children closer. Still, no one intervened.

As he rounded a corner, he slipped in his stocking feet. A group of men at the reality kiosk stopped their discussion and saw him slide into a railing. Having caught up, I grabbed the back of his T-shirt. My fingers touched the thin cotton, but the fistful of material slid from my grasp. He was stronger and faster and pulled away, heading for the exit.

Maybe it was the sight of a small woman chasing a large, muscular man. Or maybe my shouting finally made sense. But when this shoeless runner headed for the exit, a man in a dark green golf shirt tackled him to the ground. When they hit the floor, other would-be vigilantes joined in. There would be no escape for this thief. As they wrestled, the woman from the jewelry store arrived with mall security. Satisfied I could do nothing more, I left the men to be heroes and walked back to my friend.

She was chatting with two young women stoically guarding the shoes—just in case. The laces were stretched out, as if in surrender, having given up long before their owner. "Did they catch him?" they asked.

"Yes," I said, slightly out of breath. "*We* did." I pointed to the security guards frog-marching a stocking-footed man to the office.

"Way to go, girl!" my friend said. "I didn't know you had it in you."

Neither did I. Although I always suspected as much.

When I'm not chasing bad guys, I'm a mild-mannered freelance writer from Guelph, Ontario. My essays have appeared in various anthologies and been broadcast on CBC's national radio. www.charmian-christie.com

STRENGTH OF FAITH

"My lord, adjudge my strength, and set me where
I bear a little more than I can bear."

~ Elinor Wylie (*One Person*)

ONE OF GRANDMA'S SWEET LESSONS

By Barb Webb

Who would have ever thought the obligatory task of building a strawberry pretzel cake with my grandmother would endow me with my most valuable lesson in life?

As I recall, the kitchen dripped with the afternoon's summer heat and I'd much rather have been swimming down at the creek with my best friend, Jolene. Instead, Mama volunteered my services to prepare dessert for the evening's church supper. An awful topper to this dismal day. On my distinct list of things I'd rather not suffer through, church socials vied for the number one spot alongside having a cavity filled and being forced to eat collard greens.

Resigned to my hellacious labor, I watched Grandma rustle through the icebox and cupboards, pulling out a variety of items. Every minute or so, she'd stop to wipe the sweat from her brow with a hand-stitched handkerchief, then continue on until she assembled a mountainous stack atop the oak table in the center of the kitchen.

Grandpa carved the table before he passed on to what Grandma referred to as "Paradise." For years I thought Grandpa up and moved to some tropical island like the one I'd read about in our school-assigned reading. I sure hoped he didn't have any wild pigs to contend with, or nasty boys like those in *Lord of the Flies*.

Finally, Grandma stepped over and placed a wooden rolling pin in my hands. "First comes the fun part, Sugar."

I couldn't see any bit of fun past using the heavy pin as a baseball bat, maybe. Jolene would surely be up for rousing a team up, lickety-split. Thinking about Jolene conjured visions of cool creek water. No fair that she got to enjoy the splendors of the world while I slaved in this fiery inferno.

Grandma plucked a bag of pretzels from her pile on the table and ripped it open. Then she dumped them on the table just as plain as could be. I think my jaw might have bounced off the floor watching her.

"Come on over here now, Carrie Ann. I want you to crush these with that there rolling pin. Do you think you can manage?"

Boy, could I ever! In my short life, I'd never been invited by an adult to do anything contrary to my Mama's rules of etiquette. I was half-tempted to hug my grandmother and squeal with delight. I bobbed my head in affirmation and Grandma smiled back before she turned to busy herself with some other task.

Happily, I jumped into my assignment like our tabby taking to a silver vine until a smear of pretzel chunks and dust blanketed the surface of the table. I stepped back and admired my handiwork, almost oblivious to the sweat rolling down my back. *Almost.* As much delight as the defiant act brought, I'd still rather be swimming in the creek.

Grandma moved over to inspect my work. "That's a right fine job you did. Now gather them up in that there." She pointed towards a speckled bowl at the end of the table. "And when you're done, bring them over to the stove."

As she wobbled back over to the oven, I scooped the crumbs into the bowl. Sweeping them off the table wasn't nearly as satisfying as grinding them to a pulp.

When I filled the bowl and only a thin layer the dust remained on the smooth wooden surface, I carried the pretzels over to Grandma. A blast of heat from the gas oven knocked the air from my lungs. Good Lord in heaven, no wonder it was so piping hot in here. Grandma had the oven going *and* the front burner on.

I stretched out my hand to pass the bowl, trying to distance myself as much as possible from the blaze.

"Come on over here and pour those into this pot I'm stirring."

Inching forward, I narrowed my eyes to slits to avoid the sting of the heat and proceeded to deposit the contents of the bowl into the yellow liquid Grandma swished with a long wooden spoon. Butter, from the looks of it.

"Slow down, child. A little at a time."

"Sorry."

"It's okay, now. There, that's better."

Grandma stirred as I poured in the crushed pretzels a little at a time until the bowl emptied. By that point, my shirt was soaked through and drops of sweat nipped my eyes. Why in the world did Grandma go through all this heat and hassle for a church supper?

I stepped back from the oven, but the roomed boiled up like the interior of a volcano. Or so I imagined.

"What should I do next, Grandma?" Go outside and fetch some cool water from the pump? *Pretty please.* Even the Georgia-July sun would be preferable to this suffocating hot box.

"Go on over there and start slicing up those strawberries. Use your pretzel bowl to put the tops in and the white bowl for the berries."

I walked back over to the table and went about following orders. The strawberries were ice cold to my touch and I wished I could bury my body in the bowl to escape the drench of the kitchen. After using a nearby dish towel to mop my face, I cut berry after berry and plopped them into the mixing bowl. While I completed my chore, Grandma hummed a Revival tune, spread the pretzel mixture into two glass pans, and busied herself with the rest of the items on the kitchen table. I watched her make fresh whooping cream, then stir a variety of other things I couldn't quite identify into the cream. One ingredient looked like the cream cheese Mama spread on her morning muffins. Cream cheese and whooping cream seemed an odd concoction to my 12-year-old mind.

Without really noticing, I began humming along with Grandma until my fingers were stained red and my bowl was full. The heat in the room hadn't lightened, but my mood had.

Grandma spread the cream mixture over the pretzels layer and then came over to inspect my work. "Oh, you did a fine job there. Let me have that."

"Here you go." I passed the white bowl over. She poured a cup of sugar over the berries and tossed them in the bowl before ladling them in a thick layer over the contents already in the glass pans.

When she finished, she let out a huge sigh and fell back to lean against the kitchen sink, waving and flapping her arms around as if to air them out. The effort only served to create another string of moisture across her brow. "I swear this heat is going to be the death of me yet."

"It sure is hot," I readily agreed. Which continued to perplex me. Grandma could have made a simpler dessert, one that didn't require turning on the stove, or even had Mama pick some treats up and spared me the chore of helping and Grandma's health from ailing. Why all the fuss and bother?

We both rested a moment and I drew up the courage to ask her what was weighing on my mind. "May I ask you a question?"

"Why certainly, go on, child." She waved her hand towards me in a gesture of encouragement.

"Grandma, it's hotter than a dog's butt in a pepper patch today. Surely there has to be something else we could bring to the church supper. Mama could have probably picked up one of those fancy cakes from the store on the way home, even."

For a second I feared she'd grow angry and scold my intrusive inquiry, thinking me not adult enough to ask such questions. The smile spreading across her flushed cheeks, though, spoke otherwise. "Maybe, Sugar. But this here is a right suitable treat for the church supper table."

Glancing over at the fresh strawberry concoction, I had to admit it looked divine, although bakery cakes always suited me right fine, too. I didn't quite see the difference. It's what Grandma said next that enlightened my child's view and stuck with me throughout all of my adult life.

"Sugar, let me tell you, you can always take the easy way out, but there ain't nothing in life here worth sweat'n over, except the Lord."

When times are rough, things looks grim, or I'm simply in need of a reminder, I recall my grandmother's words of wisdom. Then I pull out my recipe file and whip up a batch of strawberry pretzel cake.

It truly is divine.

As a true Gemini, she has dual writing personalities: Barb authors nonfiction as Barb Webb (www.BarbWebb.com) and paranormal romance as Anne Leland (www.AnneLeland.com). She currently resides in Georgia with her husband and three children. Her current releases include The Mom's Guide to Earning and Saving Thousands on the Internet, McGraw Hill Publishing, January 2006.

THE PLATE

By Frank Baron

It was the lowest emotional point of my life. Despite her three stints in various rehab facilities, my wife's alcoholism was out of control. I had two young sons who needed me to be more than an "average" dad. My business was failing. I was hounded by creditors at work and at home, and flinched whenever the phone rang. I lived on coffee, nicotine, and antacids. Only the love for, and of, my sons, kept me from succumbing to despair.

One night, when both boys were asleep and the phone had been mercifully quiet for an hour, I collapsed in my chair and tried to read. That took too much concentration, so I turned on the television. The canned laughter, contrived plots, and vacuous lives seemed a cruel mockery. I turned it off.

The silence pressed against my ears. I didn't want to think; didn't want to consider tomorrow looming—another day like today, and the day before, and the weeks and months before that.

For some reason I began to talk with God. It wasn't a prayer really, just a chat—something I used to do as a child.

"God, I think I'm cracking here. There's too much for me to deal with and I'd sure appreciate it if you could help me out. My plate is too darn full."

Immediately, I heard a response. A pleasant, matter-of-fact voice said: "Can do, Frank. Here's a bigger plate."

I smiled, then chuckled, and in short order was laughing like a loon. It was perfect! I didn't have too many troubles to handle—I just needed a bigger plate.

It's no coincidence that my life improved from that moment on. Of course, my problems didn't disappear. But when they get to be a bit much, I just order a bigger plate. And God delivers.

Frank Baron is the author of What Fish Don't Want You to Know. He can be reached at his website: www.frankbaron.com.

OUR FACES ARE NOT OUR OWN

By Janet Ross-Pilla

How many of us have animated conversations with our own reflections? No, what we carry in our mind is the fixed image of the last thing we saw before leaving our vanity mirrors. We are oblivious to the animations being absorbed by all we greet—smiles, winks, frowns, wrinkles, emotions. When my daughter smiles, what she feels presented to the world is a full, balanced and complete smile that fills her face. What the world sees is a different story.

Since infancy, she has loved to laugh and does it freer and more heartfelt than anyone I have ever known. Leaving for college created a void of sound in our home and hearts because the music of her laughter was gone. I called her often to get my "fix." The phone call I received on June 12th, 2003 held the potential of silencing that wonderful sound forever.

The call came from the horse breeding ranch where my daughter, Jocelyn, worked. Her boss said there had been an accident. My husband and I should go to the hospital; Jocelyn was asking for us. Her boss was too calm when she told me of Jocelyn's trouble with the horse she had been told to train. The woman's composed demeanor might have reflected concern for the hour's drive ahead of us to get to the hospital where my daughter was taken. I tell myself now that perhaps she didn't want to alarm us. I do believe neither she nor anyone at the ranch could have grasped the extent of Jocelyn's injuries. How could they? No one saw it happen. The doctors at the first hospital she was taken to didn't have any idea either, or maybe were just not telling her father or me the complete story.

In the emergency room, the neurologist guided us to a visitor's lounge after a brief visit with our daughter. He turned the television off and politely asked the few visitors to leave so we could be alone. This alarmed me, but not as much as the hospital chaplain, who had been clutching my arm since I rushed through the doors a lifetime earlier. Before the doctor could speak, my husband turned to the chaplain and asked, "Is there some reason why you keep following us? I mean, should we be more fearful than we already are?"

She let go of my arm and tried to assure us through a quick nervous chuckle that this was her job as with every trauma patient's family, "Just in case you should need me." We all sat down on the tips of the vinyl-covered chairs and leaned toward each other like the huddle before a big game, except games do not twist my stomach into macramé.

"I've done preliminary tests," he began. We leaned closer. "She has what we call sixth and seventh nerve palsy." He was calm and gentle. He spoke in increments. I was at the mercy of his words; they were too slow. I wanted to tap the back of his head like when I give mechanical things a whack to get the electricity flowing again. Instead, I took in a breath that audibly vibrated along with my body. He bowed his head and went on. "The sixth nerve damage is evident in her inability to move her left eye beyond center." I began to rock in sharp forward motions. "The seventh nerve damage is evident in her inability to move the whole left side of her face." A moan emerged from somewhere. Had it come from me or my husband? The doctor continued, "She could not raise her eyebrow on my command, or smile . . ." By that time I was nestled into recesses of my mind, rocking and shaking. He couldn't see the baby girl with the sweet smile who I cradled in my arms. "Only time will tell," he concluded.

After Jocelyn was airlifted to the nearest number one trauma center, there were either chaotic moments with nurses, doctors, fluids, needles, X-rays, or a total absence of life and sound. I clutched one of her hands; her father squeezed the other. Importance came in waves in the emergency room of St. Paul's Regions Trauma Center.

My husband and I trailed behind the gurney as they rolled her up to ICU. It was there that I started grabbing doctors and chasing nurses, looking for answers to impossible questions. The trauma doctors in charge of head injuries were most accessible at first. They were many and everywhere at once. As soon as one would stand still long enough, I asked questions, many questions. They did not seem to have time or answers, at least none that I thought applied to what I was asking. The only time I received a definitive reaction was when I asked about the nerve damage to her face. The looks I received were those of a cross between indignation and abhorrence.

"There is no reason to worry about that now," one doctor said. Then he turned on his heel and left.

I was very confused. How could I not worry about my 20-year-old daughter's beautiful bright eyes and contagious smile? What were these people thinking?

I found out. Then I felt like a fool for caring about the vanity that our faces carry and present to the world. The damage that the horse had caused when she kicked my daughter in her head and into a wall was enough to have killed her many times over, but her spirit fought back. Her strong will had kept her conscious and calling until help came.

The reason our questions went unanswered was that the doctors did not know themselves how she was managing to stay alive considering the extent of fractures to her skull—eight and counting. That wasn't taking into account the multiple jaw fractures and swelling of her brain. So my daughter's charming smile was, as it should have been, the least of anyone's concern. I wasn't sure if each doctor thought the doctor before him or her had explained Jocelyn's condition to us, or if they were purposely holding information back. It didn't matter; no one could cleanse my feelings of being the worst mother ever for caring about my daughter's face, her smile, and the joy it has always brought me. The world and its vanity could be damned if she would only live, I thought.

I had many days in ICU to damn my own vanity before coming to terms with what it is about my daughter that gives me joy. It isn't just her smile. It is the essence that is her, the aura that connects her to God, The Supreme Being, Creator Spirit, Allah, or whatever name we give to the powers that watch over us all. It is her spirit, the sound of her laughter, and her love of and appreciation for life that penetrates my heart. A Zen master might ask, *What did she look like before she was born?* I could now answer, *She was a blank slate waiting for the day she could come into her senses—her soul.* She was born; she cried for the loss of safety that my womb had provided; she smiled at the world enabling newness to become Grace.

Strength came to me. Not from God, although I prayed. Not from any inner source, although I possessed it. Not from the medical profession, although they were competent. It came from the strongest energy surrounding me. It came from a survivor—my daughter. Certain crises in our lives also enable newness to become Grace. When I hear of the pain and loss of others, I think, *But for the Grace of God goes my daughter.* Her smile, whether half, whole or crooked, is not who she is. It is not what my pains of labor brought into the world. Her laughter rings true through the hearts of all who listen. She walks the earth leaving a welcome path for others to follow. She understands and speaks truths of life and they are hers to own because, more than many, she knows the alternative. She smiles a winning smile that to the world fills the right side of her face, but is still contagious and large enough to wrap around the world and meet itself on the other side.

After six months, the sixth nerve that controls her eye movement recovered enough to allow her the freedom of driving again without double vision, and her ophthalmologist holds hope for a full recovery of that nerve. Every time she sees him he expresses the miracle that she represents. He says he is glad to see her smiling at the grass from life's side. The nerve that controls the muscles to the left side of her face has been slower to show signs of improvement. Will that nerve heal and return a full-moon smile for the world to share? As that first doctor said, "Only time . . ." And with every half-moon smile, I thank God she has time and life in abundance—and she is courageously back in the saddle of her own horse.

Janet Ross-Pilla is a writer of fiction, including screenwriting. Awards for her writings include: finalist in 2005 Moondance Competition, Storyteller Award from the Hollywood Black Film Festival. Published stories appear in Summit Avenue Review and Ariston. She can be contacted through www.janetross-pilla.name.

NANNA

By Mary Broadbent

When I am feeling all alone,
in the darkness of the night,
I remember
Nanna saw an angel.
I believe because she believed.

When I am in doubt
if there really is a heaven,
I remember
Nanna saw the Lamb of God.
I believe because she believed.

If you are ever full of fear,
and see no goodness in the world

Remember,
there is a new angel
to scare away with kindness
any evil in the world.

Nanna walks with angels.
She is at peace.

I believe because she believed.

Mary Broadbent is a writer and educator living in New Hampshire. You can visit her website at www.marybroadbent.com.

BEING THERE

By Judy Gruen

Four years ago, a friend of mine lost both her parents in a three-month span. To add to this emotional juggernaut, she was planning her son's bar mitzvah at the same time. I told her, "I simply can't imagine how difficult this must be for you."

Soon after, I not only imagined it, I lived something close to it. That May, as I was ordering invitations for my eldest son's bar mitzvah, my mother was discovered to have end-stage cancer. Wrongly diagnosed with severe arthritis, Mom became alarmingly feeble, her pain unremitting. Further tests done at my sister's and my insistence revealed the harsh reality. Her incompetent doctor told us, "Take her home and make her comfortable. Gather the grandchildren around." He gave her a few weeks to a few months at best.

My sister and I were in a state of shock and despair. Cancer had already claimed our father, aunt, and grandmother. Our only brother had been killed in a car accident more than thirty years before. We could not fathom losing our mother, who had always been so strong both physically and psychologically, and whom we each loved beyond measure.

My bond with Mom had become increasingly intimate in recent years, enhanced in large part by our spending more time together, frequently over our special meals on Friday night or Saturday, our *Shabbat*. Nearly every week, Mom would come over and sit on the same spot on the tapestry-patterned living room couch as the kids snuggled next to her to show her their school projects, tell her about their week, or have her read them a story. Mom was also a lively favorite at our Shabbat tables, which were frequently populated by as many as a dozen guests. After retirement, Mom had studied diligently to learn enough about Jewish history and culture to become a docent at the Skirball Museum in Los Angeles. Her impressive knowledge and enthusiasm about the subject regularly enlivened our conversations. It also made me even more proud of her achievements.

I began my campaign to get Mom to come over as often as possible two years before this time, when my mother-in-law, whom we have since lost, was critically ill.

"We only have your dad and my mom left," I told my husband. "The rest of the week is too hectic for visits. We've got to get them over here for Shabbat." I had no idea how much more precious this time would become, no inkling that it would be so limited.

After Mom's devastating diagnosis, my sister and I were thrust in a whirlwind of preparing for hospice care in Mom's home. Given her prognosis, we also had to rush to settle certain business affairs. We tried each day to absorb the shock of it all, our expectations of a long future for Mom shattered. My life was surreal: On any given day I could be calling the hospice nurse to inquire about morphine dosages, while also waiting for the bar mitzvah caterer or photographer to call back.

The day I picked up the invitations, I headed out with heavy heart to visit Mom. I wondered how I could show the crisp invitations to her without my breaking down completely. For a brief moment I thought about not showing them to her at all. But how could I not show them? I hoped against hope that Mom, despite what the doctor said, might survive to see the first of her grandsons step up as a bar mitzvah and read from the Torah. Yet part of me feared that I might be sitting *shiva,* the traditional week of mourning, during a week anticipated for joy and celebration.

With a searing pain in my heart, I showed Mom the invitations. I also continued to share the bar mitzvah plans with her as they progressed. She liked to be in the know, even though she fully realized that she might not live to be at the event. Each day, I steeled myself to remain strong in her presence, allowing myself to cry alone in the car on the way home. Sometimes I was able to stick to this plan.

But Mom's deterioration was rapid and inescapable. It seemed nearly impossible for her to make the bar mitzvah, and she stopped asking about the details. While she didn't tell me directly, she confided in her hospice nurse that she wished I could move the bar mitzvah up.

When the nurse told me how deeply Mom worried about this, I was crushed. Mom understood that there was no way to move it up. But something had to be done. My husband and I came up with another idea: If Mom couldn't come to the bar mitzvah, we would bring a trial run of the event to her.

We invited the entire family to Mom's house for the following Sunday for brunch and to hear our son, Avi, rehearse his chanting of his Torah portion, or *parasha.* Our rabbi also came and wrapped Avi's brand-new *t'fillin* on his arm and head for the first time, explaining the significance not only of these phylacteries that Jewish men over the age of bar mitzvah wear during their morning prayers, but also part of the meaning behind Avi's *parasha,* called *V'etchanan.* In this chapter of the Torah, Moshe recounts his disappointment that despite his fervent pleas, God would not allow him to live to enter the land of Israel. Once again, the 3,000-year-old Torah resonated with our lives today in a way that was too deep for words.

It's a good thing we rushed to put together this trial run. If we had waited even one more week, Mom would have been too weak to appreciate what was happening. We took our last photos with her and the family that day, but I can hardly bear to look at them and be reminded of the last days of her decline. I much prefer earlier photos that are in many rooms of our home, photos that capture her true life spirit, her radiant beauty, and her elegance.

Mom passed away exactly two weeks before Avi's bar mitzvah. My week of *shiva* coincided with the first nine days of the Hebrew month of Av, historically a time of tragedy for the Jewish people. When I got up from *shiva*, I rushed to finish the details of the bar mitzvah for which there had been no time: menu planning, seating arrangements, getting suits tailored.

Fittingly, Avi's bar mitzvah fell on the Sabbath known in the Jewish calendar as Shabbat *Nachamu*. This is the first Sabbath immediately following the 9th day of Av, the saddest and most tragic day in all of Jewish history. On this Shabbat, we read a section from the book of Isaiah that promises comfort to the Jewish people for all the tragedies that have befallen us: "Comfort, comfort My people, says your God," Avi read, and the promise of comfort for my loss, and for the ongoing heartaches of our people, echoed in my heart and mind.

Many friends offered their own solace to me before and after Mom passed away, assuring me that she would be at the bar mitzvah, no matter what. I know they were right. The day could not have been anything but bittersweet for us, but our pain was mitigated—at least in part—by the joy in our son's rite of passage into Jewish manhood, and by the distinct sensation of Mom's spirit filling the room, emanating from her well-deserved seat in the World to Come.

Judy Gruen is an award-winning humorist and columnist for Religion News Service. Her most recent book is Till We Eat Again: Confessions of a Diet Dropout. Read more of her columns on www.judygruen.com, and write to her at judy@judygruen.com.

LEGLESS BUT UNDEFEATED

By Claudia Ann Sodaro

Some people have healthy legs and rarely use them. Brett had legs he couldn't use.

That blistering hot day on July 19, 1978, an invincible Brett, at 19, was looking forward to his lunch break while working for the railroad in Brunswick, Maryland. Riding atop a six-ton Pettibone Crane aroused feelings of power, manhood, and strength in him. His startling fall forward onto the tracks turned that machine into a monster, one capable of devouring and destroying Brett's life. As the crane rolled over his body, he heard a snap like a stick. It severed his spinal cord. He felt like an accordion being forced to play its last note for the dust and dirt of the earth.

Paralyzed from the waist down, he yelled, "Am I bleeding, am I bleeding?"

Just from the back of your head, came the answer.

His next sight was one of blue skies and clouds. He listened to the womp, womp, womp of the helicopter blades lifting him higher into the sky and landing him on the roof of Shock Trauma Center in Baltimore. He studied those clouds, believing they'd be the last sight he'd ever see before touring heaven or hell.

Thoughts raced through his mind: Am I going to die? Will I live and be paralyzed forever? He stared at hospital-room walls that gave no answers. *How am I going to tell Mom and Dad?* he wondered with anguish. His parents struggled with the pain of accepting that his younger brother, Dennis, had cerebral palsy and walked with canes. After Brett perceived that he'd never be able to walk again, the thought of his parents learning this fact was more emotionally crushing than the weight any heavy piece of equipment could impose on his body.

As he came to grips with his paralysis and its limitations, his life flashed before him and could be summed up in the Eagles' song "Life in the Fast Lane." All that changed as quickly as today becomes tomorrow. With a trachea tube down his throat, a newly inserted catheter and a rash developing all over his legs, he spent the first week in the hospital waiting for nightfall to bring the release of tears, sorrow, and frustration.

Eventually he shared those tears with many of the nurses who cried along with him. A sense of humor, his best quality, emerged once again as Brett realized that what others saw in him was painful for them, also. One morning, when a nurse asked him about the rash on his legs, Brett told her, "One blessing about being paralyzed is that you are numb, so it sure doesn't bother me."

A smile, he actually got a smile.

Going home was the hardest adjustment for him because the house wasn't set up for wheelchair access. He had to be lifted into and out of his wheelchair each time he left or returned home.

Brett developed a severe case of hiccups that lasted for a year and a half. Seizures of his diaphragm and a swollen spinal cord were determined to be the cause. A search for a cure brought him to Johns Hopkins Hospital. He felt guilty complaining of hiccups and vomiting when he was surrounded by people dying of cancer, but for him the discomfort was maddening.

He made a promise to God that if He would cure his hiccups, he would serve Him the rest of his life. They did subside with the aid of tubes inserted into his lower back and anti-seizure medication. He remembered feeling like "a banana being peeled away until my innermost core was exposed." Keeping his promise to serve, Brett attended church regularly and worked with youth ministry.

Some 15 years or so later, he played guitar in church with a group called Second Birth. Bluegrass gospel music was their specialty, and it attracted the attention of one lovely lady named Bonnie.

"Man, that's a pretty woman," Brett said to himself as she walked away, having just complimented his musical abilities. He invited her to a bluegrass festival, but they drove an hour past the Gettysburg, Pennsylvania exit they needed to take, and have been talking—and have been in love—ever since.

Bonnie and her two children, Bryan (7), and Kevin (5), became the light of Brett's life. He eventually married her and they bonded as a family. However, his injured legs landed him in the hospital more times than he spent at home with them. Sores and infections had to be treated and overnight stays were often necessary.

Brett wanted an end to these constant interruptions in his life; he chose to have his legs amputated from the thighs down. When young children in the hospital saw him, they would ask, "Where are your knees?"

He wondered how his children would react to this dramatic change in his physical appearance. They had grown accustomed to dangling legs in his wheelchair for the past two years.

His first day home, Bryan and Kevin eyed him with concern. Finally getting up the nerve, the older of the two asked the big question, "Daddy, where are your legs?"

Brett said, "I tied balloons to them and sent them up to heaven."

The answer made absolute sense to the children. Their big smiles revealed that and their dad was home with them where he belonged. Brett told Bonnie, "I went from a six-foot-four-inch tall guy to a four-foot-six midget all in one lifetime." A five-foot-seven Bonnie continues to tell Brett, "You always wanted a woman you could look up to and I always wanted a man I could push around."

A recent photo of Brett, which I was drawn to at a friend's house before we were ever introduced, shows a glowing, smiling man, sitting in his wheelchair, undefeated, with two large yellow clown-type shoes extended from his stumps. His favorite gift continues to be the joy and smiles he provides for others. If Brett can give so much without feeling limited, how much more can I give, realizing God's limitless blessings?

Claudia Ann Sodaro lives in Tarpons Springs, Florida with her husband Chuck. A published writer and composer of music, she volunteers as Leepa-Rattner Museum of Art docent and preschool storyteller at East Lake Library.

WALKING BY FAITH

By Brett James Sigler

Though I'm paralyzed from an accident,
God, help me not to waver.
Lord, I stand on the promises
made by you—my Savior.

Walking by faith and not by sight,
God is patiently teaching me.
Though my legs are gone now,
I still walk closely with thee.

Life from a wheelchair can be alienating
and I may feel out of place,
but like your servant, Paul,
grant me strength to run the race.

Life's physical barriers are a challenge.
I have learned to appreciate
problems are but hurdles
if I take a leap of faith.

At first glance, some view me as handicapped,
but a disabled world's what I see.
For they're lost without Christ,
and I wonder who's handicapped, them or me?

For in my weakness God is made strong.
What a small price to pay.
For Christ laid down His life all alone,
so in His glory I walk onward today!

AUNT CAROLYN'S FAITH

By Kimberly Gasuras-Lewis

I had just fled with my two children, 12-year-old Kyle and 4-year-old Kiana, to my parents' home a few miles away after an especially bad beating by my husband. I had taken his abuse for the six years we'd been married, but I knew in my heart this time I was not going back. The kids were upset over what they had just witnessed, but happy to be going to stay with their Yai Yai and Pappaw (Greek words for grandmother and grandfather). Even though I knew going back to Bob was out of the question, the fear of the unknown was very frightening. Where exactly was I going?

I was extremely depressed, disillusioned, and lost. While I had always had a strong faith in God, right now my faith was minimal. How could this be happening to me and my children? What had I done to deserve this? Here I was, at age 31, moving back in with my parents with two children in tow. Just before this latest blow-up in my marriage, I had quit my job to try my hand at writing full-time, but who could focus on writing with court dates coming up, living out of suitcases, trying to find a full-time job with insurance, and dodging my soon-to-be-ex-husband's every stalking move?

During my bleakest moment, my mother's younger sister, Carolyn, called from Oklahoma. Not only did her husband leave her seven months prior, after deciding he wanted to start drinking again after years of sobriety, but he took her off his insurance the day he left. She would not divorce him because of her Pentecostal beliefs, so he filed. This was not the bad news; there was something much worse.

"Kim, I know you're going through a tough time right now. I am praying for you and with faith in God, you will get through this hard time in your life and you and the children will get through it safely," Carolyn said.

"I know; it's just so hard. I'm afraid he's going to kill me. He always said he would if I left him," I said, my voice cracking as I tried to hold back the flow of tears that was always just under the surface.

Carolyn reassured me that no one was going to let that happen. She reminded me that I had family all around me, and God watching over me. Then, as gently as possible, she told me what was going on in her life.

"I found a lump in my breast months ago. I prayed it would just go away, but it didn't. It grew and began to hurt. Since I don't have health insurance, I put off going to the doctor until a few days ago," she said, her voice unwavering.

"I guess I waited too long, because it is cancerous and it has spread to my bloodstream. My doctors say I have about three months to live," Carolyn said, her voice still steady.

I couldn't hold back the tears any longer.

"I don't want you to die," I said through sobs.

"Please don't worry about me. I will be fine. I have prayed and gave it to God. He will decide when he wants me in heaven. I start chemotherapy on Monday. Please pray with me," she said.

Please, Jesus, protect Kim and the children and help them get through this tough time in their lives, she prayed, for me.

I told her I would have Mom call her when she got home, and I hung up. I couldn't believe the feeling of peace that had just come over me. I had been stressed out for so long and now I just felt better, hopeful, somehow. It had to be the prayer. I was gaining my faith back because of Carolyn. She was worried more about me than herself. All I had been able to think about was myself and my problems, but her situation was much worse. Yet she prayed for me and my children.

While my mom was able to make the trip from Ohio to Oklahoma several times over the coming months, I had to stay behind to take care of Kyle and Kiana. I had also begun a new job registering patients at our local hospital and had enrolled in college to complete my degree in social work so one day I could help other women that were suffering the way I had been.

Carolyn and I talked and prayed on the phone many times as she went through her chemotherapy with grace, style, and perseverance. She didn't even lose her hair as so many patients do. The three months the doctors had given Carolyn to live came and went, and a miracle happened. The cancer went into remission.

Even though most doctors do not like to admit anything they cannot explain medically, they all agreed there was no other explanation for her to be alive than a miracle of God.

While Carolyn was opposed to divorce, she was very supportive of mine.

"The man of the house should lead the family to follow Jesus. Bob was not doing that. You cannot stay in a relationship where your life and the kids' lives are in danger," she said many times to me as I went through with court (he got six months in jail) and completed the divorce proceedings.

Carolyn and I talked, cried, laughed, and prayed together over the phone for the next few years. Carolyn continued to minister to others and focused on keeping healthy, while I began a new life with my children. I completed college and got a job with our local Children Services Agency and gained back my self-esteem. I don't think I could have done it all if it wasn't for the example Aunt Carolyn put forth with her show of strength, courage, and her unwavering faith in God—her belief that all things work out in the end the way they are meant to be.

After four years in remission, the cancer was back again with a vengeance. It had spread to her bones and Carolyn died a few months later. She said it must be God's will and died with a smile on her face because she knew she was going to heaven.

At Carolyn's request, her body was flown back to Ohio so she could be buried beside her mother. The day of her funeral was a beautiful fall day, with all the colors and smells of that time of year. I read the poem "Safely Home" that Carolyn had asked me to read during her funeral. My favorite passage reads, "There is work still waiting for you, so you must not idly stand; Do it now while life remaineth—You shall rest in Jesus' land." It was the way Carolyn lived her life, and the lesson she taught by example: not to live idly by, letting obstacles stand in your way of living the life God meant for you to live.

Aunt Carolyn may be gone, but she lives on in my heart and in the person I have become. Because of her encouragement, faith, and example, I know that I can make it through anything that life hands me, as long as I keep the faith.

Kimberly Gasuras-Lewis is a freelance writer living in Bucyrus, Ohio, with her two children and her very new husband, Ron. She writes feature articles on a regular basis for the Bucyrus Telegraph-Forum and has been published in Ohio Outdoors and Recreation Newspaper.

WHEN LIFE GIVES YOU GRAPEFRUIT

By Cindy Appel

There's an old saying that goes, "When life gives you lemons, make lemonade." But what can you do when life gives you grapefruit?

My two daughters and I had arrived home just ten minutes before the storm struck. My youngest, worrying about our big dog that usually stayed outside, opened the back door for her mere moments before the first hailstones fell in what turned out to be the worst such storm in our area's history.

"Oh no, not again," I cried. Our house had been totally re-roofed only three months previous due to damage from the last big hailstorm barely one year ago. The year before that, the roof also had been damaged due to hail. Was this going to be an annual event?

For the first few minutes, the hailstones that rained down upon us were only golf ball-sized. Our trees' branches seemed to be slowing some of them down before they could collide solidly with my old car—its body full of little dents and dings from the year before, but its new windshield still in mint condition. I thanked God for the much-needed rain, but prayed that the hail would let up before any real damage could be done.

But was God really listening to my prayers? I wondered that as baseball-sized hail came crashing down only moments later. Soon ice chunks were pelting us mercilessly, and then—could it be? Hailstones as big as grapefruits battered our poor mulberry trees, severing small limbs as they fell. The lovely new windshield became a spider's web of cracks and lines.

It sounded as if giants standing in the clouds were having a contest to see which one of them could toss a bowling ball down upon the unsuspecting earth the hardest. *There goes the roof and the car,* I thought as the three of us stared out our front window in disbelief. Later that evening, my husband arrived home from work with his truck windshield practically lying in his glass-dusted lap.

It looked like a series of drive-by shootings had occurred when we took a quick glance at the cars up and down our street. But we had been fortunate. In other parts of town, boarded up front windows gave homes a sad, black-eyed appearance. We had valiantly fought the grapefruit-sized hail, but the grapefruit won.

"This storm definitely qualifies as one of life's 'lemons,'" I moaned, feeling only slightly less self-pity than the kid who pitches his opponents' game-winning home run. What good could God bring about by destroying two 13-year-old vehicles and a brand new roof? We wouldn't be driving junkers and band-aiding an old house together if we could afford better. It seemed God wanted to keep us in poverty forever, and, if that wasn't enough, He wanted to make sure we didn't harbor even a seed of hope of ever living a more comfortable life.

I turned to the Bible for solace. From the sixth chapter of Matthew I read, Store up for yourselves treasures in heaven where moth and rust do not destroy . . .

"Or hailstones either," I said bitterly.

". . . For where your treasure is, there your heart will be also."

I found little comfort in that particular passage because I kept seeing the word "treasure" as "necessity." Without a functioning car it was next to impossible find and keep a better-paying job, I reasoned. And without the better-paying job, we couldn't afford to pay for another roof—making it more than difficult to sell our old house and move away from this hail-stricken place.

But then my eyes wandered further down the page. No one can serve two masters. Either he will hate the one and love the other, or he will be devoted to the one and despise the other. You cannot serve both God and Money.

And then it jumped out at me: Who of you by worrying can add a single hour to his life?

True, I had been worrying needlessly. We were all fine. The roof hadn't sprung any leaks and the windshields could be fixed. I even could see well enough through my car's windshield to drive. It was just my pride that caused me to wince when I parked my ancient and hail-pummeled automobile with the cracked window besides a smooth and shiny, brand new car in the church parking lot that next Sunday.

After all, a car is just a way of getting from point A to point B. I go to church to serve God, not money. I thanked God for all the good things He had placed in my life—love, peace, grace, and forgiveness—things that couldn't be squashed by a chunk of ice. I saw then how God's love was truly my "treasure."

Lemons and grapefruits in life can come in all shapes and sizes. So, when life gives you grapefruits, quit complaining and make fruit salad. And be sure to thank the Man Upstairs.

Cindy Appel's articles and essays have appeared in over forty publications. She is the author of four romance novels and numerous short stories. Excerpts can be found at her website online: http://pages.sbcglobal.net/cynthianna.

PRAYER FOR STRENGTH

By Amy Brozio-Andrews

In the darkest of my nights
My soul is sodden with despair.
Too overwhelmed to look to heaven,
Yet I know You must be there.

Alone and cold, small and frail,
Forsaken and afraid,
Struggling to find some strength,
The stuff of which I'm made.

The smile of a stranger,
The kind word of a friend,
The small hand of a child,
When my world feels at its end,

To these tiny kindnesses
I hold tight with both hands;
Hope will blossom in my heart and
Peace will come again.

Amy Brozio-Andrews is a freelance book reviewer and the managing editor of Absolute Write.

ADD PRAYER IN TIMES OF CRISIS

By Mary Emma Allen

"All I can do is pray," Maria apologized. "I don't have much money to give or stuff to send to the flood victims. I can't travel there either." Then she repeated, "But I can pray," in a voice that seemed to be seeking approval or indicating she might have been criticized for this.

According to James 5:16, we are exhorted to pray for one another. The writer of this book in the Bible's New Testament further explains that fervent prayer avails much.

When I lay practically immobile in a body cast with a broken back for six weeks, wondering if I'd walk again, a friend sent me a card with this verse from the book of James. I was too weak to think deeply about its meaning, but in the years since, I realize how much prayer can mean.

During this time of healing and weakness, an umbrella of prayer from family and friends covered me. They were concerned about my well-being and continually gave prayers to God that I would heal and walk again. Amazingly, I regained the use of my body. Eleven years later, I have very few reminders of the accident.

Prayer played a role, we feel, in our son-in-law's recovery from cancer. When he was diagnosed, my mother-in-law called our daughter (her granddaughter) and said, "You must keep a positive attitude and pray. That's very important."

Mum had followed this strategy throughout her life, from the Depression years, raising eight boys, and surviving bouts with colon and breast cancer. She was a true believer in prayer.

I recall my grandmother praying when her son was in stationed in the Pacific during the latter part of World War II. "Alfred's gone to war," she announced, with tears in her eyes. I'd sit beside her in the evening while we read from her Bible. Then Nanny prayed, "Thank you, God, for all my blessings and for my family. Please watch over Alfred, wherever he is, and keep him safe. Bring him back to us soon. And watch over the others who are serving with Alfred."

"Alfred knows I'm praying for him," she'd say.

She was proud he'd enlisted to serve his country and fight for freedom. However, a mother couldn't help but worry. When she could do no more, Nanny always added prayer. Her son came home safely.

As you're doing all you can for flood survivors throughout the south, in their new homes and as they rebuild, add prayer. If you cannot do so much as others, add prayer. When you are at a loss concerning what you should do, add prayer.

Add prayer to your life in times of crisis. Add prayer when others are going through crisis. It may not solve all problems, at least in ways we think they should be solved. But prayer can bring a measure of peace . . . for ourselves and others.

Mary Emma Allen writes for children and adults from her multigenerational New Hampshire home. Her work appears in numerous anthologies. Read more about her writing and teaching at: http://homepage.fcgnetworks.net/jetent/mea; e-mail: me.allen@juno.com.

A WALK IN THE CLOUDS

By Julia Temlyn Prindle

I've dreamt that dream before: the one where I'm falling faster than gravity from unspeakable heights. But this is not a dream, and though I am not falling, every step is one step closer towards the same plunge that dreadfully haunts me in the night. Sixteen years old, facing, no—overcoming—an obstacle I never dreamed possible. Here, in the rainforest of Ghana, West Africa, I am about to cross one of the latest wonders of the world. Composed of a series of seven bridges, this jungle canopy walkway is one of only three in the entire world, and it is my opportunity to face my extreme fear of heights; a chance such as this may never come along again.

Thanks to a youth mission trip, I'm out in the middle of the Ghanaian rainforest, contemplating my fate. Nothing but rope suspension cables fixed to trees, ladders covered with heavy wooden planks forming a deck to walk across, and heavy rope handrails, are about to keep me from plunging into an abyss of lush, verdant trees, and trickling rivers that engulf into gushing waterfalls.

Funny, I did not feel as much apprehension or sickness about this trek as I did when I was challenged to ride Disney-MGM Studios' Twilight Zone Tower of Terror, a similar feat of height, with an elevator drop of 13 stories. This jungle canopy seemed only natural. No one was twisting my arm, forcing me to do this. It was as though God was asking me to prove my faith, to trust Him to take me to earthly heights to prepare me for spiritual heights.

As I inch across the bridge, I recall the hike up this mountain that brought us to the elevation of 100 feet. We had hiked for more than a mile, up steep rocks and grassy knolls, to a plateau. There at the plateau stood a tiny restaurant, quite resembling a Floridian-style café, perhaps like those found in the Keys. We sat outside, unable to order the food because of the thrifty mission style of preparing peanut butter and jelly sandwiches for road trips. At times during the month when we were on our own, taking a break from our group work, enjoying being tourists of this definitive country of Ghana, we would go to local restaurants, where a burger was served with goat cheese, and French fries closely resembled England's "chips." I find a wooden table with my comrades and settle down for a hearty lunch, hoping it will provide me with some strength to face this challenge of heights.

Unwrapping mine from the silver cellophane, I notice something different nestled inside the Ghanaian sweet bread—a favorite type of bread that we often bought from street peddlers—while sitting on our bus at stoplights. No, this is definitely not peanut butter and jelly. This is something new, something I had never tried, never even dared to try: sardines. Sardines, lettuce, and possibly even some sort of mayonnaise. Hmm . . . I take a bite, swallowing my pride as I've done many a time during this month-long trip. "Not too bad," I agree with my friends. The sardines were so finely sliced that it tasted not unlike a tuna sandwich. My mom would never believe I had tasted this new sandwich, but then again she would find it hard to believe many things that had already happened and that were yet to happen during this trip. I finish my sandwich and reach for my royal blue canteen, guzzling my safely boiled water—a must for Ghanaian water drinking because parasites were known to inhabit the water. Glass soda bottles were reused; we were advised to use straws when drinking out of soda bottles, or in extreme circumstances, learn to drink with our lips curled up inside our mouths, so that our mouths, resembling an elderly person without dentures, were barely touching the neck of the bottle. I take a deep breath and stand, ready to hike a bit more before reaching the peak, struggling to keep to my nerves in check.

Attempting to keep my mind on the matter ahead of me, and take in every single moment of this adventure, I concentrate on the bridge I am preparing to cross. I wait until the person in front of me has stepped onto the platform connecting the first two bridges. I take my first step, and feel the bridge wobble a bit underneath my feet. "Don't look down," I remind myself. I breathe deeply once more, steady my feet, say a quiet prayer, and continue walking, creating my own rhythm and pace. So far I'm doing fine, but then again, I've made it only halfway across the first bridge. I'm more than 100 feet above the ground, growing dizzy from looking at those trees and rivers far below. Behind and ahead of me, my friends tell me not to look down, so I look up, and consequently see the seemingly many more bridges that lie ahead, beckoning me to venture closer, mocking my fear, cringing at my bravery and anticipation. My foot inches near a crevice formed by the ropes, and I quickly snatch it back, afraid of getting it tangled in the beautiful, yet ensnaring weave. I step onto a circular platform surrounding a tree trunk, one of those same trees that deftly support the ends of each of the seven bridges. I lean against the trunk and await the signal for my journey onto the next bridge.

Only one person at a time may walk across the first; on the second and subsequent bridges one must walk halfway across before another can start his or her journey. My friend Jimmy waits patiently as I begin to cross the second bridge. I cautiously inch across, one foot in front of the other, so as not to make the bridge sway. When I have made it halfway across, Jimmy joins me, only not sauntering as I, but stepping lively, as if this bridge were a sidewalk on the firm ground. I feel it swaying beneath me, ruthless, relentless, unyielding. Panicking, I stop dead in my tracks, crying and forcefully telling him to stop walking so fast. Some of my friends, waiting ahead of me on the next platform, begin singing an inspirational song, "The name of the Lord is a strong tower; the righteous run into it, and they are saved," in an attempt to comfort me, and their purpose is successfully achieved. I breathe a sigh of relief as I near the next intersection of trees, thankful for the momentary rest they allow.

By the third and fourth bridges I've grown more confident. Determined, I stand in awe of the creation that surrounds me, breathing in the life and beauty that God has placed at this altitude. Had I not taken this step in faith I never would have come this far, and I would have missed out on such glorious, wondrous beauty. As if to add to my confidence, I realize that I am no longer climbing so high; the bridges climb steadily to more than 160 feet, then steadily lower again to their original altitude of 100 feet.

I've faced my fear, and looking down into the rainforest and jungle, I smile at God's creation, imagining Him smiling back. My friends cheer for me as I glide onto the seventh and final bridge. I have someone take my picture on that last bridge, knowing that my mom will never believe my journey to these heights without photographic proof. As I shuffle onto the embankment, into the little shack that signals the end of the bridge, I glance back at those gnarly ropes suspended from the watching arms of the forest, with tears in my eyes, not out of fear or even relief, but knowing that I have accomplished something enormous, knowing that I still have much more to accomplish in my life, and whether I fear or am eager, I know that by God's grace I can do all things!

Julia Temlyn Prindle is a writer and editor who has weathered many storms in her life, and finds that what doesn't kill you makes you stronger. Learn more about her at www.temlynwriting.com; e-mail: julia@temlynwriting.com.

GOD'S SOLACE

By Suzan L. Wiener

His hands reach out
to those who need His touch.
He'll be there because
He loves you so much.

Don't feel lost;
don't feel alone.
For with God,
you're not on your own.

He'll dry your tears
and lift your heart.
God brings joy
to a level of art.

Know you're loved
in every way
and God won't ever
lead you astray.

Suzan L. Wiener has had numerous poems, stories, article,s and shorter pieces appear in many major publications, such as Canadian Writer's Journal. Her unrhymed love poetry e-book is available at Lionsong Publication's website: http://lspbookstore.netfirms.com/fiction/poetry.htm.

CANCER: AN UNLIKELY
LEARNING EXPERIENCE

By Matthew Zachary

When I speak to audiences, I always start my speeches the same way: "My name is Matthew Zachary, and today is my best day."

I'm a musician, a composer, a husband, a brother, a son, and a Jew. I'm also a member of an elite club—one no one wants membership in. As of January 10, 1996, I became a cancer survivor.

When you're diagnosed with cancer—when you hear the words, "You have a brain tumor"— you suddenly find yourself less concerned with the small things in life.

That's the good side. The bad side? Everything you'd expect and then some. The realization of your own mortality, the fear of death, fear of what the treatments will bring.

For me, the fears went one step further: Would I play the piano again? The doctors said no. But I wouldn't accept this as an answer.

When I was 21, music was my life. I was studying music in my senior year of college, playing piano wherever I could on the side, and composing almost every spare minute of my days. Since the age of 11, I'd eaten, breathed, and slept music.

Then along came a brain tumor—a rare, malignant brain tumor. A medullablastoma the size of a golf ball, the kind most commonly found in children under 12 years old.

Until this point, my life had been pretty normal; I had my family, faith, friends, and music. Then I'd begun to experience troubling symptoms. I started to have trouble with my playing, and noticed problems with my left hand's dexterity and motor coordination. At first, I shrugged the symptoms off and simply pushed myself harder, practicing longer, trying to tell myself it was all nothing. But my body soon told me that something much more serious was going on. I suffered from agonizing headaches and fainting spells. My speech became slurred. And I continued to lose ability and function in my left hand.

And then that news—not just that I had cancer, but that I probably wouldn't play again. The chances for my survival with ability—much less vision, hearing, or balance—intact weren't good.

My answer to the doctors? "That's not good enough." I vowed to play again, no matter what. I chose treatment options that gave me the best chance for recovering the use of my hand and ability—sometimes even at a lower chance of survival. I had eight hours of surgery to remove the tumor (during which my cousin, a conservative rabbi, held a minyan at the Wailing Wall in Jerusalem), and went through dozens of full-body, high-dosage radiation treatments. I lost my hair, more than half my body weight, and the ability to eat solid food. I managed to graduate with the rest of my class on time in 1996, despite my illness.

And through all of it, I was determined: I would survive, and I would play again.

I prayed—I turned to my faith. There is something to be said for the healing power of prayer. Throughout adversity, one must maintain a strong spirit, no matter how difficult. With a positive mental attitude, some gut-determination, and little bit of hope, you will find that you can surprise yourself when you least expect it.

I found new meaning and depth in the Jewish holidays. Rosh Hashanah, for instance, has always represented a rebirth to me. It is the end of one chapter and the beginning of another. No matter how tragic or triumphant the previous chapter was, we must learn from our experiences in order to better ourselves and to make the coming year as fruitful as possible. I found new poignancy in and understanding of Yom Kippur as well—when we stand before God at our most humble, vulnerable moment, as our sins are weighed and we unassumingly pray to be inscribed in the book of life for the coming year. So I indeed felt humbled and reminded that life was in fact about forgiveness (especially towards ourselves).

Then came the recovery period. I slept most of the time, often 23 hours a day, but even in those few minutes I had each day, I'd practice. I'd scribble down music notes when a melody came to me—and, surprisingly, they did. Even with the pain and the tiredness, the music in my mind had still survived. Day by day, month by month, year by year I practiced, re-teaching myself the music and technique my fingers had once known without effort.

It's been ten years since my survival. I returned to my music, to the jazz-inspired compositions of innocence and emotion that I'd envisioned all my life. I released my first album, *Scribblings*, based on those long-ago scribblings during treatment and recovery. In 2000, I recorded my second album, *Every Step of the Way*, about the journey back into light and health. To mark my ten-year anniversary in remission, I will be releasing my third solo piano album, *Absolving Destiny*, in the spring of 2006.

I'm always writing, playing, and recording. I get out, live my life, and each day—no matter what challenges it brings—is my best day. I speak to audiences of patients about survival, to audiences of doctors and nurses about caregiving, about connecting with those they treat as human beings.

Most important, when I speak to those audiences, I perform the songs that came to me along the way—the songs that speak louder than any words about the fact that life can and will go on—often, even richer than before.

I tell people, although it's painful at times, when there are no answers, do not ask, "Why?" Do not ask, "Why me? Why not someone else?" Life is what you make of it. Instead, I tell them, ask, "Where?"—"Where am I going next?"

Cancer isn't exactly the learning experience I'd prescribe to most. But in a strange way, it is an experience I'm grateful for. Cancer gave me the ability to look within, and to find my own strength—to truly know what I'm capable of. And as a musician and composer, it gave me the comfort of knowing the music that was so important to me would always be a part of my heart and life. Ten years later, the two—life and music—are still too deeply intertwined for me to separate, as intertwined as life and faith. The challenge to survive can be a humbling experience, for life is indeed as precious and frail as faith itself.

I wake up each day and give thanks for my life. I am proud to be a Jew and I am proud to have faith in a way that I cannot put into words. I believe that having faith helped me to prepare me for the challenges of survival and the success I have today.

My name is Matthew Zachary. And today is my best day.

Recording artist, composer, and public speaker Matthew Zachary brings hope and inspiration to thousands through his two hit solo piano albums as well as his acclaimed speaking and concert appearances nationwide. Matthew is also founder and chairman of Steps For Living, a nonprofit organization that uses music and the arts to increase the quality of life for anyone affected by a diagnosis of cancer. For more information on Matthew, visit www.MatthewZachary.com, www.StepsForLiving.org, or send e-mail to sfl@stepsforliving.org.

A DIFFERENT KIND OF MARATHON

By Jean Marie Wiesen

I run as fast as I can. I can't stop. No. I have to keep moving; nothing can stand in my way. The finish line lies over the next rise of the rolling hills. The ground feels soft under my feet, cushioning my stride. The sun beats down, unforgiving, relentless. Sweat drips from my temples, splashing onto my shoulders. I can feel it running down my arms, and my legs feel slick. The breeze I feel on my face does nothing to cool my body. My efforts will not go unanswered; the Lord is my strength, my core, my center. He will never fail me, of that I am sure.

I'm thirsty, my throat is dry, and my lips are parched. My stomach aches; it tightens more as I push along, and it's threatening to cramp. *No, not now, I have to keep moving.* Why am I doing this, edging my body beyond its limits? What good can come of it? Is there a point? Yes, there has to be; otherwise, why am I here? What am I supposed to learn? I don't know, I can't think. Legs, don't fail me now. My pace has to remain steady. Focus, yes, that's the answer. Maintain focus at any and all cost. Am I running toward a goal or from fear? I don't know. It doesn't matter. I *cannot* stop.

My grandparents cheer wildly as I move along the winding course. A number of friends support my efforts as well. Danny's there too; I miss him so. He smiles and tells me not to be afraid. It's odd; I don't actually hear them. No, I *feel* their words of encouragement. Sounds are muted; however, they're integrated into my very being.

My chest hurts, my legs burn. Drawing more air isn't helping. I've maxed out on additional oxygen. I put my head down, I lean into the hill, I dig deep, I dig deeper. My legs are pumping as hard and fast as they can, my arms swing close to my sides. I'm covered in sweat, my heart pounds in my ears; all is still around me, no sound. What happened? My entire body is about to burst. I've hit the wall. I can't get through it, over it, or around it. Now what? Oh, Lord, please help. I can't do it without you. Give me your hand—I'll take it and never let go. I promise, Lord. No! Don't leave; take me with you. Lord! No, you can't leave me here. I'll die. I'm thirsty, Lord; I'll die. Wait! I am dying.

It's okay now; something shifted. Running doesn't hurt my body anymore; I'm in the zone. I'm floating, I'm safe. The pain has subsided. I'm going to make it. Wow. Thank you Lord, I knew you wouldn't abandon me. I can feel your touch, your warmth—ah, the sun feels good. I've stopped sweating. It's okay now. I can breathe, I'm relaxed . . . thank you, Lord. This is amazing—I've *never* felt such peace. That was a tough wall to break through, now I'm gliding with no effort. I have all the breath I need.

Wait, I'm choking. My chest hurts again. I cough. Ouch! What was that? Something is being pulled from my throat. God, it's painful! I cough and can't stop; the more I cough, the pain increases. I feel lousy. It all feels wrong. My body jerks. My head feels stuffed with cotton and nothing makes sense. What happened to the peace and serenity? Where . . .

"Hey, we thought we lost you. Welcome back. I'm Maureen, your nurse for the day.

"Don't fight so hard. We're pulling out the breathing tube. It's okay—if you can't breathe on your own, we'll put it back.

"No? Well then, try taking a few slow breaths."

I cough more and struggle desperately for air. I'm convinced all my oxygen was drawn from my lungs along with the tube. Have to breathe on my own, have to dig deep again. Lord, if I've ever needed You, now's the time.

Where am I? The calendar on the wall to my right is barely in focus. I strain to read it: June, 1996. What happened to the first part of the year? Where am I? I shut my eyes and reach inside my mind for answers. Nothing. I try harder. Club Yale? Yes! My home away from home. The information slowly surfaces; flying with a head cold hemorrhaged my eardrums and destroyed my balance. C'mon mind, give me more, please. Neurosurgery a few years ago? That's right! And I landed in the 1 percent category that gets aseptic meningitis from the surgery. Oh Lord, I recall the head pain now. Nearly four long years of hell . . . my head doesn't hurt? Is it possible the coma worked? Ah, yes, I'm an experiment. A rat in a maze. The doctor said the pento-barbituate-induced coma had a 53 percent mortality rate. I did question my sanity in agreeing to this.

Wow, I'm alive! I beat the odds. My brain still feels muddled. I know where I am, but I still can't figure out how long I've been here.

My heart races while I attempt to fill my lungs. I close my eyes; I want to return to my earlier serenity. I want to feel the warmth of the sun. The present reality doesn't belong to me. How do I know the pain won't return? Can I risk staying here? Danny, I want to go with you—take my hand. We were meant to be together. I wish you had not waited until you were so sick to tell me how much you loved me. Ah, I'm floating once again. I'm safe and warm. Peace returns . . .

"Hey, you just got back, don't leave again. We need you to stay with us. And when you can, I'd love to hear where you've been for the last four days. We didn't think you'd survive—you were only supposed to be under for 20 hours. I believe you've been the recipient of lots of prayers. Yes, that's right, rest now. The worst is over."

Jean Marie Wiesen is an EMT with Westport Volunteer Emergency Medical Services in Connecticut. She is the author of the WWII novel Threads in Time. She is also a photographer and socializes/raises guide dogs for Puppies Behind Bars. Visit her at www.jeanmariewiesen.com.

Role Models of Strength

"Who better than those on the next step up, to guide your climb?"

~ Aviva Rifka Bhandari

PEACEKEEPER'S COFFEE

By Doug Setter

It was a long drive to Okachani. More than two and a half hours in a convoy of the Canadian M113 APCs (Armored Personnel Carriers), which rattled and shook as they kicked up clouds of dust along the dirt roads of the former Yugoslavia.

The 4:30 a.m. start was no big deal. Neither was the long drive and diet of road dust. It came with the job. But the attitude from the locals . . . that was starting to wear on our sense of humor.

When we got to Okachani, we passed by the usual war-torn roofless brick houses with their weed-infested yards. Some of the intact houses had Serbian villagers still living in them, determined to stay. As our carriers rumbled past, they gave us a curious look, a scowl, or ignored us altogether while they tended their gardens and eked out their existence. We would wave or just act like they were not there. Sort of a mutual tolerance.

Today our job was maintenance patrol, which was a nice name for cleaning up after someone else. It was a tiresome routine of repairing damages or replacing materials stolen by the locals. The soldiers kept grumbling about the constant clean-up. I kept hearing, "Just let the two sides go at it and sort it out. Isn't that what they want?"

I was a sergeant in charge of an eight-man section responsible for a defensive area in the corner of the village. This defensive area was a couple of houses that we had previously cleared of glass, debris, and bloody mattresses. We had then fortified the buildings with sand bags, chicken wire and lumber. We would routinely check on its sturdiness, then grudgingly clean up debris and replace stolen corrugated iron, wire, plywood, and sand bags.

"Look at the bloody mess," someone cursed. "Let's just shoot the . . ."

I cut him off.

"Let's just get the job done," I snapped. "The day's not getting any cooler."

Months ago, I had all of these high ideals about helping second- or third-world countries, protecting the down-trodden and saving all the homeless children. We were going to set everything right and make the world a better place. Now, I was not so sure. Not quite the noble liberator that I thought that I was. Every report that I heard of torture, infanticide, or execution was starting to wear at me. Every time some drunken villager pointed an assault rifle or pistol at us or told us to "get out of my country," I thought what a waste of time this was getting to be. And our own (Canadian) media relentlessly criticized us every step of the way. It was sticking straws *into* this camel's back. Maybe the U.N. or someone was benefiting from this misery.

I had even grown numb to the loud griping that I was hearing today as the soldiers hauled the sheets of corrugated iron. Other days I would tell them to keep it down. But today, between constant clean-ups, restacking sand bags, and make-work projects from headquarters (like making flower beds), I really could give a flying leap.

I turned my attention back to unloading the APC. The soldiers were getting careless with flinging off the supplies. Too much flying metal, dust, spit, and swearing. I was about to shout something when this young woman showed up. I never had seen her before, and had no idea from which shell-ridden shack she came out of. But there she was, with a tray of small ceramic cups.

Right here, amongst the crumbling buildings, bullet-holed walls and broken glass, was this Serbian villager with a tray of what smelled like coffee. Hostess-style, just like she was serving some friends at a tea party.

She was a slim lady with well-kept dark hair, dressed in a dark sleeveless top and light-colored shorts. Lines on her worry-etched face and missing teeth made her look older than her probable late twenties. Despite the sadness in her eyes, she spoke cheerfully in Serbo-Croatian as she gestured the tray towards me. It was a curious sight, but my mother had always taught me that it was rude to refuse hospitality, so the "show no favoritism" rule could bend some.

"Over here," I hollered at my section. "C'mon for a coffee break."

"Hvallah (thank you)," I said, gratefully accepting one of the small cups full of floating coffee grounds. I sipped it carefully as the soldiers in my section each grabbed a cup, like kids after candy. The stuff was warm and bitter and I do not like coffee. But I swallowed it back, just the same.

I replaced my cup on the tray with another "hvallah" followed by some theatrics to describe "delicious." Some of the guys gave a satiety performance of "mmmmmmm, coffeeeee" that rivaled Homer Simpson with a doughnut.

She cheerfully said something, flashing that sweet, missing-tooth grin and walked away amongst the rubble. Her head was held high and her walk was proud. How could she be like that when she had next to nothing?

For all we knew, that might have been the last of her coffee. Something that she normally reserved for her own family's meager meals. Then there *we* were, six healthy, fit Canadian solders, with food in our bellies, money in the bank, and a few thousand dollars of dentistry in each of our yaps.

We must have been thinking the same thing. For the next few hours, sweat poured off us like running water as we worked hard and steady into the late afternoon. And not a single gripe came from anyone.

Doug Setter served as an infantry sergeant for a U.N. peacekeeping mission in Croatia (former Yugoslavia) in 1993. Doug has written a crime column for the Vancouver Review and his articles have appeared in Outdoor Canada, Inside Kung Fu, North American Survival Guide, Vitality Magazine and The Maple Leaf. He has served as a military paratrooper, completed five marathons, competed in kick-boxing, and holds a Bachelor of Human Ecology. He currently lives in Chilliwack, British Columbia, and divides his time between personal training, writing, and instructing for the military.

THE ACE I GOT DEALT

By C.J. Piperly

The day my daddy's plane went down in the ocean, he wasn't flying one of his photo reconnaissance missions over war-wracked Vietnam. He was a naval aviator, flying back to the base on Guam one night with two of his buddies after a trip to the mainland.

One of the fuel lines on the plane malfunctioned, and they couldn't use the fuel in their second tank. Daddy said it was "like running out of fuel with a full tank of gas." Rapidly losing altitude, they radioed their status and position, donned their chutes, and opened a trap-door-type hatch in the belly of the aircraft. Tom Peters, a civilian technical advisor in their squadron, slid down the hatch first. Daddy waited a few beats, then slid down second. Commander Edwards was to slide down last.

Daddy's chute opened properly and he splashed down in the Marianas Trench—the deepest part of any ocean on the planet, well-populated with shark and jellyfish.

At that moment, my mom was at the home of one of Daddy's fellow officers. While Mom chatted with the officer's wife, their phone rang. The officer picked up, but Mom didn't pay much attention until she heard the officer say, "So they're all in the drink, then?" Her gut turned to stone—those words were every Navy wife's worst fear.

Daddy had gotten his life raft inflated, and he had a light and other small tools from his survival vest, but it was a long, miserable wait in pitch darkness with 12-foot waves crashing over him. One of those waves carried a poisonous man-o-war. Its tentacles took Daddy across the throat, leaving their stinging toxins in his skin. That same wave swept the man-o-war away as quickly as it had come, but Daddy was now in serious need of medical attention. Breathing got tougher and tougher.

Four hours after he'd had to ditch in the ocean, the rescue helicopter found him. Though they continued searching for days, no rescue team ever found Tom Peters, or Commander Edwards, or the plane.

All Daddy could eat for more than a week was chicken soup. He attended memorials for his buddies, barely able to speak his condolences to Tom's and Commander Edwards's widows. Worse, he and my mother knew any sympathy they offered would sound hollow to the grieving women. In addition to his own mourning, Daddy was left to wonder, *What's so special about me? Why did I get found and they didn't?* And Mom had the same torturous, unanswerable questions: *What's so special about me? Why did my husband come back and theirs didn't?* Mom's told me that to this day, they sometimes still wonder about those questions.

Living at the naval base in Guam, a speck in the South Pacific, also offered snakes, giant bugs, and typhoons. On more than one occasion, Mom and Fred, their dog, had to hunker down in furious storms alone in their trailer, without Daddy. When typhoons came, all the pilots were ordered to fly the airplanes to a safe, sunny location, and all the wives were left to ride out the storm. There were also rabid animals and, if the supply ships were delayed, scant supplies. (Mom once had to wrap Christmas presents with Band-Aids because the island ran out of Scotch tape.)

So many other things have tested my parents over their lives. Mom's father committing suicide. Both of Daddy's parents dying of cancer. Five years of frustration in not getting pregnant—only to have their first pregnancy end in miscarriage. A massive, near-fatal hemorrhage immediately after I, the result of their first successful pregnancy, was born. Mom's struggle to recover from alcoholism—and both of them never once letting me or my brother see that anything was wrong. And being the only ones in the family able to make arrangements for and execute the wills of seven separate elderly relatives, none of whom had children of their own.

These hardships could have crippled them, turned them bitter, driven them mad. But they found solace and strength in each other. Not a small part of that was keeping and appreciating their sense of humor. They were so in love, and still are to this day, that not one thing won against them.

Whenever my adolescent self did the spoiled-brat routine, or complained that my friends' parents let them do anything they wanted, my mom would always tell me, "I'm the ace you got dealt, kid." At the time they were just words, didn't mean anything. But with the 20-20 lens of hindsight, I've learned that my ace was really both of them together, as a unit.

I got dealt such an amazing hand with these two. My ace gave me not only them, but other powerful cards—and showed me exactly how to use them in the game for maximum effect. I'm not always smart enough to use those other cards the way they taught me, but I learn, and I remember. I especially remember their strength when they wanted to give up, and how they discovered that even their weakest points ended up being strong enough.

They're the best thing that ever happened to me. They're the ace I got dealt. And I stand in awe.

By Frank Baron

Like most Canadians who were alive 25 years ago, I was captivated by the Terry Fox story. Terry had his right leg amputated when he was 18 because of cancer. He wanted to do something to help others with the disease. At the age of 21, he decided to run across Canada, from the east coast to the west, and raise money for cancer research along the way. On April 12, 1980, he dipped his artificial leg into the Atlantic Ocean in St. John's Newfoundland and began.

He averaged 26 miles (42 kilometers) per day, a full marathon, and called his effort the Marathon Of Hope. Soon, his progress was featured on nightly newscasts coast-to-coast. Every Canadian became familiar with the brave, boyishly handsome young man with the hippity-hoppity, mile-eating gait. Crowds gathered whenever he neared a new town or city to cheer him on and donate to his cause.

On September 1st, near Thunder Bay Ontario; 143 days, 5,373 kilometers, 3,339 miles into his amazing journey; Terry was forced to stop. His cancer had returned, this time in his lungs. We wept along with him when he announced the news. When he died a few months later, at the age of 22, a nation mourned. He was, and will ever remain, Canada's favorite son.

He left an ache in our hearts, but also a wonderful legacy. Every September, in hundreds of communities across Canada and the world, people take part in the Terry Fox Run. They run, walk, or bike 10 kilometers in his memory, to raise money for the cause he loved. Eighty-seven cents of every dollar raised goes to fund cancer research and to date, more than $360 million has been raised world-wide.

I'd often contemplated taking part in a Terry Fox Run but never did. I donated money over the years but didn't participate in the event itself. When I had my heart attack in November 2004, I realized I had to make some lifestyle changes, including (gulp) exercising. I started walking and worked myself up to a couple of kilometers (1.2 miles) most every day. When the buzz began about this year's walk, the 25th anniversary of Terry's run, I decided I would take part.

What follows is a recounting of that day.

Sunday, September 18th. The 25th Annual Terry Fox Run.

Awake at 6:15 a.m. This is Very Wrong. Had my alarm set for 8:00. Athletes need their rest. I tell myself to go back to sleep. I refuse. I toss and turn. It's no use. Try to convince myself that my body, like that of all finely-tuned athletes, is merely raring to go. Then I face reality and realize I can't fall back to sleep because I'm nervous. So I get up.

9:50 - It's a fine, sunny day and we hop into the car to head for the starting point. Sons #1 and #2 have decided to join their old man. We are also accompanied by one of #2's urchin friends. I suspect they've come to laugh at me but I keep my suspicions to myself. No point jump-starting the little bassets. There are a zillion cars and we have to park about three blocks away. I fret about this extra walking distance, haunted by an ironic vision of me collapsing three blocks from the finish line. #1 reassuringly tells me not to be an idiot.

10:15 - We've registered, gotten ribbons, and are at the official Start. The main pack started at 10:00. Police have closed the roads on this part of the route. The bikers and many of the runners are already out of sight but there are about 2,000 people and an elephant in the mob ahead of us. I rub my eyes but the elephant does not go away. Apparently the local zoo is taking part, too.

Kilometer 1 - There is a sign marking the distance with some encouraging words written below. That's nice. So far, so good. It's kinda hot and I can feel sweat forming between my shoulder blades. #1 is carrying the water bottles and camera in a backpack. He's a good boy. I take a sip of water.

Kilometer 2 - The road curves and I lose sight of the elephant and much of the main pack of people. A rather chubby woman pushing a child in a stroller is about 20 feet in front of me. I decide to pass her.

Kilometer 3 - The sweat is beading on my forehead now, too. I swipe at it now and again. Still feel pretty good. I've nearly pulled even with that chubby-but-plucky woman pushing the stroller. I consider staying put, using her draft to pull me along, but decide that would be cheating. Besides, I've been doing that for a kilometer now. Heroically, I dig down for another gear, pull even with her, nod and smile, then surge inches ahead.

Kilometer 4 - I may be paying for that burst of speed. Legs are barking a bit but not too badly. Have to circumnavigate, for the third time, evidence that an elephant has been here recently. It's not like sidestepping a bit of dog poop. Have been taking regular sips of water. Mustn't dehydrate. All the pros say so. Cannot stifle groan when I see the next long portion of road is uphill.

Kilometer 4.5 (approximately) - The pros said nothing about having to pee from all that stupid hydrating. Luckily, we are still in a rural section of town. I veer off the road and behind some bushes to unhydrate. #1 snickers from the roadside and makes jokes. I cannot kill him because he is carrying the supplies.

Kilometer 5 - Half-way! And a little less than an hour has passed! The tortuous uphill portion is nearly over and there's a rest station set up here by volunteers. Bless their hearts. They offer water, wedges of oranges, and bite-size bits of chocolate and granola bars. The volunteers are all women, mostly either teens, or in their 60s. I stifle the urge to hug them all, fearing I may lean on them too heavily and be unable to stand upright again. Or worse. I can see the headline in the local paper: *Walk Participant Crushes Local Matron - Blames Fumes From Elephant Poop.*

Kilometer 6 - My longest training walk was 5.5 kilometers, so this marker is significant. I take stock of the old bod. Legs aren't bad. Feet seem okay. Heart doesn't feel like a Keith Moon solo. I squint behind me. Is that a chubby woman pushing a child's stroller? Sheesh. The woman is indomitable.

Kilometer 7 - I don't know what they've been feeding that darn elephant but it's sure not agreeing with him. I must have gone half a kilometer out of my way so far to avoid its tons of undigested matter. Son #2 and his buddy have spent the last three or four kilometers running ahead a few hundred yards, then back, then ahead again. They jump around, swat overhanging tree branches, and just generally goof off. I hate them.

Kilometer 8 - Am approaching one of the main intersections downtown and a nice policeman has stopped traffic in all directions for me to cross. The lads are somewhat ahead of me now, having already crossed. I am momentarily confused, unsure whether he wants me to go south, and then west, or west and then south. I pause, thinking. There are lines of cars paused, too, in all directions. The policeman's smile falters a bit while I am thinking and he suggests, "Why not cross on the diagonal? I got them all stopped." I smile back and agree. It feels weird crossing a main intersection diagonally. A few drivers honk supportively as I make my way to the other side. Everyone is so friendly.

Kilometer 9 - A theory I'd been working on for the last 15 minutes or so has evolved into a certainty, one with potentially tragic ramifications: The sidewalks are uneven. Some of the cracks separate slabs of sidewalk as much as two millimeters off level. A person could be dragging his feet along, thinking it's all nice and even, then catch his toe and go tumbling ass over tea kettle. I mentally draft a scathing letter to my local councilman and tell Son #1 to make a note and find out who our local councilman is.

Kilometer 9.5 (approximately) - Despite the treacherous sidewalk cracks, it now appears certain I'll finish. I feel a bit giddy. I tempt the sidewalk gods by breaking into a lumbering jog for five or six steps. #1 frowns and tells me he'll kill me if I have another heart attack now. I agree the timing would be unfortunate this close to the finish and settle back into a trudge.

12:15 - The Finish Line! We did it in two hours. Not bad. Volunteers applaud and offer water bottles but I'm hydrated to the gills. We high-five each other and wander around. A band plays. We find a pavilion full of hot dogs and help ourselves. Not daring to sit down, lest I not be able to get up again, I lean against a fence.

I'm not euphoric. I'm too tired for euphoria. But I'm satisfied. And fairly sure I have no elephant doo-doo on my shoes.

Frank Baron is the author of What Fish Don't Want You to Know. *He can be reached at his website: www.frankbaron.com.*

LITTLE NIÑO

By Allison Cooke

Dear Little Niño,
your gentle smile
contrasts your circumstance,
this mean environment.

I look around
and I want to ask,
"What is it
that makes you smile?"

You run and laugh,
so enchantingly,
on dirt streets
in sandals too large for your lively feet.

You scrounge for your meals,
and it shows
in your frail body,
but still you share with me.

I'm here to help you
but you insist
on helping me,
and that is your strength.

Allison Cooke is a 17-year-old high school student living in Ontario, Canada. Besides writing, she enjoys playing the cello and taking care of a menagerie of small animals. This is her first published piece.

ABOUT JORGE:
WALKING THE TALK

By Lisa M. Abbate

May 2005. Machu Picchu, Peru. Stun-glorious is a made-up term I use in my mind to describe natural beauty of a staggering magnitude. If my secret word combo was in the dictionary, the best way to define it would be to include a picture of the sight before me, of Machu Picchu and the surrounding mountains. Craggy, massive, green, pristine—and a river runs through it. This archeological site, considered sacred by many and sometimes called the "Lost City of the Incas," which sprawls on a wide mountain ridge some 8,000 feet above sea level, was abandoned at some point. No one knows why. I imagine it was someone's secret garden until it was rediscovered in 1911.

I'd always wanted to visit Peru, and there I was, traveling with a group of like-minded people, of seekers, if you will, and like many of Peru's visitors, we were exploring, studying and discussing the many sacred sites that we visited on this exceptional journey. But we had something, some *one*, few people visiting this country had. We had Jorge. I was in the presence of a man who is said to walk in both worlds, and this guy was no Peruvian flake.

We were sitting in a small stone enclosure at the edge of a cliff at Machu Picchu. Jorge Luiz was teaching me to see the energy of the mountains—the *apus*—surrounding Machu Picchu. "Hold out your index finger and move it towards you, until you see two of them." *Act casual*, I thought, *interested, but not giddy*. I was eager, but nervous. After all my practice and experimenting alone, in various places near where I lived—the woods around Walden Pond or the shores of Lake Champlain, perhaps I was finally in the presence of someone I could really learn from. I was allegedly in the presence of a bona-fide shaman. I tried to relax so I could focus on his instructions and not miss the moment.

I use the word shaman to describe Jorge because it provides a point of reference, and it isn't exactly *untrue*, but in his culture, his spiritual tradition, he is known as a *chakaruna*—a bridge between worlds, a connector to the authentic self. I don't know what a *chakaruna* is supposed to look like but I wouldn't have guessed this. Whenever I saw Jorge, he was in standard-issue casual attire—khakis and a cotton button-down. And sunscreen on our long days in the sun. I'm guessing his age to be late forties or early fifties; it's hard to tell with that youthful-looking Peruvian skin.

He spoke extensively, but rarely about himself, so I had to do a little digging. Jorge grew up as a part of a large family; I don't know exactly how many siblings but it sounds like there were many. They lived modestly, austerely, in a one-room dwelling. A grandfather was a herder of llamas and alpacas; his mother came from a long line of healers. In his youth, Jorge had no interest in becoming a healer or exploring his own spirituality—he wanted none of it. Later on, an inquiry from the BBC was a catalyst for his becoming who he is today.

He did well in school and got a job as a tour guide, where he developed a love of textiles and art of the cultures of Peru, and became a passionate collector. Our group of twenty-something people stayed in one of his hotels, and I had the opportunity to peruse some of the countless artifacts that he has acquired through the years—found, bought, or received as gifts. He really has enough to house his own museum.

One day, while Jorge was in his twenties, the BBC showed up. They were doing a program on native beliefs and religions, and wanted to meet the holy people, the shamans of the region. Would Jorge track down some of these people—the ones who were the most genuine—and find out if they would be willing to participate? He agreed, and his world got bigger. In his travels and his searches in Peru and Bolivia, Jorge found the histories and meanings of the artifacts he collected to be very different from what he thought he knew. He found higher and deeper truths about the universe, about humanity and the many civilizations that lived in Peru throughout human history, and about his own inner world.

I gazed at the mountains. Nothing. After several attempts, though, I perceived something. Just above the mountain range, I could see, well, something that was like a mist, but it wasn't a mist. Or a tad opalescent, but not quite. Perhaps like what you might imagine a halo to be, that extended, uncurled, across the top of the range. I'd seen a similar phenomenon in my practices back home, but was never sure if I was really seeing something because it was subtle, and I had no one to share my experiences with. I described what I was seeing to Jorge—actually we both described what I was seeing at the same time.

I am skeptical of spiritual healers and self-help "gurus"—people only have something to teach if they have really learned, transformed, even, and are sincere in their desire to pass on their knowledge. How many are the real deal, and how many are out to make a buck off of the vulnerability of others? Of all of the books on healing, personal growth, shamanism, and the stories by the alleged "finders" that the seekers seek, I always wonder what percentage is true experience, not embellished by the writer or publisher for the purpose of selling more books. With Jorge, I sensed a substance behind his words. This was a man who walked his talk. Through Jorge, we experienced some of the rituals of his spiritual and ancestral lineage. We blew coca leaves to the wind in ancient ceremonies designed to open our hearts. We hiked into remote areas, where tourists typically didn't go, where he introduced us to ancient rock carvings, explaining some of the meanings of the symbols. He was always teaching. The message, sometimes direct and sometimes subtle, was often about connecting with the authentic self, and celebrating life.

There are three fundamental Incan laws: *munay* (love, attitude of love for all creation), *llancay* (work or service, expression of the love of all creation) and *yachay* (wisdom of connecting to the spiritual self). I learned from Jorge, and I believe his time with our group was, in part, his endeavor to serve all three of them.

At one point, he brought a woman aboard the bus we traveled on, a young woman he knew who wanted to go to the U.S., and introduced her. She wanted to leave, but needed a job, and a work permit, and would anyone be able to give her a job in the States and help her get on her feet?

My digging also turned up this: At Christmas time, Jorge Luis has the children from the village and surrounding areas to his hotel on Lake Titicaca for a day of art and celebration. And he does a lot of other work with children, my friend tells me. One of his art projects with kids is to give them pillows, and has art teachers help them draw on them their dreams of what they will be when they grow up.

At another site, an old Peruvian Indian woman who lived nearby, whom Jorge had helped get medical attention in the past, came to see him. She seemed distressed. I watched as he took the time to sit and speak with her a little way from where our group stood, and I could see that she was comforted by his words and his presence. Then she walked with us a while across the rugged terrain, we in high-tech hiking boots and she in her wide skirts and nimble, dusty, cracked-skin feet. She never stumbled. Some of us gave her money when she left.

I get the impression from my exchange with Jorge that, with practice, I will see more of the "energy body," or aura, if you will, of the *apus*. Perhaps I will see more color, or a wider energetic field. I don't know; I haven't gotten that far yet. Jorge also spoke to me of the happiness, the contentment, he felt when gazing at the mountains and their energy. "Keep trying, and the joy will come." The next morning, when we all left the hotel at 5:15 to hop the bus back up to Machu Picchu and watch the sun rise over the *apus*, I knew what he meant.

Lisa M. Abbate is a writer and freelance editor. She can be reached at www.wordmountain.com.

PERCEIVING THE POSSIBLE

By Ellen Lewis Lief

When I was 12 or 13 years old, I wanted to do something for someone else. Maybe because my father was a socialist, or because my mother was a Pollyanna, I felt that anyone who "had" and wasn't sharing with the "have-nots" was making a serious mistake. It's funny that I thought of myself as one who "has." Now that I'm grown with a family of my own, I understand how close to the edge we lived then. But I certainly had food and shelter and love and all my faculties and lots of youthful energy. I knew that I could be useful to someone.

I called the Volunteers of America organization. I was an avid reader, and I liked to read aloud. The volunteer bureau hooked me up with a blind couple who lived in San Pablo, California. She had no sight at all. He could tell light from dark, but that was about it. My mother drove me to their house on Saturdays. Sometimes she stayed, sometimes she dropped me off.

Their neighborhood had few trees. The lawns in front of the small houses were just patches of weeds, or bare dirt. Most of the houses could have stood some fresh paint. Their house was clean, modest, and dark inside. It was sparsely furnished. That, I learned, was not so much because it was all they could afford, but because it was more practical for them. They were a very sweet couple. Good-natured, warm and generous. He loved to say, "'I see,' said the blind man!" It was his favorite joke.

I read articles from the local newspaper, some mail, recipes. The woman was particularly interested in transcribing her recipes into Braille. She taught me the Braille alphabet. I remember that there are six dots: two rows across, three down. The position of the dots in the rectangle makes the letters. The letter "a" is a dot by itself. Although I'd come to their house to be of service to them, I was learning a valuable skill that I wish I'd retained. It was a bit upside-down that she was teaching me, but it felt perfectly natural. Perhaps I knew that because it was good for me to help them, it was good for them to help me, too.

They loved children and longed to raise a family of their own. After a long time of trying, they finally succeeded in adopting a little boy. He was about four years old, blind and deaf. The adoption agency said he was also "retarded," but his new mom wasn't so sure. She felt he just hadn't had a chance.

They were so happy to have that little boy. He sat at the kitchen table with us, skinny and shirtless, banging a wooden spoon on a pot and nodding his head. She loved him so much; her face lit up when she talked about him. He'd been there maybe a month when I met him. She communicated with him by touching him. He loved her, too. He would lean into her touch to be closer to her. They made a happy family.

At the time, I wondered how a blind mom and dad could take care of a blind and deaf little boy. But I wondered it in the way kids wonder about how grown-ups do any of the things they do—like drive, or smoke, or build skyscrapers.

Now I wonder about it in the way a new parent wonders how single parents do it, or parents of twins do it, or single parents of twins. It's more than wonder. It's awe. When you find yourself having difficulties, it is hard to imagine how someone who has even fewer resources than you have and even more challenges can possibly manage. I guess we use ourselves and our experiences as our touchstone for what can and can't be done. I feel lucky that the family in San Pablo is part of my experience. I know that what might seem to be impossible, is possible.

Ellen Lewis Lief, an unemployed, or perhaps retired, technical writer struggling to live up to the name "homemaker," lives in California's Great Valley with her two daughters, two cats, two bettas, several fish named Bob, thousands of dust-bunnies, and one and only husband.

LEGACY: THOUGHTS ON COURAGE AND INSPIRATION

By Patti Wigington

My great-grandmother was born in the woods of Kentucky in 1891, just one more mouth to feed in a long line of dirt farmers. The cabin her family lived in was small—about 15 feet by 12, if the foundation stones that remain today are any indicator of square footage. There was no floor, except the hard-packed Kentucky soil, and the family was so poor that Gert didn't get her first pair of shoes until she started school.

By the time I was born, Gert was nearly 70. I don't recall hearing her talk about her childhood much, but I do remember that she was one heck of a good cook. The problem was that she could cook only for large groups of people, so if we went to visit her at my grandparents' house, she'd fix enough to feed a small army. I remember her as being very loving toward me and my younger brother, and I always liked going to see her because she did all those things that great-grandmothers do—sneaking candy to us when our parents weren't look-ing, or giving us a dollar just because she could. Great-grandma privilege, I sup-pose you'd call it.

My mom grew up with Gert as a part of her life, and told me about Gert's two marriages. The first was to my great-grandfather, and the pair of them tol-erated each other enough to produce two handsome sons and a lot of animos-ity. After two and a half decades of misery, they finally got around to getting a divorce. Later, she remarried—this time to a decent fellow who actually loved her—and remained married to him for another two and a half decades, until his death. I frequently heard stories of Gert's life in Chicago, where she owned and operated a successful restaurant—apparently her pizzas were the toast of the South Side, and rumor has it that she sold her secret sauce recipe to the com-pany that later evolved into Chicago Uno. She was a woman to be reckoned with: a businesswoman in a big city in a time when women weren't supposed to be businesswomen. Yes, Gert was one tough cookie.

She passed away when I was 13, and it wasn't until long after she'd died that we began to uncover the trail of secret heartbreak and pain that had shaped her life.

About ten years after her death, I began doing some genealogy research, and unearthed information about Gert's early marriage. By early, I mean 14-year-old-and-daddy's-got-a-shotgun early. This revelation was previously unknown to anyone including her son, who was my grandfather. We had no idea where Gert had been or what she'd done between her 1906 marriage to a fellow named Vol-lie and her marriage to my great-grandfather in 1913. By doing a bit more digging, I was able to uncover even more earth-shattering news: Apparently a few months after this quickie wedding, Gert had given birth to a baby girl.

More information began to unravel, and a picture of Gert formed that was quite different from the strong, confident woman I had known. I learned that her mother had died shortly after birthing yet another child when Gert was four, and that her father had promptly ridden off to Missouri and returned three months later with a new young wife. Gert's new stepmother was fairy-tale cruel, and when she gave birth to daughters of her own, treated them far better than her seven stepchildren. At about the age of five, Gert's job was to help with the food preparation for the family and other farm workers, rolling out biscuit dough. She was so small that she had to stand on a box to reach the tabletop.

Her father had little time or interest to devote to his children. I have a photo of him; he appears stern and distant, clutching his bible. My mother tells me that when he died in 1936, Gert didn't go home to Kentucky for the funeral. In fact, she rarely went back. The little girl who had rolled biscuits for her unloving father and his shrew of a wife had fled Kentucky as soon as she could, by marrying early and getting out of the hills.

That youthful romance, as appealing as it must have been to a teenage girl in 1906 Kentucky, was as doomed as the home she left behind. According to a cousin of mine, descended from Gert's sister, the bridegroom was actually a nephew of Gert's stepmother. His name was Vollie Carey, and I have a mental image of him being a smooth talker, a fancy city boy ready to sweep farm girls off their feet with his debonair ways and seductive lies. Whatever he was, I don't know. After their wedding, Gert and Vollie got on a train to Chicago, and on the journey Gert made the happy announcement that she was with child. Vollie got off the train to buy cigars somewhere between Hawesville and Chicago, and never bothered to get back on.

She never saw him again.

Gert got to Chicago, moved in with her sister, and eventually delivered a healthy baby girl. Because she had to go to work to support herself, she put her daughter in a temporary foster home. Unfortunately, there was some sort of misunderstanding and when Gert went to collect her baby, the child was gone. She'd been adopted by some other family.

Gert spent years trying to find her missing daughter, even enlisting the aid of her brother-in-law, a lieutenant in the Chicago Fire Department, but had no luck. There's no record of any dissolution of her marriage to Vollie, but in 1913 she married my great-grandfather, the son of German immigrants. In spite of the constant fighting and bickering, they had two boys, both of whom went on to fight in World War II. She never mentioned her baby girl, their half-sister, and carried the secret to her grave.

Knowing this story now, as an adult, it makes me wonder. What did she see when she held me as a baby? Was it painful for her, or did it bring her joy? I'd like to think it was the latter. Looking back at the heartbreak she must have felt—and seeing it from the perspective of a parent myself—I often wonder how she had the strength to go on. How did she get up and drag herself to work each morning? How did she continue to function when her soul had been torn in two?

I suspect it was quite simply because she had no other choice. When life deals us big lumps of tragedy and pain, we either shut down or we go on. There's no in between. We do what we have to do, and if that means we force ourselves out of bed and go to work and become successful and then cry ourselves to sleep at night, then that's what happens. We adapt, we overcome, we go on.

I look at her life—what I know of it now—and I am honored to have her blood in my veins. Somewhere out there, there may be someone descended from a baby accidentally adopted one day in Chicago nearly a century ago. Someone who has Gert's blood in them just as I do. Perhaps some day they will do some digging into their own family history and discover that their grand-mother was adopted. Perhaps they'll figure out who her biological mother was, and maybe even track me down.

If they do, I hope I can honor Gert by making sure they know of her forti-tude and her courage. And if they don't, it's okay. Because her legacy was to in-spire me, and I plan to make sure that my children know her story, and that their children do as well.

I only hope that if I am ever faced with such despair, I can meet it with the strength and bravery that she did so many years ago.

Patti Wigington is an award-winning writer with a central Ohio newspaper. Her free-lance articles have appeared in Gaea's Cauldron, Twinshelp, and Pediatrics for Parents, and she is a contributing editor for Garden and Hearth.

LARGER ARENAS

By John Vanek

The guard scowled at me, then at my competitor's pass, then back at me. He snickered something about snowballs in hell. Although I stood more than six feet tall and weighed 200 pounds, he apparently saw the gray hair peeking out from under my "U.S.A." cap and didn't like my chances for a medal at the 23rd Olympiad in Los Angeles. Begrudgingly, he finally stamped the pass. I returned his scowl and attempted to maintain the appearance of a world-class athlete as I sucked in my middle-aged paunch. The guard, of course, was right. My friend, an Olympic coach, had given me a competitor's pass and this once in a lifetime chance to walk in a world that few will ever know. The escalating threat of terrorism would soon eliminate the magical freedom that I enjoyed that summer day in 1984.

Placing the competitor's pass around my neck, I strode into the locker room, where the pungent aroma of liniment and sweat assaulted me. Giant men, who dwarfed my every dimension, spoke in whispers, if at all. Breathing was audible. If the wooden benches had been pews, this could have been a church. Some heads were bowed; others stared like statues. After years of preparation, the best wrestlers in the world were here to prove it one more time.

I savored the moment—a sports fan transported to Oz—as I floated from the locker room into an enormous arena roofed in a rainbow of flags. I wandered from match to match, watching victory thrill some and defeat agonize others. When the gold medal match in the super heavyweight division of Greco-Roman wrestling was announced, I positioned myself next to the mat.

As the American hoisted his 240-pound frame into the ring, a sudden silence filled the arena, as if the "mute" button had been pushed. His baby face and mop of dark hair seemed out of place, small and fragile above a warrior's body. When the word "indomitable" was coined, they must have had this man-child in mind. In the unlimited weight class, he had already defeated opponents twice his size, using strength and quickness. Then, the announcer boomed, "Jeffrey Blatnick – U.S.A." and the crowd's roar rattled the rafters.

Many people remember Carl Lewis, who duplicated Jesse Owens' 1936 grand slam track and field performance at the 1984 Olympics. And who can forget Mary Lou Retton, the perky teen who dazzled us with her smile and style, winning the woman's gymnastic championship with perfect "10s" in her final events? Yet, Blatnick's Olympic teammates selected *him* for the ultimate honor: carrying the American flag in the Closing Ceremonies. How many people remember his name? Who cares about wrestling? For me, Blatnick's story is not about wrestling or Olympic medals; it's about the human spirit—a story of journey as much as destination.

All anyone can hope for in this life is to find a passion. Jeff found his in wrestling. He won two NCAA championships and qualified for the Olympic team. The U.S. boycott of the 1980 games in Moscow froze athletes' dreams in the Cold War, but Jeff kept training and winning until fate blind-sided him. In 1982, he found a lump in his neck and was diagnosed with Hodgkin's lymphoma—cancer of the lymph nodes. After surgery to remove his spleen and numerous radiation treatments, Jeff began rebuilding his dream when most would have simply rejoiced at being alive.

Now, one victory from the gold medal, outweighed by 35 pounds, his father's words echoed, "You've come too far to let anything stop you now!" The bell rang and Blatnick attacked. As I stood ringside, the surging roar of the crowd drowned out the sound of the two giants crashing together, then onto the mat, but I felt the rumble through my bones, as urgent and primal as an earthquake. Near the epicenter, I almost expected the mat to thunder open and swallow them both. Counterattack followed each attack. Aftershock followed aftershock. When it ended, Blatnick collapsed to his knees, hands clasped in prayer position in the city of angels, tears on his cheeks. He had prevailed, 2 – 0.

Fate, however, scheduled an unexpected rematch in 1985, when his Hodgkin's disease recurred. After 28 chemotherapy sessions, Blatnick won his rematch with cancer, but retired from wrestling competition. Never a victim, always a victor, Jeff chose opportunity over obstacles. He turned his life's journey into a journey for life by spreading his philosophy of "winning in adversity" as a motivational speaker, a member of The President's Council of Fitness and Sport, and a fund-raiser for numerous charities, including the American Cancer Society.

Looking back over the years, I marvel at how our concept of "hero" has morphed into a caricature. Today, superstars come in the flavor-of-the-month, as numerous as gold stars in a kindergarten. Greatness is measured in dollars, celebrity, and outrageous behavior. The world may someday forget his name, but I pray that his spirit is never forgotten. When Jeffrey Blatnick mounted the pedestal in 1984 and the American flag danced from the rafters to the strains of our national anthem, I looked into the eyes and the heart of a "super man." As officials placed the gold medal around his neck for his victory in the ring, I wept for his triumph in a larger arena.

John Vanek has published in Heartlands, Natural Bridge, Pebble Lake Review, Fourth River, JAMA, and Chicken Soup for the Caregiver's Soul. He has a poem in the permanent collection of the George Bush Presidential Library.

A HERO'S MEDAL

By Olinda Wheatley

My friend and hero Bob McGuire was a gentle man, a big brother to my family. Everyone looked forward to visits with Bob, even the squirrels in his backyard—he fed them cookies on a regular basis. He was active in the community. He gave freely of his beautiful tenor voice, his patriotism, his sense of humor, and his devotion to family and friends. He married his high-school sweetheart, Mary, when he returned from World War II. For many decades, Bob was reluctant to talk of his war experiences. I consider it an honor that he shared some of his story with me before he died.

Bob was Staff Sgt. Robert E. McGuire in the Tank Corps during World War II. He escaped injury the day the tank he occupied was hit by mortar fire. The next day, he drove another tank—and when that one was destroyed, he was taken prisoner.

In 1945, somewhere outside of Nuremberg, Bob and a friend escaped from Stalag 13C, a German prison camp. They rested and slept during the day, hiding wherever they could. They traveled by night, heading towards what they thought would be freedom.

On their journey during one of those days, they fell asleep in the woods. Bob awoke to find a gun held to his face by an SS Trooper. He was recaptured, along with his friend. They were arrested and brought to the Palace of Justice in Nuremberg. From there, with other prisoners, they were forced on a road march and walked on the famous Autobahn Highway.

When the weather turned foggy one night, Bob and his friend made another escape, but were captured again. This time, they were taken to an SS camp. They were made to stand outside the headquarters building, waiting for the Oberstadt (top officer) to come outside. Although Bob didn't go into detail, he implied that any infraction of the officer's whim or of camp rules would pose a threat to a prisoner's life.

While the prisoners waited, a guard noticed that Bob was wearing what is known as the "Miraculous Medal," with a picture of Mary, the Mother of Jesus, engraved on it. The Medal's inception was in 1830, when Catherine Labouré, a French nun, experienced a vision of the Mother of Jesus, who requested Catherine have a medal created, with a specific design also revealed in a vision. This medal is now worn by millions of Catholics as a sign of their special devotion to Mary for her intercession with prayers regarding health and safety.

The guard told Bob to remove the medal. Bob refused. The guard grabbed the medal and pulled it off. He smiled and in German said, "Mutter Gottes" (Mother of God). He then dropped the medal on the ground and with his foot covered it in sand. Bob was angered to have his medal forcibly removed and treated with such disrespect.

When the Oberstadt came out, he yelled and screamed at the prisoners, then interrogated them. The guard waited until the Oberstadt was finished and back in the building. The guard then used the bayonet attached to his rifle and pulled the medal up out of the sand. He returned the medal to Bob, said again in German, "Mutter Gottes," and made the Sign of the Cross—an expression of faith in basic Catholic tenets. Bob thanked the guard as he accepted his medal, greatly relieved to have its safe return—and amazed that the other man had apparently been trying to protect him.

Bob believes that the Medal, and the guard, saved his life that day. He wore that medal until the day he died.

At Bob's wake, members of his local chapter of the American Ex-Prisoners of War told us about his courage under fire as a tank commander, surviving some of the fiercest fights of the war, even when he was outnumbered and out of ammunition. He received a Purple Heart and many other medals for his bravery, but one medal meant more to him than all the rest.

The Miraculous Medal now hangs around his widow's neck, a constant reminder of strength and grace.

Olinda belongs to the Romance Writers of America and Sisters In Crime, Indianapolis chapters. She has published fiction and nonfiction in newsletters and newspapers, and her published novel is Pasta Perfect: Reunion.

MY QUIET RELATIONSHIP WITH DAD

By Meryl K. Evans

The Cochlear Implant Online website tells the story of Rachel, a high school student who is deaf and uses a prosthetic electronic device to deliver sound information and help her communicate. Rachel's younger sister, Jessica, is also deaf and has an implant. While reading about Rachel's story, I was surprised to read the following:

"Many of my teachers had a fear of having a hearing impaired student in the classroom in the beginning of the school year or semester, and many times they didn't know how to accommodate me as a hearing impaired student in the beginning."

I never thought about this in all my years in school. I never got the impression that a teacher feared dealing with me. Every year on the first day of school, I met with the teacher privately to let her know that I was hearing impaired and read lips.

I sat in the front row or wherever was the best place to see the teacher. Of course, I hated it. I wanted to be in the back with the other cool kids. Even as an adult, the front row phenomenon bugged me, as my co-workers or friends rarely sat in the front row. It amazed and disappointed me that adult life was a lot like high school.

Many years after I graduated, an eighth grade teacher with whom I stayed in touch told me something about my dad. Whenever he met my teachers at open house, he would tell them about my hearing loss and that I lip read. He also told them—that other than to make sure I sat in the front—not to treat me any differently than they treated the other students.

Wow. That's something I expected from my mom. Of course, Dad cared about my education and that I led a normal life, but he usually let Mom do the talking. Dad had a quiet influence on my life even though he was an outgoing guy with a lot of chutzpah. Dad had a way with sales people and bargained with them to lower the price on big-ticket items. If a fast food restaurant had a collection of goodies he wanted for my kids or me, he'd get the whole thing in one visit.

He often took me out to breakfast on Saturday mornings. A waitress stopped by and asked Dad if he wanted cream and sugar with his coffee. He said, "Yes, I'll have a hug and a kiss."

Sometimes after breakfast, we went by the downtown post office so he could check box 2044. After getting the mail, he'd pick me up and put me down on the tall marbled table while he opened the mail. I'd talk loudly so I could hear my voice echo in that colossal place with black and white checkerboard floors.

The fact he was a life insurance salesman was no surprise—he talked to strangers as if they were old friends. When it came to me, however, he made a big impact with little attention in spite of his being a stocky guy with a confident voice. In fact, whenever I saw actor William Shatner on TV, he immediately reminded me of Dad. Shatner played strong and confident characters.

In spite of his outgoing nature, he and I never talked much. It wasn't for lack of trying. While I was growing up, he attended many of my sports games and even coached. He often played catch with me so I could keep up my softball skills. He shared his love of baseball by taking me to Texas Rangers baseball games. When I cut back on sports, we didn't interact as much.

Less than a week after I received my cochlear implant (my "bionic ear"), I returned to the hospital because I had severe vertigo and dehydration. Living an hour away, Dad drove with Mom to see me. I was surprised because it wasn't as if I was seriously ill. He usually let Mom call him with updates.

Mom was always there when we needed her. Her car has logged a lot of miles driving 60 miles to Plano from Fort Worth plus more on the trip back. So it wasn't a shocker that she came to the hospital. On the car ride home from the hospital, I thanked Dad for coming and told him it meant a lot to me.

Later, I found out from Mom that she asked Dad if he wanted to go to the hook-up (the first time the cochlear implant gets turned on). He said he didn't want to go because he knew everything would be fine. But when I was in the hospital, he wanted to see me for himself because he was worried about me.

Though Dad and I may not exchange a lot of words, we speak volumes through our actions. When I was little, I could count on Dad to make sure my hearing aid was in working order and had fresh batteries. When we went on a fishing trip, he taught me new words. He filled out hundreds of contest entries to win a bike for me. Whenever my family and I went through a rough patch, he was always there to lend support and make it more bearable. Shortly after I gave birth to my second child, he said, "Thank you." This was no ordinary thank you, but the kind like I had given him a most precious gift.

No, it should be the other way. *Thank you, Dad.*

Meryl K. Evans (www.meryl.net) is the Content Maven and editor-in-chief of a few newsletters, a columnist for PC Today, and a native Texan in Plano, where she takes pleasure in her family's foibles.

THE PLANT

By Ruth Cooke

My role model for strength in the face of adversity is an ordinary houseplant. The plant is commonly known as "Mother-In-Laws' Tongues," and is a succulent capable of surviving in the arid environment that central heat and a forgetful caretaker provide, but that's not why I admire it.

I've had this particular plant for about 26 years. It came into my care during my freshman year at university, when my dorm-mate knocked it off the windowsill. She was about to throw it out when I rescued it.

The plant had broken into two parts—the outer leaves, attached to the roots; and the inner crown, with no roots attached. I replanted the rooted part and put the crown in a glass of water, hoping that it would eventually grow roots.

The crown did grow roots, and in due time I planted it in soil, and it thrives to this day. However, I was surprised when the rooted part didn't do as well. Within a short while, it withered and died.

I keep the plant around to remind me that when I suffer disaster, even one that knocks me to the ground, flat and broken, I have a choice. I can hold onto my old roots and let go of my crown, the part that grows. If I do so, I know that I will quite probably wither and die like my plant. Or I can grow new roots, adapting to the situation, and keep on growing and changing and thriving.

Every so often my plant divided, and I am blessed with offshoots of the original plant. I carefully repot them and give them to friends and family with this story. I hope that they, too, will learn that the key to survival in difficult circumstances is not holding tight to what we have, but adapting and learning and growing.

Ruth Cooke is a mother, writer, and pastor living in Ontario, Canada. She recently graduated from Emmanuel College in Toronto with a Master of Divinity and a Master of Pastoral Studies.

TOM

By Kim Ramsey

"Hey, Elephant Girl! Learn to walk!" The girl took a few clumping steps, copying me for the entertainment of her friends.

Their laughter followed me down the hall. For a brief second I thought about shoving the girl who had yelled into her locker, but I forced back the impulse, along with my tears. Stuff like this was a normal part of my school day. At least the year was almost over.

That was the day I met Tom. After school, I took the bus home with Dawn, the one actual friend I had. We were outside when a dark-haired boy wandered into the yard and sat down. Dawn rolled her eyes and muttered something under her breath before saying, "Kim, this is Tom. Tom, Kim."

He and I said hi in unison and started talking. Despite Dawn's obvious dislike of him, Tom stayed the rest of the time I was there. Before I left, he called me pretty. Even though he blushed and added, "In your own way, I mean," I knew it was a sincere compliment. I wasn't quite sure how to take it. I didn't get many of those.

The next day, school was more of the same. But somehow it didn't seem as bad as usual. A guy thought I was pretty. A cute guy. That made it a little easier not to care about the whispers in the hallway.

For the next few weeks, every time I went to Dawn's, Tom showed up. And every time, he said something that made me feel good about myself. Shortly after school ended, Tom asked me to be his girlfriend. As soon as I realized I'd heard him right, I agreed.

The first time I went to his house, I learned that he lived with his grandfather. "What about your parents?" I asked. Social skills weren't among my better points.

Tom looked at me for a moment, then shrugged. "I've lived with my grandparents since I was eight. After my stepfather threw me down the stairs, he told my mother I couldn't live with them anymore." I stared at him as he turned back to his video game. How could he be so casual about something like that? He didn't mention it again.

Tom broke up with me after a few weeks; I didn't understand why. Things "weren't working." I hated him. That was progress for me; usually I felt like I deserved to be treated badly. Tom actually tried to make me mad at him; he wanted me to get the clue that I had a right to be angry when someone hurt me. Of course, I didn't know that at the time. After a while I stopped hating him and we became friends just in time for my junior year, his freshman. There were still whispers and giggles when I walked down the hall, but with Tom's help, I was beginning to believe it didn't matter what other people thought of me. By my senior year, I actually liked myself.

But halfway through that year, it came crashing down. My best friend's boy-friend "persuaded" me to do something I was neither ready nor completely will-ing to do. After promising to keep it a secret, he told everyone who knew me. In other words, most of the school. For weeks, I was "that slut who tried to break them up." I didn't try to correct his story. I deserved what I got, right?

Not according to Tom. He made the guy stop talking about me and got the rest of the school to find more interesting gossip. And he waited, knowing that what he'd heard wasn't the whole story. Six months later, after I'd started col-lege, I finally managed to tell him my side. "It wasn't your fault," he told me. "That guy's just sick. You can't keep feeling bad about this. If you do, he wins."

Thanks to Tom's reaction, I found the strength to tell my parents what had happened and to confront the guy who did it. My parents believed me, the guy admitted—to others as well as me—what he'd done, and I felt stronger.

In the time I'd known him, the only mention Tom had made of his parents was when he told me why he lived with his grandfather. I met his father once, never his mother. Over the next couple years, he trusted me with more about his past and I marveled in just how strong he was. The guy who taught me it didn't matter what other people thought had spent part of his childhood hiding from his stepfather, who beat him because he was there. I'd learned that rape wasn't my fault from someone whose parents often left him alone with a baby-sitter even after he told them where the sitter had touched him. The one person in Tom's life who'd shown him true caring, his grandmother, died when he was nine. Somehow he had strength to grow beyond his past. More amazing, he had strength to spare to help his friends.

Time went on. I got engaged to someone else. Tom didn't tell me until long afterward how much that hurt him. His grandfather passed away; for once, I was able to be there for him. A few years later, despite coping with college classes, problems with his live-in girlfriend, and some legal problems he wouldn't tell me much about, Tom helped me find the confidence to leave an emotionally abusive marriage. We lost touch after my husband got help and I agreed to give him another chance.

I saw Tom recently for the first time in years. He's happily married and has a good job. A good life. Tom taught me so much about strength. I hope that whatever happens in my life, I'll remember what I learned from him.

Kimberly Ramsey is a married mother of two. In 2002, her phonics-based reading series, Stories from Somerville, was published by Oxton House Publishers, LLC. She has had two short stories published on Viatouch.com's StoryStation, and is currently at work on a young adult fantasy series.

WHERE HAVE ALL
THE HEROES GONE?

By Patti Wigington

Hero.

It's a word that seems to be bandied about with alarming regularity these days. Ask a group of schoolchildren who their heroes are, and the answers are frightening. It will range from the current flavor-of-the-week pop tart to athletes, from a rapper with a big Hummer and a lot of bling to movie stars, but it's rarely someone who's done something that actually qualifies as "heroic." Making a million bucks a day is not heroic. Being acquitted of criminal charges is not heroic. Winning the VMAs does not make you a hero.

What happened to kids looking up to police officers and firefighters as heroes? When I was a kid, all the boys wanted to play Army Men, because army guys were heroes. Now the police are portrayed as the enemy, firefighters make less money each year than the guy at the Kwikee Mart, and the military is controversial not because of the people who serve within it but because of the war they are being sent to fight.

Remember back when you could turn on the news and see random acts of bravery? People who did things not for the glory or for the fame, but merely because it was the right thing to do?

Do you remember the man who stood in front of a tank in Tienanmen Square in China? Do you remember the awe you felt when you saw that photo on the front page, one small brave figure alone in front of a giant military death machine?

Or what about the unforgettable images that emerged from Oklahoma City a few years ago, when firefighters crawled from the wreckage of a destroyed federal building, clutching bloodied infants in their arms?

Or the rescuers who worked tirelessly to pull some Pennsylvania miners from a collapsed shaft?

How about the men like my grandfather, and possibly yours as well, who flew over Germany, Italy, and France in the summer of 1944, because they were told it would help them save the world? What about the young men and women just like them who now sit in a desert on the far side of the world because we asked them to protect freedom and democracy?

Is there a soul among us who will ever forget the footage of police officers, firemen and paramedics covered in the dust and debris of the Twin Towers that unforgettable September morning? Or the businessmen and taxi drivers who helped total strangers escape the destruction? Or the group of airplane passengers that same day who forced their captors to crash into a field, rallying with the simple words, "Let's roll"?

Where have all the heroes gone? Believe it or not, they're out there. Every day. I turn on the news, and I see average people performing extraordinary acts of bravery. I see people clinging to rooftops but asking their would-be rescuers to go check on their invalid neighbors first. I see store clerks paddling canoes down flooded streets to pluck stranded strangers out of trees. I see a group of white teenage boys carrying an elderly black woman they don't even know to safety so she can get medical care.

It's not only on the television. I see my neighbors joining together to help people a thousand miles away, people we've never met. I see a group of school children collecting pennies to send off to a city that they've seen only on a map. A trailer sits beside a church down the road, getting ready to carry diapers, bottled water, sleeping bags and canned food to the ravaged south.

Tragedy brings out the worst in some people, but fortunately, it also brings out the best in many more of us. It bands us together with no regard to race, religion, or income level. We become part of a collective consciousness, and as human beings, we refuse to sit and watch others suffer when there is something we can do to help them.

Five or ten years from now, when we ask school kids who their heroes are, maybe the answers will be different. Maybe instead of naming off American Idol contestants or basketball players, they'll remember what they've seen over the past few weeks. They'll recall their parents and neighbors joining hands, opening their hearts and their homes to people they've never met. They'll remember the day that they brought in jars of change so their PTO could buy cases of Pedialyte and Pampers. They'll remember seeing people who had lost everything still finding the strength to help others in the same predicament.

And maybe, just maybe, it will inspire our children to someday become heroes themselves.

Patti Wigington is an award-winning writer with a central Ohio newspaper. Her freelance articles have appeared in Gaea's Cauldron, Twinshelp, and Pediatrics for Parents, and she is a contributing editor for Garden and Hearth.

LOOKING UP TO A SHORTSTOP

By Chris Manning

No, that's not the batboy. He's David Eckstein, the starting shortstop for the defending National League champion St. Louis Cardinals.

In the era of six-foot-three shortstops like Derek Jeter, you'll have to excuse David if he seems a bit out of place. Don't worry, he's used to it. It seems as if every biography of David has him listed at a different height, but according to the St. Louis Cardinals, he is all of five feet, seven inches. A disadvantage? Definitely. But some say it's easier when you are the underdog: When someone takes you lightly, it is that much more justifying, and more motivational, to make them regret it. David made a lot of people regret taking him lightly.

David has eclipsed what anyone ever thought he'd be able to accomplish in baseball. As a senior at Seminole High School in Sanford, Florida, he was one of the best players in the state, but no major colleges even considered recruiting him for their teams. Some coaches asked how they could give a scholarship to a "little guy" who had to use every ounce of strength to throw the ball to first base. To them, David just didn't look like a "big-time ballplayer." Instead of thinking the world was against him, he decided to keep working hard, trying out uninvited for the University of Florida Gators—and making the team.

His work ethic and his knack for making the right play at the right time eventually earned him a scholarship. He followed this up by being named one of best college players in America, as well as earning a College World Series appearance for the Gators that same year. Even with all of these accomplishments, the majority of the major league teams ignored David when they scouted for players. One team, however, couldn't overlook his heart, his determination, and his will to win, all of which made him so successful in Florida. The Boston Red Sox drafted David in the 19th round in 1997, sending him to their rookie team.

Even though this was the lowest possible place he could start, David knew he had to take every opportunity he had in professional baseball. After being passed over many times, this was his one chance. He made the best of it. In his first two years of minor league baseball, he hit better than .300, making him one of the top hitters in the league. David also got on base more than 40 percent of the time. If he had been doing this in the major leagues instead of the minors, he would have been a household name.

However, his size always seemed to overshadow his skill. Instead of promoting him for his accomplishments, management doubted his height would measure up in the majors. Finally making it to the Red Sox Triple-A team, which was one small step away from the major league, David struggled to adjust to the higher level of competition. Red Sox management, though, thought he was simply too small to be successful, so they put David on waivers; if no one wanted to take a chance on him and offer him a major league contract, he would be finished playing professional baseball.

The Anaheim Angels didn't let that happen. They looked past his small frame and saw his talent. In 2001, David began his major league career by getting at least one hit every game during his first nine games. He went on to break, or be at the top of, many Angel and American League records. The heart of the Anaheim Angels, he played a big role in his team's victory over the San Francisco Giants in the 2002 World Series.

Shortly after his World Series win, he wrote an inspiring children's book called *Have Heart*. In it, he writes about how even though he was overlooked and under-appreciated his entire childhood, his hard work was rewarding—and paid off.

So the next time someone looks at you and thinks you aren't good enough, or big enough, tell them David Eckstein said yes, you are.

Chris Manning played baseball at the high school, college, and—briefly—professional levels. He has spent his A.B. (After Baseball) days raising his two children, Parker and Piper, with his wife Ashlee. He is the author of One Team One Dream. *Visit him at www.1teamonedream.com.*

STRENGTH OF COMMUNITY

"We all have strength enough to bear the misfortunes of others."
~ François Duc De La Rochefoucauld (*Maximes*)

WHAT REALLY MATTERS

By Julia Rosien

Some people on my small suburban street knew me when I wore braces and pigtails. They remember my rusty orange bike with the banana seat and the way I tossed their evening paper on the front porch. But for most people on this street, I'm just another nameless neighbor. We share a sidewalk, smile politely at each other, and notice when a "For Sale" sign goes up. For the most part, we're strangers.

I grew up here, but moved away during the first years of my marriage only to return with my own children years later. My parents still live at the top of the hill. But people don't linger on their front porches as much as they used to. I thought maybe the world had turned to its computers and workplaces for a sense of community until the night fire struck a neighbor's home a few doors away from us.

"Someone help me!" A man's screams pierced the night. "My baby's inside and I can't get her out."

Our quiet suburban street erupted with people searching for the source of terror. The roar of fire and exploding glass from a second story window stilled our voices as we watched in stunned silence. Flames licked the eaves of a neighbor's house, and the acrid smell of smoke and the blare of sirens filled the summer night as neighbors stood shoulder to shoulder.

Dressed in only his boxers, a man held a young child in his arms. Two other children sat near his feet on the damp ground, staring straight ahead. The man's heartbreaking "no, no, no . . ." almost drowned the crackling fire, but not quite. I counted the children. The oldest son sat beside his younger brother, who was wrapped in a blanket. The child in the man's arms was the 3-year-old who plays hopscotch on the driveway. The baby was missing, his 1-year-old daughter.

Firefighters jumped from trucks and raced towards the house. Wielding hatchets, some ran into the burning building while others unhooked hoses and cranked open fire hydrants. A firefighter stumbled from the building seconds later and fell into the bushes beside the door. The father ran towards the house screaming for his daughter and pushed past the coughing firefighter, but another pulled him back. His bare chest heaved as he clawed at the florescent yellow jackets of the firefighters.

My mind jumped from one horrifying thought to another as a firefighter emerged from the smoke, carrying a baby in his arms. She was motionless. We moved, not like individuals anymore, but like amoebae, surging around father and daughter. The firefighter knelt down, breathed into the baby's mouth, and moved back while her father held her head, his tears falling on her sooty face. She sputtered and then screamed.

We sighed collectively, our shoulders sagging in relief.

The father pressed his daughter against his bare chest and thanked God, any and every God. A neighbor stepped forward and covered the pair in a woolen blanket.

Children from the neighborhood began to appear on doorsteps. Our older two children peeked from our second floor window and called to us. Pulling on sweaters, they stumbled across the dewy grass, fear contorting their faces. They huddled close as another window from the fiery house exploded outwards and sliced the night sky.

The whoosh of water replaced the eerie crackle of flame. Neighbors who normally only wave hello or goodbye turned to each other to lay an arm across shaking shoulders. We stood there in the wet grass and damp night air watching as firefighters worked and police cars arrived. Concern, not morbid curiosity, drove us to stand freezing and chatting with each other in the middle of the night long after the crisis had passed.

No one expected a 3-year-old to crawl from her bed, walk to the bathroom, and climb a counter in search of a lighter she'd seen her father hide. Who could have predicted she'd go to her brother's room and run the top of the lighter across his acrylic blanket and giggle as sparks erupted into flame? Her brother, a shy 10-year-old, lay paralyzed with fear while flames engulfed his bedding and burned his legs.

The father had raced up and down flights of stairs carrying three children to safety one at a time. But when he returned a fourth time for his baby daughter, the wall of smoke pushed him back. A house he'd lived in for years became an elaborate maze with switchbacks and dead ends. Crying over his baby, half-naked and shivering, his world shrank to one strangled intake of breath.

Watching his daughter fight for that saving breath narrowed my vision, too. My world, our world, the one without modems and cell phones, fences or closed doors is right where it's always been, even if I couldn't see it. Warm hands tucked into larger trembling ones, cold toes curled into a blanket while sleepy heads drooped, and a community sharing despair and bliss in the space of a breath.

Julia Rosien is a senior editor at ePregnancy Magazine, as well as a freelance journalist who's contributed to various publications including Wedding Style, The American Bar Association, The Christian Science Monitor and CBC Radio. As well, she teaches journaling and creative writing online and at a brick and mortar community college. She also holds memberships at various professional organizations, including the Professional Writer's Association of Canada.

THE POWER OF ONE

By VL Marshall

It takes only one
To stand out and bloom from the rest

Only one ray of sunshine
To open a blossom to its new day

One tiny bee
Can build a garden of possibility

One little bird
Can seed a glorious field in splendor

One person
Can begin to hope for the world

One handshake
Can start the engine going

One smile
Will soften the hardest of hearts

If it takes only one
Try to be that person

Build tomorrow
With today, one day, one moment, one effort

And watch a new sunrise
Appear in that one doing

Like a tiny bee
Pollinate the garden that surrounds you.

Vikki Marshall is a writer and nature photographer from California. She is currently working on two novels and a book of short stories about the plight of individuals in Africa.

HEART OF THE MOUNTAIN

By Stephanie Cordray

I grew up poor. Now, when you read something like that you think you know what is going to come next, but you don't. This is not going to be a story about living hand-to-mouth and clawing my way to success. You see, I didn't know I grew up poor. I didn't feel and certainly didn't look poor. It wasn't until I was out in the world beyond where I grew up that I learned just how poor I was.

I grew up in Dingess, West Virginia, where you could expect to be completely cut off from the rest of the world several times during a winter. If you weren't ready by mid-November you'd best pray for a mild one because you don't ever want to be stuck in those hills unprepared.

I had nine brothers and sisters. With Mom, Dad, and myself, we were a family of 12. We never lacked for anything we needed. The problem with a label such as "poor" is a lack of understanding—the understanding of mountain people. Poor is when you have nothing and hope for nothing. We didn't have a lot of luxuries, but you have to understand that not only were they luxuries, they were largely useless. We had a TV, but it was rarely on. If the electricity wasn't out from winter storms, there was a lack of reception. When I left that small town, it was this dearth of luxuries that caused many to label me poor. As we became more aware of the world around us, my mother brought in more gadgets as they became available in stores. We always looked at them dubiously out of her sight. We made the appropriate noises of appreciation with big smiles on our faces and put them in a prominent place in our rooms. They were rarely used for their intended purposes.

Even houses that had running water had outhouses. If you have no electricity a good part of the year, you can't flush the toilet. Common sense demanded that you have an alternative method. In the winter it was better that the power and running water were off anyway. Pipes full of water freeze.

Every spring we had a garden. Hill country meant it was small because flat land was a scarce commodity, but we call them farms. Any plot of land that was big enough to grow vegetables and raise a few chickens is called a farm, no matter the size. So that others can have the right perspective and not think of rolling fields of corn like you might see in Ohio, think of it as a garden. As produce came into season, we canned. Now, canning where I come from isn't the shiny stainless steel kettles on the range. That would have taken too long to put up what was going to be needed for the winter months. No, we had big metal tubs on fire pits in which we submerged the newly-filled jars for the last phase of the canning process. My mother made the best bread and butter pickles in three counties. We put up wood and coal, made candles, and stocked kerosene. We always had enough of everything.

We had grocery stores in the city. A city to us was what others would have called a small town. I'm not sure what they would have called where I grew up. If we had anything besides turkey for Thanksgiving, that meant winter came early and we couldn't get to the store. Raising turkeys took more room than we could give up from the garden space and wild turkeys were a scarce commodity in the hills where I lived.

When you grow up in coalmine country, bad things tend to happen a lot. We had some luxuries: TVs, radios, washing machine, refrigerator, and other assorted electrical appliances. Most were put up for show except for the few times when they could actually be used . . . except for the ones I took it into my head to take apart to see how they worked. Some of those never worked again, although I was quite good at taking them apart and putting them back together in working order by the time I was ten. The refrigerator and freezer stayed on the porch. We didn't worry about food being stolen. Everybody knew if they needed, it was given freely and without hesitation. I remember my mother cooking food, and helping when I was old enough, for families who didn't have any. I remember learning how to sew and making clothes for families who were in a bad situation.

When I left Dingess for the big city of Chicago is when I learned that I grew up poor. I certainly wasn't stupid or inbred, which were some other labels I collected over time. The thing that was taught to me in the way I grew up was always be prepared for bad things to happen. I learned to do that with everything in my life.

Although I was certainly naïve, I knew the classics and was better read than most of my neighbors, who all looked down on me. When the blizzard of '77 hit us, I was prepared. Cars were buried under so much snow you couldn't find them without digging in the general area where you thought you had parked. People who thought they knew how to handle a Chicago winter were helpless.

I rolled up my sleeves and raided my pantry. I had hot stews, cookies, bread, and other home-cooked foods ready to take around the neighborhood. By the time the street was scraped clear of snow, I had made some new friends who no longer thought I was so deprived. They greeted me with a new respect because this simple mountain girl taught them something: Never judge anyone because of what they have or don't have, how they look or don't look, and, above all, never think someone is stupid just because they speak a little slower than what you're used to.

The way I grew up gave me a strength of mind and purpose that has stood me in good stead no matter where I lay my head. I've been a lot of places over my lifetime; some I loved, some I hated, but I always had whatever I needed. Sometimes I feel like I'm becoming spoiled with all the luxurious things I often take for granted these days. However, I know that whatever comes I will be prepared, which is the true luxury in a world that sees upheaval and change on a daily basis.

This is the legacy my mother left me. All her life she was prepared for anything . . . except an illness that couldn't be cured. She was taken away from us in 1998 by cancer she had fought for four years. I remember going to her during that time. She asked me to give her the strength to die with dignity, the strength that she had given to me so freely that has kept me strong and prepared for life's hardships no matter what they were. Even as her body became frail and weak, the strength that was the core of her shone through her eyes until they closed in the final sleep. I held her hand and her body just as she had often held mine when I was small and afraid. It's the only time she ever asked anything of me, but what she asked I gave freely and without hesitation just as she had done for others all her life.

She was the heart of the mountain, but the heart didn't die with her body. The mountain made her, not she it. The mountain will be forever, but she sent pieces out into the world in the hope that others could be taught to give freely and without hesitation.

Over her lifetime, Stephanie has been an ESL teacher, American Red Cross caseworker, editor of a community newspaper, substitute teacher, pizzeria manager, and counselor. She's always been a hillbilly.

Canberra's Bushfire - January 2003

By Gillian Polack

Fire balls. Twenty meter flame walls roaring into suburbs. Nearly 500 homes burned to the ground; a region devastated. The sewage processing plant, Mt. Stromlo Observatory, a power station, churches, schools, and recreational areas, all destroyed. This was the big picture.

It didn't happen the way it sounded. It was not a fire for the movies. There was no clear beginning, middle, or end. No hero triumphant.

It was only when we had time to stop and live again that neighbors started comparing stories. And we exchanged the stories in an entirely different coming together. Our city turned into a village.

There had been fires in the mountain ranges for a while. Southern Canberra was used to a veil of smoke and hearing news about fragile ecosystems being destroyed. So when the air was smokier on Saturday, our first reaction was unhappy, but not overly concerned. The sky was a dirty white in the morning, the cloud cover tinged with stale smoke. Then it grew darker and the clouds changed to a grimy orange, and then to a near-ochre color.

In the early afternoon, it became rust-red, and people in my suburb went outside to investigate. We brought out hoses and buckets. An alert ran across the bottom of the television screen just before 5 p.m., warning that certain suburbs were on fire alert. All of these suburbs were just the other side of the mountain, so we kept an eye on things, but did not panic.

Then embers started to rain down. The closer you were to Mt. Taylor and Oakey Ridge, the more debris colored the air. The yellow and black air—patterned by the fire's refuse. And that wind! It gusted and swirled, changing direction every other minute. We brought out more hoses and tubs of water. A new garden recreation became hitting spot fires with buckets of water before they could spread.

We talked to each other. For some, this is when we discovered the extent of the fires for the first time, because not everyone affected had a direct view of Mt. Taylor. The red sky was the reflection of the flames in the clouds. The whole mountain was alive with fire. Tolkein's Mt. Doom. All we needed was Frodo and the One Ring.

Some people evacuated, quietly, without fanfare. Those who didn't were often short on concrete knowledge of what was happening. All we knew was the strange air and the embers. The world had shrunk without us knowing. Tiny clusters of worried people swapped gossip.

It was a night without stars, and almost without breathable air. And it was only mid-afternoon. When the sky lightened again to red, Canberrans moved.

Some people moved straight to the fire front. Groups of teenage boys grabbed their family shovels and helped bury embers to prevent the fire spreading. Other people moved to the properties where horses were kept and shifted the horses to safety, one by one. Still more people collected blankets and clothes and delivered them to the evacuation centers. They didn't deliver to the Phillip center—it had been evacuated.

Only the frail, the elderly, children and asthmatics were confined indoors, vulnerable and disempowered. For these people, the world was still tiny.

Another message appeared across the bottom of the TV screen, announcing an emergency bulletin to be shown at 5:45 p.m. The TV station didn't interrupt the important repeat of a program on Princess Diana. So TV watchers waited to see what we should do. Radio listeners were already out and about, helping fight the fires, or evacuated.

Our area never knew what that emergency bulletin said. We lost power shortly after 5 p.m., when the power station was destroyed. Three homes in Lyons burned when a transponder exploded. Gas tanks also exploded, punctuating the local sound horizon with short sharp bursts.

With silence, came light. The world was suddenly new, and peaceful. The sky was the clearest it had been all day. Then the sun set.

Many suburbs were evacuated by then—at least 10,000 people were homeless. These people took a while to tell their stories. These were the people who would not know for at least 24 hours if they had a home to return to.

But for the rest of us, in the suburbs that were threatened rather than destroyed, it was a strange evening. Some houses were empty. Cars were few. There were no traffic lights and no bird noises. The illumination and televisions of the car yards came on for a time, and the people living closest joked about sitting in the murky air and watching outdoors TV. When these faded, there was no light at all. Except, faintly visible, a dark pink moon.

With many telephones out, no power, and a surprising shortage of radios, many of us fumbled in the dark for candles and torches. Some neighbors knocked on doors, offering candles for those who didn't have them. Some neighbors even knocked on doors offering chocolates.

During the early part of the evening quite a few people paid visits. So many of us were surprised to reveal later, "I spent the evening with neighbors I hadn't met before."

The later part of the evening was dark and alone. We drew together for comfort where we could. Families grew from two to five souls or from four to eight to accommodate friends from Duffy or Chapman. People played cards, chatted, read by torchlight. Almost no one slept. The smoke was still too close. The grittiness of it had crept through our closed windows and into our pores. And that was Saturday on the slopes of Mt. Taylor.

On Sunday there was another rash of door knocks. Those who had operational telephones handled nonstop calls as the rest of the universe rang in. We all swapped stories about calls from Japan, New Zealand, the USA, the UK. The phone calls were expected but nice. They brought us back from our tiny worlds into a bigger world.

It was the door knocks that were extraordinary. We updated each other on what Saturday had done—whether the family had stood on the roof of their house to watch the pattern of the fire, or watched from the street, or had been confined to the home, with asthma.

We discovered and explored the size of what we had been through. We were in shock. We were crying. We were angry. Each of us handled Sunday differently.

All of us shared. Households without battery-operated radios were given an abundance by friends and neighbors. People with too much milk gave to people with big families and no milk. People with cars found neighbors without and took them to buy imperishables and water and batteries. Some lucky souls who had power back within two days started a new trend. Instead of pot-luck dinners with friends, we had refrigerator-luck dinners. There were some very odd menus.

These door knocks set the pattern for the week. The frail and the isolated found help. Those who couldn't drive were given shopping expeditions or moved in with friends. We chronicled the safety of everyone we knew. A new Canberra preoccupation was thinking how much clothing we actually needed, how many household goods we really used, and how many should be given away to those with no house insurance.

It was not charity. It was friendship. More than that, it was a remarkable solidarity—Canberra was a village for a while. An unusual village. The golf course and at least one recreation center harbored horses. The Dinosaur Museum had a healthy crop of children being minded for free. Some offices had cats hiding under desks, waiting to be allowed home. Some hotels gave free accommodation for the stranded, and many more private houses retained their new extended families. And the Canberra public service was a tower of strength, moving us from catastrophe to normalcy at an extraordinary pace.

The memory of the flames lingers. The smell of that fire will take a long, long time to clear.

Gillian Polack is an Australian writer and historian whose first book, Illuminations (Trivium Publishing, 2002), was published in Louisiana.

HOPE FOR A SAFER PLACE

By Shelagh Watkins

When love shines through
In a world of little solace,
There's hope honesty will prevail
Without fear of losing face.

If all children could be saved
From hunger and starvation,
There's hope they'd gain the strength
To build a stronger nation.

When all nations put down arms
And finally give up the fight,
There's hope for a lasting peace
If they could only unite.

As we become a nation
That doesn't hate because of race,
There's real hope that one day
The world will be a safer place.

Shelagh Watkins, who lives in Wales, UK, has many interests, including artwork, computing, and all forms of writing, but she particularly enjoys writing for children. Her first novel, Mr. Planemaker's Flying Machine, was published in 2005.

THE LITTLE ANGEL

By Carolee Eubanks

Sometimes angels are grand and majestic creatures with feathery wings, but sometimes they're a couple inches tall and made out of bent wire.

It was a pleasantly steamy Santa Fe afternoon. My business trip complete, I was now officially on vacation for a few days. I rolled up the rental car windows and cranked the air conditioning. The stereo blasted. I didn't have a care in the world—it was just me and the beautiful scenery and some amazing weather to enjoy.

As I drove along the main road approaching downtown, a sparkle in a small store window caught my eye. And something purple—I love purple. Impulsively, I pulled into the parking lot to investigate. Set deep into the adobe wall was a mysterious glittering window covered in rich purple velvet, with little angels, prisms, and pendants sparkling in the sunshine.

I had to check out the store, just for a second. I hopped out and slammed the car door. I poked my head inside and glanced around. Interesting, but not really my sort of place after all. I headed back to the car, where the engine idled, awaiting my return. I could hear the music thumping along behind the sealed window. Bet it's nice and cool in there by now, I thought. I went to open the door.

It was locked.

Inside were the keys of the rental car that I'd picked up 60 miles away in Albuquerque. I'd locked myself out of the car while it was running! I couldn't believe my own stupidity. I didn't know a soul in Santa Fe, and my purse was in the car. I might as well not have had a dime to my name. Everything I needed to get out of this predicament was just inches away, inside the deliciously chilly car that was sealed up tight.

I slinked back inside the store and wandered around for a minute, trying to decide what to do. Finally, I asked the two ladies behind the counter if they happened to have a wire coat hanger anywhere. They searched, and when they came up empty, they walked to the small motel next door and borrowed one from their laundry room.

I tried bending, twisting, and tugging with that coat hanger, to no avail. The car was too new for that method of breaking and entering. I paced around the small gravel parking lot, trying not to panic, and finally re-entered the cool darkness of the air-conditioned shop.

With a sheepish look, I stepped back up to the counter and asked if I could use the store's phone. They were happy to oblige. They even let me give their number as where I could be reached. And when the rental car company got lost and phoned me there, the ladies in the shop came and found me outside. I think I got more calls on their phone than they did that afternoon, and they graciously allowed me to spend my afternoon commandeering their store, with not so much as an irritated glance.

I examined every item in the tiny store at least ten times each.

Two hours had come and gone when at last the rental company driver arrived with a spare key. One simple click and I was back in my car. First I turned it off, belatedly hoping to keep it from overheating in the desert sun. Then I grabbed my purse and went inside the angel store one final time.

Another letdown awaited me as I dug out my wallet. Two dollars and change, and no credit cards? That's all I had on me? I had been planning to make some grandiose purchase to show my gratitude to the shop owners, but all I had was what my brother would call "chump change." Deflated, I browsed yet again, this time paying close attention to the prices. There on the wall, among ceramic dragons and pewter wizards, I found a small angel Christmas ornament made from bent wire. She held a little pink wooden heart. The purchase would leave me with four cents. That would have to do. I approached the cash register.

"I'm so sorry I can't spend more here," I apologized. "This is all the cash I have on me, and I really appreciate all your help."

"Aww, I think you've been through enough today," the lady said with a smile. "Take her. She's yours."

I was stunned. But wait, I thought. My purpose was to give something back to you! I demurred, but she insisted. I profusely thanked her yet again and departed, accompanied by my little angel, back on my way downtown at last.

I returned to Santa Fe not long ago and planned to stop in to visit them. But the shop was gone; only a vacant window glared back at me. I'll never have the chance to let them know what their kindness meant to me—how lasting an impression they made on a total stranger.

But I still have my little wire angel. She hangs in a position of honor, on the wall by the door to the garage, as she has everywhere I've lived in the many years since. I keep her there as a reminder to me each time I leave the house to be kind to others in my day's travels. And to always remember to take my keys with me when I get out of the car!

Carolee Eubanks is a freelance writer and mom who currently lives in San Diego and usually lets her husband be in charge of the keys.

RELIEF EFFORT BLOSSOMS

By Jamie Engle

Tonight, I took down the signs: Women's, Men's, Boys', Girls', Infants', Bedding, Toys, Toiletries. Only two signs are left. What started with a question from a neighbor about a charity donation left on my front porch blossomed into an effort of neighbors, several Girl Scout troops, family, and strangers from Texas and across the country.

"Is that something you're donating?" she asked, pointing to the box.

"Yep, truck's coming by today."

"Can I have it? Two people who work with my husband are housing Katrina evacuees and they really need clothing and other items for them," she said.

"Well, these are heavy winter sweaters, so you don't want them," I told her. "Let me see what else I can find."

They left and I went back in the house to check my e-mail. One Girl Scout leader sent an e-mail to all leaders. "I can't stand to sit and watch anymore," it read. "Let's do something."

I replied, telling them I knew of people who needed clothing, toiletry items, and a whole bunch more. I compiled a list and forwarded it, asking them to bring donations to my house. I also told them we'd sort and box for two hours on Sunday and Monday; any volunteers would be appreciated.

Our Junior Girl Scout troop was collecting items for a garage sale scheduled for the next weekend, to help fund the troop for the year. With the troop's enthusiastic permission, we cancelled it and donated all the garage sale items to the evacuees. We decided to undertake the Hurricane Relief Effort as our service project.

When my daughters came home from school, we talked about Katrina and the effect it was having: how thousands fled their homes and had nothing left. They wanted to know what they could do, and I explained about the relief effort we'd be hosting at our house.

"Why does it have to be here?" asked Alyssa, my youngest daughter.

"Because we're closest and I'm the one who knew people who needed help. Sometimes, when something needs to be done, you just have to do it."

She understood, and went upstairs. Half an hour later, she came downstairs with her arms full of things to donate.

"Don't worry, that's not all of it," she said. "I have about two more trips to make."

The older girls followed. "Same here," they said.

Later that night, I called my brother and explained what we were doing. He had a website live on the Internet within an hour. Only one thing was on it: our relief effort information.

The girls, and everyone I talked to and e-mailed, expressed how glad they were to be doing something instead of watching helplessly. Having specific people to aid galvanized everyone into action and gave them a sense of purpose.

The next day, donations started coming in, and we put their bags and boxes in the dining room. Hearing that evacuees were enrolling in Texas schools, I asked the local schools if they needed any supplies. They did, and school supplies, backpacks, and zippered binders were added to the needs list on the website.

It wasn't long before donations filled the dining room. We piled bags and boxes in the living room, but there was still a pathway. The momentum grew and we began to feel energized.

We went to the local Wal-Mart, hoping to secure a donation of school supplies. Angela, the assistant manager, was eager to help: "Just tell me what you need," she said. Words we wanted to hear, but we were surprised how fast and easy the response came. We weren't so lucky with other stores, but we were excited to have Wal-Mart's help.

The living room filled and we started lining the hallway with donations. One couple surprised me by driving up from downtown Dallas to deliver their donation, saying it seemed like the private sector was more organized than the organizations. More surprisingly, we had several people who drove more than 20 miles to volunteer for the relief effort.

We prepared for sorting and boxing. The couches and tables started out empty, but as we sorted items, the piles grew. And grew. And grew, spilling over onto the floor.

"Don't put that in the box," said Alyssa. "It has stains on it. How would you feel if you had to walk around wearing stained clothes?"

At the end of two hours, our 13 volunteers had sorted and boxed nine moving boxes full of clothing, shoes, toys, and stuffed animals. Couches, tables, and the floors were still covered with donations to be boxed, but we now had the rhythm down and a system in place.

The cul-de-sac filled with cars. Forty-five people showed up the next day to help sort and box. Many brought donations with them; some brought extra moving boxes. More families bearing donations showed up throughout the day—so many that we lost track of the number of people contributing. The pathway shrunk to: take a step, lunge over a bag, take a step, dodge a box.

The noise level rose as everyone got busy sorting and boxing—all ages working together toward a common goal. At one point, I stood there in awe, just looking at the massive piles, the boxes filling up, and the wonderfully huge number of volunteers all working so hard. I hadn't even let myself hope for such an outpouring.

By the end of two hours, more than 50 more boxes of clothing, shoes, toiletry items, cleaning items, toys, and more were packed, inventoried and ready to go. In total, there were almost 80 boxes of various sizes, mostly large and extra-large moving boxes. When my neighbor saw the boxes piled high in our garage, her eyes filled with tears.

"I never expected so much," she said.

"See what happens when you tell my mom?" said Michelle, my oldest daughter. Michelle was a rock through the relief effort, not fazed at all by all the people and commotion, just quietly leading and working the whole time. "I wanted to help the hurricane victims but didn't know how," she said. "This is right; this is what we should be doing."

My daughter Kristen decided to take over the school supply drive as her Girl Scout Silver Award project. She filled each backpack with a set of donated school supplies, a zipper binder and a book, readying them for delivery. A book in every backpack was one of our goals, then we realized we couldn't be sure if a boy or girl got the backpack. We decided to put a pile of books next to the backpacks, so each student could choose one.

We delivered the stuffed backpacks to the school. Kristen was assigned to escort the newly enrolled evacuees around the school. She watched as one girl picked out a backpack and opened it up. The girl smiled wide when she saw all the goodies inside. She picked out a book and added it to the backpack. She walked out into the hall, hugging her backpack close to her body, like a treasured possession. Every time my daughter saw a student carrying one of "our" backpacks, she smiled. "For the first time, I really see why it feels so good to help others," she told me.

Two signs are still up: for books and school supplies. According to the Dallas Morning News, 50,000 to 60,000 evacuee students will be enrolling in schools across Texas, 2,000 here in north Texas. We're now working with the school districts to distribute filled backpacks.

Donations from across the country came pouring in: 50 books from a bookseller in Michigan, some from family and friends, some from strangers. One woman found us through the Internet and e-mailed that she was having items shipped directly to my house. I saw the delivery truck pull up and the driver got out his dolly. "Why would he need a dolly for one box?" I thought. He got out not one but three boxes. I wished I could reach through the computer to give this Internet-angel a hug.

A Federal Express truck pulled up to the house. Again, the dolly was brought out. This time, the delivery was from a school in Denver: 15 backpacks filled with school supplies, one filled by each classroom in the school. As we unpacked the boxes, I pictured the smiles on the faces of all the student evacuees we could help. I hope I can find the words to thank the Denver students for their contribution, so that they can see the same smiles I do each time we deliver more backpacks.

Hurricane Katrina changed lives, including ours. Somehow, we came through it not with more fear, but with more faith in our community and people throughout the nation. My daughters have a truer understanding of what a community service project really is all about. They have a more personal connection with those they help; they have a better realization that they're helping real people.

My youngest daughter said it best: "It's good to know that if something bad happened here, someone else would be doing this for us. I know that because they're helping us help the hurricane victims."

Jamie Engle is a freelance writer, book reviewer, and Girl Scout leader living in north Texas.

BLIZZARDS AND FRIENDS

By Ken Schneider

The night before the storm was a comfortable, unusually warm evening for February. It was 1978, and I was a high school senior living in a small Ohio town. That evening, as my friends and I walked home from a school dance, we talked about the lack of snow that winter.

It had rained that night, and my old car was parked along the curb in water that had risen about halfway up the tire. The streetlight reflected off the puddle onto the rims and caught my eye. I thought about moving the car around back. "No, it's too warm to freeze. The water will drain before long anyway." I said goodnight to my friends as we parted ways and went into the house.

My father was on the road. He drove a semi-truck for a living and was home only on the weekends. My mother worked the overnight shift at a nearby hospital. That night, as she did every night, she gave us kisses and hugs before leaving for work. Though she worked an odd shift, 11:00 p.m. to 7:00 a.m., she was always there for us—at least she had been until the night before the storm.

Of course, we children—five of us ranging in age from 11 to 18—were able to take care of ourselves well enough, but we didn't know it until then. Mother had taught us many things from her years of struggle during the Great Depression. Relics from those days sat around the house as reminders of a different era. Oil lamps and candles did little more than collect dust; old quilts hung lifelessly over the sofa. Those things were merely knickknacks to us, but to my mother they had been part of her daily life as a child.

She taught us to nurture a garden in the summer and to can vegetables, jelly, and cold packed meat. We couldn't understand why she bothered; the grocery had all of those things on the shelf. Dad would buy canned goods by the case and store them in the fruit cellar—a dark, cool place in the basement where our parents sent us to retrieve the canned goods and cold packed meat for vegetable soup. I hated going down there, but I liked the soup. The frightening trip down the stairs was always worth it.

That evening mother left for work at the hospital, and we readied ourselves for bed and for school the next day. Sometime during the night, a freak sort of storm came together. A cold front to the north collided with a warm front marching up from the south. The storm combined right over Ohio, and the blizzard of 1978 was born. We woke the next morning much later than normal. Mother hadn't returned home at 7 a.m. to wake us for school.

My oldest sister, Ruth, opened my bedroom door with a banging thump and startled me from my sleep. "We had a blizzard," she shouted. "The snow drifted up the windows, and it's blocking the front door."

I looked at the clock on my nightstand, which had stopped at 3:30 in the morning when the power went out.

"The furnace stopped working, and Mom isn't home," she continued.

"Go back to bed," I mumbled, pulling the blanket over my head. "I'm sure it isn't as bad as you're making it out to be."

She slammed the door.

Like a cackling clutch of hens, my four sisters sat around the living room trying to decide what we should do. I couldn't sleep as they clattered about. It was a day off from school; what was so bad about that? I finally flung off the covers, got out of bed and looked out the window. It was bad. What would we do?

I went to the living room and sat down with my sisters. "I'm sure Mom is fine," I said. "She doesn't get off work until seven, and the storm started long before then." They agreed.

"What would she do if she were here?" I asked them.

"Light the coal oil lamp," said my youngest sister.

I shook my head at her and smiled. "Good idea," I said. "But we don't need light until tonight."

Nancy, the next youngest, chimed in. "Let's make some vegetable soup," she said. She loved that soup more than any of us. She lay on the couch with the old patchwork quilt wrapped around her shoulders—just as it was intended.

Lisa, the middle girl, chastised her: "How will we heat it up, stupid?"

Nancy smiled when Lisa said this as she already had the answer.

"Dad's camp stove!" She stuck out her tongue at Lisa.

We all agreed, at least with the camp stove idea. I went to the basement and picked out the canned goods we needed along with a jar of cold packed beef. As the girls put the soup on the stove, I checked the floor registers and felt a puff of warm air. The natural gas was still running and the pilot light was lit, which kept the cast iron mantel in the furnace hot. Though the electricity was out, enough warm air was rising that it took the chill out of the rooms above.

The temperature outside was well below zero—cold enough to freeze your face, I would later learn. But my youthful vigor and adventurous spirit clouded my judgment. I ventured out into the bright, crisp morning dressed in winter boots, an old wool hat, a heavy coat, and thick gloves, though I might as well have been wearing a light jacket. The sun that shone so brightly in the sky was deceiving. It was cold. Really cold. The snow was deep in spots, and in others there was none. The brutal wind lifted and scattered the drifts as it pleased.

Having lived in our house for 14 years, I knew everyone on the block. They all had lived there at least as long as we did. I walked down ten houses to see Mr. and Mrs. Williams, a couple in their fifties. They were faring well. They, like my mother, had been through the Depression and took the storm in stride.

Mr. Williams and I decided that we should check on the older folks. We did, and returned to Mr. Williams' house to warm up before walking to the grocery store with lists from each of our neighbors. Mostly they asked for staples like milk and bread. One woman wanted cigarettes. Silly, I thought at the time, but we complied.

Grocery stores and small markets dotted the corners of every neighborhood in my town. The people who owned them generally lived in the apartments above, so we knew they'd open for sure. We headed off to a store about three blocks away, which was normally a two-minute bike ride or a five-minute stroll. Not that day. It was a struggle to get there, even for a young man, as I was at the time. Mr. Williams and I took turns walking in front of each other to block the wind. I remember how my face burned from the icy gusts that grated my skin. We made it to the store and finished the shopping. Then we delivered the groceries to our elderly neighbors, sitting for many cups of hot chocolate heated on camp stoves and Sterno cans along the way.

One woman smeared a stinky, greasy paste on our faces. She said it was a remedy for burns and cuts. She kept us at her house for a while—mostly for the company I think—and explained how she made it. Hedge apples and I'm not sure what else. I wish I could remember what she said. It smelled awful, but it really did soothe our wind-burned cheeks.

I returned home to a chorus of laughs from my sisters about the yellow goo slathered on my skin. I sat down and enjoyed the vegetable soup that was hot and ready, and in return gave my sisters candy bars that I bought for them at the store.

By the time the storm was finished, it had blanketed the East Coast and paralyzed thousands of homes and businesses. Dad was delivering goods in Maine, Massachusetts, and New York, and was stuck there for an extra week. We found out later, when the phone started working again, that Mom wouldn't be home for a few days. The hospital staff had asked her to stay because she was already there.

Our parents had taught my sisters and me the things that we needed to survive not just during that blizzard, but also through the many hardships that our lives would bring—though maybe their most important lesson was teaching us to help others. For years, not a day went by that one of my neighbors didn't say something to me about the blizzard. It meant something to them that I was so willing to help, and now I know why they felt that way. Who else did they have? They never forgot that kindness. Those were our neighbors—people we loved and cared about—and Mr. Williams and I did what we thought we needed to do that day. Their friendship and kindness over the years far outweighed that little three-block walk I made for them. Though they never thought so. And to this day, my oldest sister gives me a candy bar every Christmas in memory of the one I brought home to her.

Ken Schneider is an aspiring writer with several magazine articles to his credit. His current work is with a noted publisher, and he hopes to have an answer soon for publication. Ken is married with one son, who is a journalism major at an Ohio University. Ken can be contacted at ksbs00@bright.net with your comments and questions.

BORROWING STRENGTH

"With enough helping hands you can walk on air."
~ Aviva Rifka Bhandari

WET AND NAKED

By Charmian Christie

Throughout childhood, my younger sister Allison and I bathed together in our parents' oversized claw-foot tub. We lathered one another's hair in mock shampoo commercials. We wrung drenched washcloths over each other, plastering hair to foreheads and laughing so hard water ran into our mouths. Once we were in the tub, Mom had trouble getting us out.

In our adulthood, an autoimmune disorder robbed Allison of her health and agility. The disease transformed her from a slim, willowy dancer to an inflexible, fragile Olive Oyl.

One autumn, an odd compilation of ailments plagued her. Her left breast was infected and swollen. She had an abscess on her right buttock and a lesion on her underarm that refused to heal. The threads in her clothing seams tore open her fragile skin.

She arrived at my kitchen door clutching Epsom salts and a bottle of tea tree oil. "I've come to use your tub," she said and handed me her things. "I have to soak my butt."

My parents still had their extra-long, antique tub, but as her body defied her, she chose to recline in my smaller version. Once again, we used the same tub, this time out of necessity, not for fun.

As she poured her ingredients under the steamy faucet, I adjusted the water. She looked at me with the fatigue that soldiers must feel after a long battle in the trenches.

"I want to keep this under control so they don't have to pack it," she said with a weak smile.

"Soak as long as you need," I said, forcing a return grin. But my stomach tightened. The year before I had held her hand as she screamed and wept in the emergency room. The nurse packed the abscess on her knee, poking lengths of gauze into a hole so deep I could see beneath her skin to the smooth cartilage below.

"I'll be outside raking leaves," I said. "Just let yourself out when you're finished."

An hour later, I walked into the bathroom, smelling like leaves and cool air. I jumped when I saw Allison sprawled in the tub. She lifted her head and scowled at me as if I had put Jell-O in her bath instead of Epsom salts.

"Still here? I thought you'd be gone by now," I said puzzled. "Isn't the water getting cold?"

"Yes, it is," she said through her clenched teeth. "In fact, it's been cool for a while now."

"Then why didn't you get out?"

"Because I can't bend my knees," she growled.

Her condition changed daily, and I hadn't considered her knees stiffening. Horrified by my thoughtlessness, I flung my shirt on the floor, plunged my arms into the tepid water, and tried to bend her knees for her. She screamed in pain, and I withdrew my arms like the pain was my own.

I slid my hands up her legs toward her bottom, to hoist her onto her feet.

"My abscess!" she screamed in warning.

"Okay," I said, yanking my hands back, holding them in the air like a surrendering soldier. "What if I lift you from behind?"

Shoes, socks, and jeans fell beside my shirt. I stepped into the cooling water. After many aborted attempts, I was soaked, the floor was covered in puddles, and Allison was still stuck.

Wiping oily drips from my face, I held my head in frustration. Buttocks, bosom, armpit—all too inflamed to touch. I slumped on the edge of the tub and looked her up and down.

"Where can I touch you?" I asked.

She looked sheepish. "I don't know."

"I'll call Mom."

When she arrived we mapped a strategy, listing viable body parts like inventory clerks. Somehow, as the flesh had melted from her bones, Allison had become a series of parts and afflictions: "the abscess," "the lesion," "her knees." But her whole person was stuck in my tub.

Mom stripped down, too. Her full bosom and round belly complimented the trapped stick figure.

"How did I make a daughter like you?" she asked, staring at her own plump thighs.

Mom lifted Allison's thighs, bending so low her breasts touched the water. I stood behind Allison while she braced her back against me. In an awkward dance, we lifted and rotated until Allison's long legs dangled over the tub's edge and I was flattened against the wall. Slippery flesh pressed together, I longed for the innocence and health of our youth.

As I disentangled myself from the shower curtain, Allison stood up in halting stages, like an arthritic old woman. She was 29.

Wet, naked, and now laughing, we toweled off. Three women in a tiny bathroom, the walls echoing the laughter, muffling the pain.

While Mom mopped water from her cleavage, I mopped the puddles from the floor. As children we'd left great pools after our splashing competition to see who could make the highest tidal wave. Feet flat on either side of the faucets, knees bent and full of potential energy, we'd snap our legs straight. Our tiny bodies shot though the water like a torpedo, forcing a wave up the tub's sloped back. Being bigger, I always won the contest with Allison but lost the battle with Mom. I had to mop up the overflow of our tsunami match.

Now, as I blotted the water with a towel, I wished it were as easy to wash the disease from my sister's body, to catch it neatly in a towel and toss it away. I'd have given all my childhood memories to wipe the disorder from her, to wring out the poison and realign her immune system like a freshly smoothed sheet.

The last puddle wiped up, I wandered into the kitchen. Allison was stretched over the kitchen counter, stark naked, bottom in the air. My mother, her bra and underwear speckled with water, was hunched forward and staring intently at an angry welt on the exposed posterior.

Brow wrinkled in concentration and nose inches from Allison's right cheek, Mom raised her head and looked at me. "Do you have a flashlight?" she asked.

The absurdity of the situation struck us with a tidal wave of laughter. We leaned against each other and howled, heads back, eyes closed. Allison's laugh swept me back to the days of dripping hair and mouthfuls of soapy water. Her distinct, strong guffaw defied her dwindling muscles. She was strong and whole in that laugh, and I scrunched my eyes tightly, as if clamped eyelids could keep us safe and happy in the past.

As laughter ebbed I gulped air like I'd been drowning in the memories. Hoots rolled into chuckles and came to rest in gentle smiles. Still grinning, I pulled the flashlight from the junk drawer and snapped it crisply into my mother's extended palm like an operating room nurse.

She resumed her inspection.

"It's healing nicely," she said.

After saying our goodbyes, I returned to the bathroom. The oil and salts formed an uneven loop around the porcelain. The tub ring, like my family circle, was fragile but unbroken.

Born and raised in Canada, educated in Australia and published internationally, Charmian Christie's writing is as diverse as her background. Her work has been heard on CBC national radio and appears in various magazines and anthologies.

MERLIN

By Yvonne Oots

It has always been the rule of thought that a story, or in this case a biography, should start at the beginning. This story will have to be an exception to the rule, or any rule for that matter. The beginning lies far back in time.

This is a story about my best friend. His name you know, his exploits documented by the greatest of scribes. For centuries, stories about him have undergone alterations to suit the taste of the times, rewritten to suit not only the writers of the day but also current beliefs. However, this is not such a story. This is a candid account experienced first-hand by this writer. A writer who knows him well—a great deal better than the writers of days long forgotten.

His name, you ask? Why, it is none other than Merlin. Yes, that is right: Merlin. You will best remember him from the Arthurian Tales, which paved the way for us to meet. Merlin and I were attending a meeting of Arthur's Round Table. It was, of course, by invitation only; Merlin was the guest of honor, and I had sneaked in. I was but a silent mouse sitting in the shadows of a corner.

Merlin, pretending that I was not there, gave his speech and released the knights to go on their way. Thinking I had succeeded in not being seen, I silently crept my way across the floor so as not to draw attention to the fact that I had heard one word from this mighty man. I was wrong. Merlin knew!

As he bent over and picked me up, I fully expected to be fed to the cat, but fortunately for me, that was the furthest from the truth. Merlin called me by name and announced that he had been waiting for me. "You should not have been so shy," he announced in his booming voice. "Why, my knights would have enjoyed meeting you." Continuing, taking nary a breath—I thought he would burst or at least turn blue if he did not stop talking to me and just breathe—he asked, "How are your legs today? It is a bad day because you are here again. Oh, yes," he continued, still not pausing to breathe, "I have noticed you before; you have been here many, many times."

Before I could say a word, Merlin kept right on telling me all about *me*—much to my surprise, and I might add, to my delight. His questions were boundless and they kept me utterly amazed that he knew so much about me.

When he finally stopped and allowed me to speak, the only thing that I managed to sputter was, "Thank you." Not allowing him to utter another word, I told him how we first met; I even remembered the time of day it was. "Thank you for being here on my bad days," I repeated.

Merlin knew that I was born with a dual spinal birth defect, Spina Bifida coupled with Spondelothesis. My childhood did have happy days of running around outside. There were an unequal number of days that bled into weeks that left me at the mercy of the endless number of body casts that were used to stabilize and strengthen my back. Headaches with dizzy spells, combined with the painful aspects of standing due to the Spina Bifida, meant my days were consumed by the long silence of loneliness. School friends distanced themselves from me upon my return, showing their curiosity but letting me know of the differences between them and me.

It was on one of those painful days that I discovered books, and moreover, the stories that lay between the boundaries of the covers. The stories intrigued me at first, as did the places the stories invited me to visit. Places that I knew of, and places nameless to me at that time.

I soon realized that I could go anywhere and be anything that I wanted to be. It was through those books that I learned to fly. I flew with eagles over the Native lands of Montana and the Dakotas. I witnessed firsthand the coronation of a great Queen of Russia. I learned the travails of a woman named Joan of Arc. I walked side by side with Sacagawea. The places and people that I could meet all within the margins of a book left me spellbound.

It was through those stories and many others that I learned to transform the dark days into magical times to explore the world. It is through the lives of those heroic beings I met along the way that I learned to look inside myself and find a strength that has never left me. The strength of the heroes in the stories taught me that I did not have to settle for being 'sickly.' That with courage and determination, there was another path that I could take.

Today I walk without pain. The surgery I endured, the year of physical therapy to relearn to walk, is a lifetime away from me now. Today I still meet with great queens and fly with the eagles over Native lands. Sacagawea and I have become sisters. She taught me the most. She taught me, above all things, to trust what I see within myself, knowing freedom is just one step away.

Today I live just one step away of where I could have been: unable to walk and unable to realize my dreams. The memory of that time is now only a reminder of what lay ahead of me, and that I alone will decide fate.

My days as a child are long gone. Until, that is, I succumb to the call of a book and once more, transport myself back to the days of Arthur, where I sit in the shadows and wait for Merlin to finish his lessons to those mighty knights. With patience, I wait my turn to show him my newfound treasure of words.

Strength lies only one step away. Sometimes it is not a journey to the outside, but to the inside of your heart. Look deep. Who knows what you will find? Maybe one day you, too, will write of the many friends you found along the way.

Today, Yvonne is a writer who pays respects not only to the legends she remembers as a child, but writes about her newfound friends of today. Taking life one step at a time.

WHAT REMAINS

By Audrey Glassman Vernick

The shopping bag is gray, from a New York department store that went out of business years ago. I don't remember how it came into my childhood home, but I know how it left. That journey began sometime in April 1989, when it was stuffed—swollen and overflowing—with condolence cards.

Like all deaths, my mother's death was awful. She was on the sidewalk, exactly where she was supposed to be, when she was hit by a car that had been hit by another. The accident happened just when things were getting especially exciting in her life. Her second grandson was about to be born and her first novel was about to be published—by the first publisher to whom she sent it.

In the long days that followed the funeral, our mailbox was filled with condolence cards. And this mattered. Each card mattered. The pile of cards was a tangible thing, a physical presence that illustrated how many lives had been affected, diminished, by our horrible loss.

Late at night I went through the growing piles and read the cards, then reread the cards. I'm sure my sisters and father did the same. When the piles grew too big, we started keeping them in the gray shopping bag. It was probably my father who pulled it, empty and folded, from the cabinet above the oven, where my mother had stored it. When the cards stopped coming, he must have put the bag away.

I imagine that he kept it in the big closet in the bedroom that had been my parents', and became just his. I picture it tucked in the corner, back where she used to hide our presents. The bag was just there, never looked at. And then, as unlikely as it had seemed during those slowed-down days of bereavement, time passed.

For my father, my mother was the wonderful first chapter of his adult life. It ended horribly, left him bereft, but he did his work and moved on. I know he still cherishes her memory deeply, but it is in its place. For a daughter, though, the end is not nearly so tidy.

Once an unsuspecting soul asked me what it felt like, how I would describe my loss, and I said it was as though a hole was torn in my guts—someone reached in and pulled out my heart and entrails—and then told me to proceed with my life.

When my father prepared to move into a new home with his second wife, he came across the cards again. His new wife had also been widowed and they both carried so much weight, so much back-story into their new lives. It was time for him to find a new place for the gray shopping bag.

And so it came into my house, the physical embodiment of The Bereaved Years. I did not know where to put it, how to treat it. I stashed it in a corner of my office and waited for the day I'd be ready to deal with it, whatever that meant. It just sat there, its cards and envelopes with their 25-cent stamps threatening to spill over, break through the torn seams at any time. One day I looked the bag in the eye and placed it in the closet—it's what we Glassmans do.

Years later, eight months pregnant with my second child, I had to transform my office into a nursery. Out came the bag, back into the room, inviting attention. Still, there was never a moment when I felt a strong and sudden desire to empty the bag onto the floor and wade through all that sympathy. But one night, when my son was asleep and my husband downstairs, I just began.

Going through that bag was not cathartic exactly—I had already had that catharsis a hundredfold. It was Catharsis Revisited. All that I had lost came flooding back, spilling over the roadblocks, the tall towers that time and the events of my life had erected. It was painful, excruciating, but it was also strangely, perversely satisfying.

Something had changed. The bulk of that bag had once been a necessary validation: All those people had been witness to our loss, to the loss of a life that was supremely significant. But numbers didn't tell the story anymore. It was time to hone, to edit, to cut away. To throw away.

So I sat and read the cards. And I cried, hard. I cried to the point of a headache and beyond. Primary sources tap right into the raw emotions of those days; they're a time machine of emotions. I was very pregnant, already loving a new little person within me, and aching for a person who was gone. I was feeling the push and swirl of a life that was almost ready to start while inviting a withered grief back to full bloom.

There were hundreds of cards. And the ones that touched me the most were from people I'd never met. My mother had been taking a writing class at the New School in New York for two years. In that time, she'd gone from a beginning writer to an about-to-be-published novelist. This was a world—the only one—in which she existed without her family.

We received so many cards from the women in that class. I don't know if there were men in the class—it was her world—but the women wrote to us. Their cards and notes were touching little masterpieces of exquisite beauty. Her classmates wrote with reverence about her sweet, kind friendliness. They were proud of her publishing achievement as if it were their own. They considered her a fine writer, an excellent and gentle critic, a wonderful person.

My mother would have never allowed herself this knowledge. She was genuinely humble and would not have noticed how much respect she commanded from her classmates. And even if she had some suspicion of it, she would have never told us; it is something we would have never known about her. I am so grateful to these women for taking the time, for being so brave, for passing along that offering to a family they never met. When we received the cards, the pain was too great to realize the beauty of that gift. But it sparkles brightly for me now.

Many condolence cards were dropped in my recycling bin that night. Years before, it would have felt like a hideous heresy to discard them, but I was able to do it without great regret. Some were passed along to one of my sisters. They're still in that torn gray shopping bag, taking up room in her house. I've kept a box, a sturdy white cardboard box that's 7 inches wide, 11 inches long and 2.5 inches deep. It contains the cards that matter to me. The ones from the writers are on top.

And now the closet where the bag used to be is filled with sweet little dresses and small sassy shoes. And the box is in my own closet. I will always keep this box. It will not be whittled down. This is what remains. My children may some-day wonder what they're supposed to do with this box, what to make of it. I trust that time will guide them to the answer. Time has a way of doing that.

Audrey Glassman Vernick is the author of the picture book Bark and Tim: A True Story of Friendship. She received NJ Arts Council Fiction Fellowships in 1999 and 2005. She writes for children and adults.

CONDEMNED AND REDEEMED

By Janine Peterson

My house was condemned. What hurt more than the sight of the gaping hole above the upstairs guest bedroom, more than the absence of the cedar shingle roof, more than the oily smell of smoke that permeated even the milk in the fridge, was the sign that had been nailed onto the front door: "This house is unfit for human occupation."

Lightning struck my family's home the night after I graduated from high school. I was in bed when the loud crackle startled me awake at 11:11 p.m. Tentatively, I stepped out into the dark hallway and approached the far guest bedroom where my mom's family—four siblings and a herd of my cousins—slept just the night before. I noticed a ghostly shape at the top of the stairs that seemed to warn me away from the closed door. Scared, I ran back to my room and jumped into bed. The figure, in retrospect, might have been my mother's father, my grandfather, and opening the door to the guestroom might have created a dangerous backdraft. I fell back asleep.

Forty-five minutes later, my mom woke me in a panic. "The house is on fire!" I sat up in bed and choked on the black, acrid cloud that poured into my room. We all ran outside. The flames reached maybe ten feet above the roof. They were the only light under the starless, overcast sky.

I later learned that the lightning short-circuited the upstairs smoke alarms, but our dogs were restless and eventually annoyed my father to the point where he walked out of the master bedroom and smelled the smoke himself. The dogs probably saved our lives. I remember wandering around in the early morning rain, watching the flames shoot much too close to my own bedroom. I remember running barefoot with my brother in the wet grass, waving down the fire trucks, as if they needed help finding the pillar of fire. I remember clutching our dogs. And I remember the sign: "CONDEMNED." We were legally homeless.

The firefighters saved most of the house, where we had lived for two years, as well as many of our possessions, though everything reeked of smoke and was covered with soot. Having moved at least nine times before, I had long defined home as anywhere I had a roof, a pillow, and my family. After the fire, I had only one out of three. At some point I realized I would need to sleep. And eat. And change out of my pajamas. But I had no idea where that would be. I watched as the photographs and journal that I saved from the flames collected rainwater on the lawn.

We had neighbors with sons about my brother's age. My brother was a sophomore in high school, and the boys were a year older and a year younger than him. Dan hung out with them and sometimes played in their pool. One Halloween they stole our pumpkin and returned it intact on November 1. Their father hated our dogs because they would bark at anything that moved down our street. Sometimes he screamed at them. Sometimes my mom yelled back.

But even though they were more acquaintances than friends, they opened their home to us. As my mom threw away all the smoke-contaminated food in our fridge, our neighbors offered our family home-cooked meals. It was that simple. We needed food and they invited us to their table. We needed beds and they gave us a place to sleep. We needed clean clothes and they let us use their washing machine. We smelled of soot and they welcomed us regardless.

They brought us, literally, out of the rain, and offered to let us stay indefinitely at their pool house, which had two bedrooms and a pool table. Our blackened possessions stank up the rooms until I couldn't smell them anymore, but at least I had a bed. It might have been just another bed to a girl who had moved and traveled as much as I had, but it was offered at a time when I couldn't imagine where I would sleep. I didn't have my clothes or my books or the photos from the years when I was taller than my brother, but I had a place to rest my head. Simply having something, even if it was borrowed, gave me strength to face what I had lost.

For days afterward we picked through the remains of our home. Everything was coated with greasy soot. My mother's hope chest was irreparably scarred, though my father was able to salvage a few decorative pieces to work into the chest he built for me several years later. A guest bathroom sink had liquefied, then congealed into a colorless ball. All of my books were gray. I found charred pieces of carefully archived second grade homework assignments strewn across the backyard. Our luggage, hard-sided plastic suitcases that had followed us across five continents, had melted into the attic floor. I kept the useless key on my key chain for weeks.

I sorted the contents of my room into four piles: one for immediate cleaning, one for long-term storage, one for short-term storage (because I now had to pack for college three months earlier than expected) and the last for the dump. My brother, meanwhile, used the quiet of our neighbors' guesthouse to study for his ongoing high school exams.

A few days later we moved to a hotel, then rented a house for six months while ours was rebuilt. I left for college not knowing to which home I would return at Christmas. But thoughts of our neighbors' kindness sustained me through that semester.

After we got the keys to our dorms, I threaded them along with the old luggage key. It was a key to where I came from. I needed to remind myself that I came from more than nothing. Lightning and fire might have burned away the physical past, but not my memories. And I will always, always remember.

Janine lives near DC. She writes about martial arts and shooting from a feminist view, and she writes about local Maryland history. Currently working toward her MA in psychology, she is also writing about teenagers.

ONE BREATH AT A TIME

By Cynthia L. Kryder

My friend Deb is dying. It is not a horrible cancer that is slowly killing this 45-year-old, vivacious mother of two, as you might expect, no tumor that can be scorched with radiation or excised with the scalpel. Instead, it is a lesser-known disease that is prematurely ending her life.

Deb and I have been friends for more than 25 years, ever since we were college coeds in the 70s, sisters in the same sorority. We are blessed to be part of a cadre of nine women, sorority sisters all, who've remained close to one another through the passage of time. Even with jobs, husbands, children, and moves that have taken some of us around the country, we still gather every spring at the Super 8 Motel in Lancaster, just as we've done for the past two decades.

We come bearing bad jokes and bottles of Merlot and zinfandel, with a few pony bottles of Rolling Rock beer thrown in for old time's sake. Like the teenagers we were when we first met, we curl up on lumpy mattresses, wear baggy T-shirts to bed, and talk well into the early morning hours, even after we turn off the lights. Over time, our conversations have matured from discussions about childbirth and potty training to menopause and sexual dysfunction. But never, ever have we talked about death and dying. Until now.

When Deb was diagnosed with idiopathic pulmonary fibrosis more than a year ago, I knew nothing about IPF. Since then I've learned volumes about this devastating disease that is weaving its insidious honeycomb throughout my friend's lungs, robbing her of her breath and eventually her life. I know that Deb is one of a handful of people in the United States who suffer from IPF and for whom the cause of the disease is unknown. I know that although prednisone might slow the progression of IPF, medical science offers no cure. I know that unless she receives a lung transplant, my friend most likely has less than two years to live. I know that even with a transplant, her chance of surviving another five years is probably less than 50 percent. And I know that donor organs, lungs in particular, are in very short supply.

Deb and I live 90 miles apart and, because of the distance, I am able to visit her only once a month. I drive across the Pennsylvania Turnpike bearing my old, red and white Coleman cooler with the rusty lid filled with home-cooked meals that perfume the inside of my car with the smell of my mother's kitchen. Living so far away, I feel helpless because I cannot do Deb's weekly laundry or take her to doctors' appointments or keep her company while her husband works. To assuage my guilt, I prepare foods I know she likes—sticky-sweet shoo-fly pie, saffron-yellow chicken pot pie, savory beef barley soup with chunky carrots—labor-intensive recipes I don't normally make even for my own family.

When I arrive at her split-level home north of Harrisburg, I know the front door will be unlocked. Deb is in the living room, seated in the quilt-covered recliner, waving to me from the picture window. Her bichon frise, Callie, barks and greets me as I open the door and she dances around my legs, almost tripping me as I climb the stairs.

When I reach the top, the first thing I notice is Deb's breathing. Because of her limited lung capacity, she takes rapid, shallow breaths, her chest rising and falling quickly. Watching her, I try to imagine what it's like to breathe this way. Unconsciously, I take short, quick breaths myself, but stop after ten seconds. It is too difficult for me, a healthy person, to breathe in this fashion. How can Deb do this day in, day out, I wonder?

Deb is not a petite person. Of average build, when she stands she is at least an inch or so taller than my 5'7" height. Now, reclining in her La-Z-Boy, she appears small and fragile. Her sweatpants and sweatshirt hang on her frame and I can barely see the outline of her limbs through the cotton fleece. She looks weary and it is obvious that she has lost weight since my last visit. As I approach her, she struggles into a sitting position to greet me.

Walking across the living room is like maneuvering through an obstacle course and I take small, deliberate steps. It is a distance of only nine or ten feet, but I don't want to risk becoming entangled in the tubes that carry her oxygen. She is breathing oxygen simultaneously from two tanks today, not a good sign, and I know that I will need to do most of the talking.

When I finally reach the recliner, I stoop and wrap my arms around her. Her back is bony and I can feel the outline of her ribs, but we hug each other tightly as she whispers, "I love you. Thanks for coming." The life-sustaining gas she is never without hisses in my ear. She smells of bath soap and her now-curly auburn hair, cut in a short, perky style, tickles my neck. I know that another friend probably came this morning to give Deb a wash and blow dry. Even with a terminal illness, Deb wants her hair to look good. The thought makes me smile and I tease her about her curls, the only pleasant result of the prednisone therapy she has endured for the past 12 months.

Our two-hour visits rarely vary these days, now that Deb is no longer able to walk more than a few steps. Callie jumps on my lap and allows me to rub her belly. I wash the dirty dishes in the sink and straighten up the kitchen. Deb and I converse about the nuts and bolts of ordinary life. I banter about my kids and my job, share the latest news of our friends. We laugh about her 18-year-old son and his constantly missing car keys and we chat about her 16-year-old daughter's boyfriend and the upcoming prom. I refill her water glass and bring her lunch on the metal tray with the painted flowers.

And finally we speak about the inevitable. We cry, but there is no ranting or raving, no self-pity or sentimentality, for even as her condition worsens, Deb holds firm to her belief that something positive will come from this ordeal. She speaks of her illness with grace and dignity, and I marvel at her composure, as well as her faith.

With Callie draped across her legs, Deb lists the good things that have happened since she became ill. Her son has learned to do his laundry and her daughter has learned to cook and clean up after herself. Deb no longer cringes when casual acquaintances wash and fold her underwear or search through her kitchen cupboards. She has learned to humbly accept the meals and groceries friends bring without feeling guilty that she can't reciprocate. She's learned to ignore the dust accumulating on the bookcase and the lint sticking to the carpet. She's come to relish the feel of Callie's creamy white fur beneath her fingertips and she finds joy in simply sitting in a chair and watching the clouds move across the sky. And she's learned to savor a piece of pie, bite by bite, without worrying about the calories.

Yes, my friend Deb is dying. But in the process she's sharing with me her newfound ability to slow down and approach life one day—and one breath—at a time.

Two weeks after entering the end stages of IPF, Deb received a double-lung transplant. She is alive today and recently celebrated her 50th birthday.

Cyndy Kryder has been a freelance writer for more than 13 years. She writes primarily about health and medical issues from her home in Southeastern Pennsylvania. This essay previously appeared at www.stories1st.org.

STRENGTH OF LOVE

"There is a comfort in the strength of love;
'Twill make a thing endurable, which else
Would overset the brain, or break the heart"

~ William Wordsworth (*Michael*)

A GIRL'S HOME IS HER CASTLE

By Jenna Glatzer

Whether she prefers crinoline and lace-trimmed ankle socks or overalls and skinned knees, nearly every little girl dreams of being a princess.

Still dizzy from the endorphin rush that Goofy provided when he asked me to dance in the food court, I had just returned from my first trip to Disney World. No longer was my teenage babysitter the woman I aspired to be; now I had loftier goals. I was going to be Cinderella. Too precious to set her feet on the concrete and socialize with the ice cream-stained masses, she retained her mystique by dressing to the nines and sitting in her exquisite castle, waving that "royalty wave" to passers-by.

The castle is what lured us there in the first place; the barrage of commercials and postcards displaying that magnificent monument left my toddler jaw agape. Parents are powerless against that wistful stare, especially when it comes from their firstborn. So, perhaps it's no great surprise that they scrimped and saved until I got to see Cinderella's estate up close—but less expected was what came next.

My father toiled in the backyard with a box of hand-me-down tools in hand, night after night, late enough to breach the rules of neighborly etiquette and cause my mother to throw her arms in the air. "Come to bed," she'd call. "You're disturbing the peace!"

No one ever complained, though. Instead, neighbors stopped by with unexpected donations of spare material or free labor. "I was working on a freight elevator in Manhattan, and the landlord said they're demolishing an old water tower," said next-door neighbor Nick. "Bet there'll be plenty of good lumber we could take."

And off they went in a rented truck, carting away enough redwood for the floor and framework, while Mom stayed home with me, practicing spelling lessons. After the frame came the wire lathe, which was next smothered in layers of stucco, textured with trowels. As weeks passed, there was no mistaking where this project was heading: My father was building me my very own castle.

No tree fort would suffice. This would be a bona fide three-tiered Cinderella castle, complete with wall-to-wall carpeting, electricity, and hand-painted flags atop "waving towers." The grandeur didn't quite compete with the castle that's still safely ensconced in the theme park, but it was a castle nonetheless, and 4-year-olds don't have much of a sense of scale. To me, the 12x6-foot structure my dad built in the backyard was a palatial fantasy den, fit for the finest of princesses.

Mine wasn't the sort of block where castles blended into the scenery. We lived in a neighborhood where all the kids played ball in the streets, and four families packed into one high ranch that was conspicuously missing a lawn. It was a block where someone was always muttering expletives under a broken jalopy, unwilling to let it retire in peace. Like all such neighborhoods, everyone planned to some day make it out, but the same faces remained year after year.

My father was a young science teacher, my mother an English teacher. She loved her work, but had to give it up when my younger brother, Paul, was born with Down syndrome. "I heard you had a little Mongoloid," the family doctor proclaimed when he visited my mother soon after she'd given birth. "You should start thinking about institutions."

That was the 70s, before the world caught up to my mother and figured out that people with Down syndrome weren't just defective products to be weeded out of the factory line. She worked tirelessly with her always-smiling son at daily "early intervention" classes, helping to build his underdeveloped motor skills by balancing him on an exercise ball, or forcing him to reach out for toys.

According to books, I was supposed to resent all the attention paid to Paul. It didn't seem to matter that Paul was my favorite human being; my father was convinced that somewhere deep inside, I must have felt slighted. That worry fueled him, and the need to erase it dictated his manifesto. For months, I believed his hair had changed colors, despite my mother's explanation that the blonde speckling was errant sawdust, and the white splotching was stucco.

He was a man on a mission to make me feel like a princess, despite the popular notion that such lofty feelings were best reserved for those who could afford a ticket to the upper class. I had no concept of designer clothes or fancy furniture, or what it would be like to have two bathrooms. What I did have, however, was a five-and-dime store glittered tiara to wear in my turreted castle.

All the local kids came to play "kingdom" with me, and I chose my irresistible 5-year-old next-door-neighbor, Marc, to be my prince. It wasn't a tough choice; he was the only boy in town who wasn't yet jaded by the fear of "girl cooties." His title meant that he got to wear a crown whenever he came in, and I would make sure to run my toy vacuum cleaner if I thought he might visit.

Marc was everything a little prince should be. When anyone used the word "retard," even when the intent was innocuous, he considered it a call to arms. The word always fell carelessly from someone's lips, then hung in the air for a moment, mutating into a tightly strung bow and arrow that would leave jagged holes in my young faith in humankind. I knew the word was an assault on Paul, even when the neighborhood kids just thought it was a generic synonym for "dummy." Marc knew it, too, and fought tirelessly to preserve the honor of his princess and her beloved brother.

That, and he taught me the meanings of all of the important swear words, even writing them for me on my blackboard so I could practice them when he was out slaying dragons. It wasn't until years later that I learned he'd spelled them all wrong.

My father remembers that we liked to run out there on rainy nights to watch for lightning from the upper windows. I remember cooking elaborate plastic cuisine on the play-stove. I remember the flags my mother painted, meticulously sculpted out of thin metal to appear windblown. I remember that they let me paint the first coat on the teardrop-shaped door, provided I put a smock over my gown. I remember loving that smock even more than the gown.

There's something about a fantasy oasis in the middle of a run-down town that's both startling and inspiring, like a tenacious flower that somehow blooms out of cracks in the concrete. Inspiration is infectious; even the local paper caught wind of it and sent a photographer to capture the unveiling.

When my father started his own car wash, his salary outgrew our humble home. We moved to one of those blocks where homeowners associations enact bylaws outlawing basketball hoops and gauche kiddie pools, and the street smells of old money. On my first day of sixth grade, a classmate asked me where I lived. When I told her, she said, "Oh. So, you're rich?"

"No," I answered. I used to be rich, I thought, but I don't have a castle any more. Even though I was 10 when we left, and had traded much of my tea-time and plastic tomatoes for Sweet Valley High books and singing lessons, the castle never turned "uncool" when coolness became important. It still bothered me that someone else would peek out of the Plexiglas windows fastened with piano hinges in the tower. Or so I thought.

The truth was worse than I envisioned. The new owners tore down what took my father months to build. Worse, they did it in favor of a standard-issue, comes-with-instructions swing set. Maybe they saw the castle as frivolous. Our old, heartbroken neighbors called to say, "It's gone," voices grave as if an old friend had died. The new owners hadn't just torn down a structure; they'd razed a dream.

That dream taught me that my worth had nothing to do with money or stature. It showed me that beauty can grow from unlikely places, and that fulfilling the plans our imagination creates is more rewarding than accumulating expensive "stuff." And it taught me that anyone could be a princess.

Luckily, my treasures weren't stored in the walls of the castle. They were stored in memories of tea parties and storytelling, and in photographs of friends with hands cupped, doing their best Cinderella waves and beaming the smiles that "real" royalty practice, but erupt in earnest from happy children. That's the legacy of a father's love that no swing set can ever replace.

Jenna Glatzer is the editor in chief of AbsoluteWrite.com and the author of 14 books, including Celine Dion: For Keeps and Hattie, Get a Haircut! Visit her site at www.jennaglatzer.com.

Sixteen Times

By Kathy Powers

I had a baby nephew, and though he lived only three days
He won my heart forever with his soft and gentle ways.
My brother, a new father, oh how hard it had to be
To lose a child just like that. Last night he said to me:

"Sixteen times I got to see him. Sixteen times I got to say
'Daddy's here now and I love you,' and I said it every day.
Sixteen times he grabbed my finger. Sixteen times he held it tight.
On the night that he was born, the stars were shining bright.

Though my nephew was a fighter and a whole lot like his dad,
In the end, it cost him all the strength his little body had.
But my brother never gave up on his brand-new, infant son.
He believed in silver linings, that this battle would be won.

"Sixteen times I got to see him. Sixteen times I got to say
'Daddy's here now and I love you,' and I said it every day.
Sixteen times he grabbed my finger. Sixteen times he held it tight.
I believed within my soul that he would be all right."

So, I never saw it coming; like a bolt out of the blue,
And one day, I had a nephew, and the next, no baby Drew.
The loss was overwhelming, but I broke through from my haze
When he said, "Sis, I was lucky. I had Drew for three whole days!"

"Sixteen times I got to see him. Sixteen times I got to say
'Daddy's here now and I love you,' and I said it every day.
Sixteen times he grabbed my finger. Sixteen times he held it tight.
And I know he's found his home in a better place tonight."

Kathy Powers lives in Spring Lake Heights, New Jersey. She has four nieces and two nephews. She wrote this poem 12 years ago, after the death of her first nephew, Christopher Andrew ("Drew") Powers, Jr. Her e-mail address is jerseypeach@optonline.net.

By Kimberly Ripley

I was 11 when I first met Gordon. My mother and father had been divorced only a matter of days, so I wasn't a prime candidate for meeting Mother's new beau. I treated him rudely despite the gifts he brought me. I didn't want anything to do with anyone who might stand in the way of what I knew would be an imminent reconciliation between my parents.

At 14, I gained a stepfather. Gordon and my mother married after three years of a turbulent relationship. By this time I had come to realize that I was gaining an ally right in my own home. Gordon didn't always agree with my mother's method of discipline. He, in fact, believed that children were interesting smaller versions of adults, and regarded their feelings and thoughts with an honesty and respect that I had never known.

Learning to accept him into my home and my heart brought me experiences I would have forgone otherwise. Gordon was understanding and appreciative of my love of the theater, and carted me back and forth to rehearsals, productions, and cast parties. He even let me have my own cast party at our house. He cooked for two days, set up an elaborate feast, and stayed upstairs while my friends and I indulged in sheer delight. When they went home, Gordon came back downstairs and cleaned the mess himself, sending me to bed.

"You worked hard," he said, referring to my part in the school play. "You need to go to bed."

He encouraged my friendships, and was one of those parents who constantly chauffeured groups of kids to dances and ball games. We'd pile into the back of his beat up Datsun pickup truck, covered with blankets, as he delivered each of my friends to their homes.

Enduring constant conflict with my mother, I reached a point one spring when I decided I'd prefer to go and live with my biological father. Knowing I would meet staunch opposition from my mother, I approached Gordon with my plan instead.

"I hate to see you go," he said. "But your happiness is what's important here."

As it turned out, my father wasn't able to have me come and live with him. Sadly, this caused a rift in my relationship with him. I was truly disappointed, but bolstered by the fact that Gordon had put my wishes and needs ahead of anyone else's including his own. This concept was new to me, but one I came to accept throughout my years with him.

When I married young and found myself in a dire financial situation he loaned me money, but never made me feel like I'd imposed. He became

"Grandpa Gordon" to my children. When my marriage failed, he encouraged and stood by me, and never once said, "I told you so."

He walked me down the aisle a second time, and welcomed more grandchildren. All the while he remained my rock and my strongest parental guide. Divorced from my mom for many years by this time, Gordon shared his joy at meeting and later marrying Carol, a wonderful woman, and they've since spent many happy years together.

Gordon never once in all these years said a negative word about my "real" father. In fact he encouraged our visits and praised his efforts. When my sister got married both Gordon and Dad walked her down the aisle. With Gordon's blessing both my sister and I have re-established our relationships with our father.

It has been documented by reams of philosophers that "blood runs thicker than water." I beg to differ with that statement. For although I love my natural father dearly, I have another father who has stood by me through thick and thin. He has taught me some of life's most valuable lessons. He remains my confidante and true friend. And he is my closest "relative."

From petulant pre-teen through adulthood I have had the honor of learning from this brilliant psychologist and professor. Yet none of my acquired knowledge touches on his profession. Instead I gained insight into what really matters in this life, and I learned that families are there to help us live it.

What did Gordon learn from all of this? That's hard to say. If I was to fathom a guess it would go something like a quote I've seen on greeting cards and wall hangings. It reads, "A hundred years from now it won't matter what kind of car I drove or how much money was in my bank account. What will matter is that I was important in the life of a child."

I was that child.

Doesn't God work in mysterious ways?

Kimberly Ripley is a freelancer and author of six books. She lives in New Hampshire with her husband, family, and very faithful dog. Visit Kim's website at www.kimberlyripley.writergazette.com.

AFTER DAKOTA

By Jennifer Lawler

Last month, I had to put my dog Dakota down. I held her while she died and, watching the light leave her eyes, thought how I could never do this again, the leaving, the being left behind.

Dakota was older than my daughter, outlasted my marriage, and was a true companion for many, many years. We struggled through countless tough times together and somehow I always thought she'd be with me forever—I'd be the curmudgeonly old lady with the big old happy malamute by her side.

I can still see her, trotting down the snow-filled road, looking back over her shoulder at me, her tongue hanging out of her mouth, smiling. She seemed to be saying, Are you coming? Let's play!

I remember the silky feel of her perky upright ears, and the way she loved me to scratch her face just below her eyes. Her joy in living was infectious. A treat, a belly rub, a game of Frisbee—it was all good, a delight. Every little thing was a joy: the smell of the rice on the stove, the cricket that made its way into the house, the stuffed toy she carried everywhere, her fluffy tail curving over her back.

When I was sad, she licked my tears away. When I spent too long at the computer, she'd burrow her wet nose into my hand, lifting it off the keyboard. Let's play, her wagging tail said. Nothing ever kept Dakota down for very long. Even when she was sick, she bounded across the velvet green grass of the park as if she were still new to the world, and danced with delight when she found a squirrel to chase.

When people asked me about pets, I'd say, I have a big ole malamute, Dakota. She's smarter than I am! She is so sleek and beautiful, I'd say. She's such a joy to be around. She is always *so there*. And then I would remember, and add, oh, I have a little mutt, too: Her name is Jasmine.

Losing Dakota was like losing my soul mate. She loved me exuberantly and without cause. With no conditions, unreservedly, not expecting anything in return. I wanted her to love me forever.

I thought, why couldn't it have been Jasmine? Why did it have to be Dakota who had to go so soon, too soon? We hadn't done everything yet. Images flashed through my mind of my sweet girl, my crazy puppy. The long road trips, the winter spent in the north woods of Minnesota, the unending games of fetch. Jasmine never learned to fetch.

When I come home from the vet, sobbing, Jasmine is there, waiting. She looks up at me with her sad eyes. She was abandoned as a tiny puppy and it affects everything she is. I look away from her sad eyes. We both have so many miles on us, so much hard work and exhaustion. All Jasmine ever asked was a bowl of food and a warm place in the sun.

All her life she has been overshadowed by the beautiful malamute. Strangers would come up to us when we went for walks. "What a beautiful dog!" they would croon. "May I pet her?" they would beg. They were never talking about Jasmine.

Sometime in the night, I remember I haven't fed Jasmine yet and I put some food in her bowl before stumbling back to bed. I hear her munching with relish and I remember how Dakota used to shove her out of the way, eating her fill first. The leftover crumbs were Jasmine's. I hear Jasmine gobbling down the bowl of food without stopping. It is the first time in her life she is allowed to eat unmolested, without her lower place in the hierarchy being reinforced.

Later in the night, she creeps into bed with me. I don't have the heart to toss her out. But it was always Dakota who slept next to me, her long heavy length stretched out against my back. Jasmine curls into a tight circle near my face and lets out a long sigh. It is not the same, but it is better than nothing, to have the warm weight on the pillow next to me. It is better than nothing.

In the morning I sit at my computer and Jasmine curls up on my feet. As I type, I feel Dakota's wet nose in my hand although I know she isn't there. Just for a moment, a brief pressure: Maybe she is here, after all, somehow? Despite the box of ashes I have put on the closet shelf? I call my sister. I can't say anything, I just cry. She knows it's me. She is trying to finish a tax report for her company, but she doesn't remind me of how busy she is. She just listens to me cry and after a little while I hang up the phone.

I look at Jasmine. She looks at me.

I reach down and touch her face. She is my skittish one; she has never been trusting. Once she broke her leg and had to stay in her crate to reduce the stress on her healing leg. She would hide the food I gave her under the bedding, I guess in case I stopped remembering to take care of her. It broke my heart at the time. I will take care of you, I would croon to her. I will take care of you. But she never quite believed me.

Her fur is coarse and short and she has floppy ears. Dakota used to grab her ears and tug. I stroke them now. Her expression is unreadable. I look back at the computer and get to work.

The next week, school starts. I walk Jessica to school every day. Dakota was supposed to be here with us; I had planned it. We were going to walk to school together, every day for years and years. It was going to be a memory that we looked back over, glad to have it. The emptiness is like a wound. I can see her tail curving over her back, the light in her eyes, the perk of her ears. She would have loved this.

A fallen leaf skitters across the street. Where is Dakota now? I wonder. I wish she were in the wind around me, or up in heaven the way I was told when I was a child. But I am afraid she is only in the box on my closet shelf.

Are you sad? Jessica asks. Yes, I tell her. You miss Dakota, don't you? she asks. Yes, I tell her. There is a long silence and then she says, I miss Dakota, too. Her pain, I think, is different from mine. She was not the one who had to say that this life of love and joy had to end, that there would be no more games of Frisbee or fetch, no more nights snuggled together, no more long walks on snowy afternoons.

One afternoon, I am getting ready to walk to school when Jasmine gets to her feet and goes to stand by the door. I stare at her. She lifts up a paw, touching the door, and looks at me. I realize she knows it is time to pick up Jessica and she wants to come with me.

But you don't like to go for walks, I say. She looks at me, then looks at the door. I get her leash, mostly unused, from the closet. I clip it onto her collar. She wags her tail tentatively, as if she is unsure how to do it.

Jasmine has always been my good dog. She has never been any trouble. She was house trained in minutes, once she understood what I was asking of her. She never eats trash out of the garbage or chews underwear or kitchen tools. She doesn't put her paws on the table or try to eat off my plate. She doesn't jump up on anyone. When I say sit, that is what she does. When I say heel, that is what she does. I used to tell stories about Dakota's outrageous escapades and then I'd say, off-handedly, of course Jasmine never does anything like that. She is such a good dog.

All she ever wanted was a warm place in the sun, and a bowl of food to eat. And that was all I ever gave her.

I close the door behind us and Jasmine lifts her muzzle to the wind. She trots up the driveway. She is a little dog, close to the ground. There is nothing beautiful and elegant about her. No one stops me to say, "What a beautiful dog! May I pet her?" She is just a mutt trotting along the street.

When we arrive at school, she sits quietly by the door, waiting for Jessica. Another student's father approaches me. "What kind of dog is that?" he asks with interest.

"A mutt," I say.

"She looks like she has some Brittany spaniel crossed with rottweiller," he says. He must know dogs; most people can't see beyond her squat, sausage body and her crooked bent tail.

"That's right. And she has some chow," I say. "She has a blue tongue."

He nods his head and says, "She's a good dog."

I look at her. She looks at me.

I am sure he means "good" in a different way from what I mean by it. I mean obedient and not too much trouble. He means "good" as in, a good dog to have. The kind of dog everyone should be lucky enough to own.

Jessica comes out of school. A puzzled expression crosses her face when she spots Jasmine. "What is she doing here?" Jessica asks.

"She wanted to come," I say.

"She *wanted* to come?" Jessica says, both eyebrows raised.

"Yes," I say, and lean down to pat Jasmine, and for a moment I forget that it was supposed to be Dakota who accompanied us home.

"Can I hold her leash, Mom?" I hand it over and Jessica gives me a big grin and the two of them go trotting off together. Jessica giggles and Jasmine wags her tail as they stoop to investigate a gutter. I suddenly realize that Jessica is touched by Jasmine's behavior. She is flattered that Jasmine wanted to come and walk her home.

This morning, for the first time ever, Jasmine springs onto the bed and licks my face to wake me up. Dakota used to do that, but I'm not thinking of Dakota this morning. I'm thinking of this annoying little ball of fur. I fend off her kisses and smile at her and say, "Hello, Jasmine." I bury my face in her neck. She has a good dog smell. I lift my head and look into her sad eyes. "Hello, good girl," I say, rubbing her ears. She jerks her muzzle toward the living room as if to say, Get up! Let's go!

I throw back the covers and she gives me a play bow. "I'm coming," I tell her. I rub her ears once more as I slip out of bed. I feel my heart opening up to her, my good dog. Even though I already know how this story will end.

Jennifer Lawler is the author of more than 20 books, including the popular Dojo Wisdom *series. Her articles and essays have appeared in* Family Circle, Oxygen, Cooking Light, Minnesota Monthly *and more. She can be reached through her website at www.jenniferlawler.com.*

FIRST BORN

By Kathryn Morrison

She is my firstborn. You know the one I mean—the child who is never allowed to get dirty. The child who has never had one drop of formula pass through those perfect lips that wasn't heated to the exact right temperature. The child who never cried for more than 30 seconds without the parents peering into the bassinet, wondering if they should call the doctor.

It was the first pregnancy, where every little twinge, cramp and strange feeling sends you running to get the *Reader's Digest Medical Guide*. Is this normal, should I call the doctor?

The first labor. Will it never end? What do you mean I'm only six centimeters? It's going to take how much longer? Thank God for that little can of gas strapped to my wrist!

The first born. The perfect culmination to the first part of your perfect marriage. The child born at least ten months after the wedding. The grandparents can breathe a sigh of relief.

The first born. Look at those tiny perfect toes. There are ten of them and ten fingers and two tiny ears and two incredibly beautiful eyes and one perfect little mouth. All parts present and accounted for, and all in the right place.

The first smile, the first "Mama," the first steps, kisses, and hugs. My first daughter. My new best friend.

Four years old. She has been out of my sight only for the two days I spent in the hospital giving birth to her younger sisters.

Four years old. Big sister to a 3-year-old and a 2-year-old. Best friend to her 21-year-old mother. Burden carrier for her 26-year-old father. Peacemaker for her screaming parents. Mommy, Daddy, please let's pray for Jesus to make Daddy well. Tears streaming down that perfect, innocent, perfectly innocent face. Sitting in the dark behind Daddy's big chair, ripping her favorite book to shreds. One long shred after another, page by page.

A warm, sunny day in November, sitting with Mommy and Daddy at the picnic table. Gentle breezes lift long golden hair from sad gray eyes. It's the first time she has seen her Daddy in two days. He wants her to make the decision; should he go to the hospital and get better, or stay home and just try harder to behave? Without a pause, she, only four years old, answers: "The hospital, please, Daddy. Let the doctors make you better so Mommy won't cry any more." My first born. My best friend.

Nine years old. Big sister to 8- and 7-year-old sisters and a 2-year-old brother. Caretaker of her sick father. Jesus helped Daddy get the medicine he needed for his mind, but now his head does funny things. It turns to the left all the time. We need to ask Jesus to fix that, too. Correcting me for my hysterical outburst when there would be no Easter Bunny money that year. Helping me protect her sisters and brother. Protecting them from me. My best friend.

Twelve years old. We have moved to the new house and into the twentieth century. 1986 and we have electric heat and air, hot running water, a real bathroom. Too bad Daddy's sick, but hey, we have a phone! I sit at the kitchen table and watch the hands on the clock creep around to the time when she will get off the school bus and be home again. I know she will help me cope with getting dinner cooked, dishes washed, homework and bath time. She will tell me funny stories about her friends and teachers at school. She will help me forget for a little while. She is my best friend.

Fifteen years old. She is running wild, drinking, smoking, and sexually active. Going straight to hell and taking one sister with her. Rebelling because that is what teenagers do. Rebelling because everything is broken. Her faith—Daddy never got better and never will. Only worse and worse. The doctors say schizophrenia, she says he is just plain crazy. One sister on her way to juvey hall, the other living to go to church. Little brother still just a royal pain. Her Mom, maybe the most broken one of all. I should stop being her friend and be her mother. Too late to pull rank on her now. She has always been part of the decision-making process. She resents me now. Finally, even the family is broken. She is banished from it. Sent away from home and friends, away to another state. Gone to live with her aunt, far away. It feels like labor all over again. My firstborn is being ripped away from me. I threw away my best friend. She is gone. She will not be coming home on the school bus. She will not be making me feel better. She is gone and I am crying in the dark like I will never stop. My best friend, my first born, is gone.

Years of tension and hostility. A very cold war begins. I do not attend her wedding. I do not want her married at 17.

The cold war thaws. I must be there for the birth of her firstborn. I work two eight-hour shifts back-to-back and drive 600 miles to get there just in time for her labor to begin. My firstborn in labor with her firstborn. My one-time best friend giving birth to her new best friend. My baby girl has a baby boy. My first grandchild is a grandson.

I get her back just in time to lose her again. I lose my daughter and my grandson to her mother-in-law. The mother-in-law had two sons, never a daughter. Now she has mine. I am fighting a battle for my sanity and cannot fight for my daughter as well. The mother-in-law lives close to her; she has money, stability, and her sanity. I cannot compete. My marriage goes to hell. I lose my firstborn to her mother-in-law. I lose my middle daughter to pot, my youngest to alcohol, my son to foster care and finally, I lose my sanity. I am alone in darkness.

There is a tiny glimmer of light. A far-away voice is calling my name. There is one left who wants to be my friend. He cares that I have not laughed in years. He takes my hand and leads me slowly back into the light. I regain my sanity. My son comes home to me. My youngest daughter comes out of her alcoholic haze. My middle daughter meets and marries her knight in shining armor.

I marry the one who led me back to reality. My firstborn no longer holds anger toward me from the past. She is happy I am finally away from her Daddy. She is happy I am happy.

She comes home for the birth of her second child. A daughter. She comes home again when her marriage falls apart. She brings a new man, a mean abusive man who is the father of her third child, another daughter. She comes home yet again to try to work things out with her husband when she leaves the mean, abusive man. Sadly, her marriage cannot be repaired.

I want her to stand on her own two feet, without me or her sisters or a man to hold her up. I will not let her move back into my house. She runs to the mother-in-law who has money and stability. Soon, the money and stability turn into suffocation.

She flees the suffocation into the arms of husband number two. A marriage designed to hurt and humiliate husband number one, and it does. He is devastated and vows to get sole custody of their two children. Now, she is horrified she might lose her children. Attorneys are hired, names are called and mud is slung. Finally, they realize no one will win this fight. Only the children will lose. They agree on joint custody. She leaves the horrible mistake marriage. Now, everyone wins. Everyone is happy.

Twenty-seven years old. She has met a wonderful man who makes her happy at last. He has children, she has children, and they have a child together. Child number four for her. Another daughter. Her last child. At last, she is settled and happy.

Twenty-seven years old. The oldest child of a paranoid schizophrenic father. Schizophrenia strikes one in four and is hereditary. She has two sisters and a brother. Which one will it be? Any of them, none of them? She is almost out of the danger years. My son is just coming into them.

The phone rings very late one night. She wants to know the first signs Daddy showed. And how long was it before he was totally out of control? Mommy, I am so scared.

I go to Florida to be with my firstborn.

Tests are run. Doctors are seen. There is fear, so much fear. We talk and talk of days gone by, of old hurts and new hope.

Finally, the results are in. Thankfully, there are no true symptoms of this dreaded disease. She suffers from depression. She will be fine with treatment.

My firstborn, my oldest and best friend, the little girl I once leaned on, needed me. And this time I was strong enough for her to lean on me.

Kathryn Morrison and her husband live in coastal South Carolina. All four of her children are well and she loves spending time with her 10 grandchildren.

THE SMELL OF LILACS

By Catherine Lanser

If you've ever smelled lilacs, you know what hope smells like. They seem to know how hard it is to make it through the winter, so they put everything they have into producing the most beautiful-smelling blossoms they can muster. As a child I would lie under the lilacs for hours and breathe them in while Dad took down the storm windows. They seemed to appear out of nowhere and suddenly everywhere you looked bushy lilacs held out massive clumps of flowers, proudly releasing their magical smell. I could almost taste the scent in the air and it made me want to skip.

As I grew up, I never forgot about the lilacs. I store them in my mind the other three seasons, and in spring I prowl the neighborhood where I live to catch the fleeting smell of lilac bushes growing against strangers' fences. Perhaps because it is so spectacular, their bloom doesn't last long. I know I have to find them in time or I will miss them entirely. Breathing in their scent carries me to another world where my only concern is getting inside in time for dinner.

At least that's how it was until Dad's stroke. After that, the lilacs reminded me of the cleansing wipes the nurses' aides used at the nursing home to clean up after Dad. They were lilac-scented, I suppose to bring some joy to a difficult job, and when I used them after helping Dad to the bathroom, I didn't think much about it. The next spring I waited for the lilacs as I always had, but their scent brought me back to the chemically-manufactured smell of the cleansing cloths. Instead of making me want to skip, the smell nauseated me.

The phone rang at 5:15 the morning Dad had his stroke. Since I had to be at work at 5:30, it didn't even cross my mind that something bad had happened. I even cheerfully asked my brother how he was, as if he always called to catch up at that time of day. He told me what had happened and I heard it in bits and pieces as my head began to buzz. Mom had found Dad in the hallway. He was calling to her and he couldn't get up. He had a bad headache and was trying to get to the kitchen cupboard for aspirin. Mom recognized that he was having a stroke and called 9-1-1. By the time the ambulance arrived, he was unconscious.

The two-hour drive to the hospital was a blur. I joined Mom, two of my brothers, and my sister-in-law in the waiting room. They told me that Dad had suffered a hemorrhagic stroke, which meant that a blood vessel had burst in the back of his brain. They were in the process of deciding whether or not to allow the doctors to perform surgery to reduce the pressure inside his brain. It could improve his chances for recovery, but it was also likely that he would not make it through the surgery alive. Without the surgery, he could die within the next few hours.

We decided that Dad should have the surgery and we gathered in his room to say goodbye. He looked as if he was sleeping and I kissed his cold, pale forehead carefully. We formed a circle around his bed and a Catholic priest joined us to perform Last Rites. We held hands, praying the Our Father while a nurse in garden clogs reached through our circle and set a box of tissues on Dad's thigh. Dad was taken to surgery and gradually the rest of my siblings arrived, nine kids in all. The small waiting room felt swollen.

A few hours later we rallied when the doctors told us that he had made it through surgery. Everything seemed like it was back to normal, even though we were far from home. For the next 18 months, Dad's brain tried to heal itself, it seemed, one cell at a time. During that time we became acquainted with a man much different than the man we had known before.

Physically, he needed assistance to walk and lost his ability to swallow food. A food tube hung out of his abdomen and we used a syringe to feed him liquid nutrition that looked like wood glue. Mentally he had changed, too. He was confused, combative, and threw temper tantrums, swinging his arms and hitting you or lunging and biting you when you got close. Other times he talked about dead people and called us by their names. We laughed when we could, yelled back when we lost our temper, and grieved every day.

During his recovery, Dad went through a phase where he was unable to tune out stimuli and he fixated on the sensation of things touching him. His clothes, his shoes, his feeding tube—they were all needles to him. He waged a battle to end the discomfort, tearing off his shoes and socks, struggling to remove his clothes, even pulling his feeding tube out. We held his hands to keep him from tugging and tried to keep his mind occupied.

I tried to keep him busy by giving him sales flyers to read because it had been a hobby of his before the stroke. After he retired he had taken over the grocery shopping and it was more than just a task to him. It was an epic quest to get something for nothing. He would spend hours studying the grocery flyers and then spend hours more shopping at all the stores in town, but buying only what was on special. During weekly phone calls to me at college, he told me how much he had saved. By the way he talked, the stores were almost paying him to shop. But after his stroke he couldn't comprehend prices and the flyers just made him think of food, his other obsession.

Even though he couldn't swallow, his cravings for food were still strong. We tried to train him to swallow with pudding and thickened beverages, but they weren't what he wanted. He longed for solid food—the McDonald's outside the nursing home window taunted him. He felt that we were keeping food away to torture him, not understanding that any food he ate would likely end up in his lungs and cause pneumonia.

Without our help, he did whatever he could to get food on his own, even with limited mobility. He used his feet to wheel himself to the nursing home dining room and caused a stir trying to steal food from the other residents' trays. At home he managed to take a bite of the Styrofoam fruit that decorated Mom's table before she pried it from his mouth.

Dad stayed at four health facilities during his recovery and at every stay he begged us to take him home. Finally after 15 months, we were able to grant him his wish. My brothers helped him through the front door and he leaned heavily on his walker as they led him to his recliner and turned him around. He fell backward into it, beaming from ear to ear. My siblings and I took turns helping Mom care for him at home as his health began to decline.

Three months later, in early March, he died at home in the bedroom that had last been mine. I was supposed to be home that weekend but an unexpected spring blizzard kept me away and instead my sister went home to help. She called me early that day, telling me that she thought Dad was dying. I told her I would come home right away and was still packing when she called back to tell me he was gone.

As I drove home, I tried to remember what Dad had been like before his stroke, but I couldn't remember. The quiet, gentle person he had been had died and left behind an amplified version of a man he had never been. I couldn't remember the soft tone of his voice over the howling of this new man.

Over the past three years, my memories of Dad have returned. I feel his fingers tickling my feet when I was just a little girl. I see him directing an army of brothers to build a screen porch in an afternoon. I hear his voice telling me he loved me. And when the spring comes, it's as if he's right there with me while I breathe in the wonderful lilacs.

Catherine Lanser is a writer who lives in Madison, WI.

A JOURNEY HOME

By Harry E. Gilleland, Jr.

There across the expansive valley—
a valley lush and green,
now decorated so gaily
with summer flowers
of many hues and sweet scents,
above which float butterflies,
dragonflies, and honey bees
sparkling under the noonday sun.
There upon the far hillside lies
my journey's end, if her I please.

Before the war, this cursed war,
our betrothal lovingly was made—
young lovers torn apart by folly of man.
Have the four long years of absence
caused that love since to be betrayed?
I pray not . . . I pray for my journey's end.
So weary am I of fighting, bloodshed,
the stench of death, the ugliness of man!

I long to bask in the glory of nature,
to never again leave this valley,
to farm this land, to raise a family,
to live in peace and harmony,
to share my life and love with her,
if she loves me yet . . . soon I'll see.

As I stride through the valley,
I see her hanging clothes on the line.
Then she sees me. She stands immobile,
as if trying to decide. Does she love me still?
Will my journey have found its end,
or will it today just begin?

Uncertain, I slow my pace . . . and wait . . .
A shout of joy! Her washing falls
from her hand, as she now walks
toward me; then she runs, arms open,
ready to embrace. We hug. We kiss.
Our tears and hearts merge—all's right
in my world. I am home! Home . . .
to a place in her heart. It's not too late!

Reprinted from Gilleland Poetry: Storoems and Poems (Lulu Press, 2005).

Harry E. Gilleland, Jr. is a writer who lives in Shreveport, Louisiana. He has published two books of poetry and a prose novella. His work may be seen at www.gillelands.com/poetry.

BREASTFEEDING BOOGIE

By Kelly Pollard

The doctor dashed in as my son's tiny head hung halfway outside of my body. He had barely witnessed the race I had endured. With the snips of the thick cord, I thought I had seen and survived the most intense life experience I would ever have to conquer. The labor and delivery had been never-ending surges of body-thrashing contractions followed by a frenetically-paced delivery, ending with my tiny son in my limp arms. There could only be lazy, rose-colored paths ahead as a new family of three. Little did I know the true test of my strength would slope and swell for months more, as my son Bobby and I tried to learn the complicated waltz of breastfeeding.

I had trained well. A dutiful appearance at a prenatal class devoted solely to breastfeeding was firmly attached to my tool belt, which was also well stocked with a bulging bookshelf of parenting handbooks and nursing primers. My mind and body were aligned in what I thought was prime condition. However, no number of words read or videos studied can prepare a new mother for the physical feat and emotional hurdles of simultaneously nursing and mastering new motherhood.

The first time I took his tiny hand in my own and meekly guided his wobbly bobble-head to my breast was an awkward balancing act that ended in my blood pulsing in nervousness and Bobby dozing off without any attempt to latch on. The nurses didn't seem concerned, so I chalked it up to one sleepy mother-baby duo and put off the worries until later. The improvement never blossomed and my spirits withered with each attempt, first every three, then two, then every hour around the clock. I was sent home with a son who had barely consumed an ounce or two of milk in two days and me a big, emotional time bomb, operating on no sleep and heavy doses of hormones and insecurity.

Through and between the constant stream of visitors bestowing meals and gifts and love on my new family, Bobby and I continued to struggle. By his first doctor visit, my fears were confirmed. He had lost one pound and his tiny body was shrinking even out of the minuscule newborn sleepers that had seemed so tiny on the store racks. He was borderline preemie and my blood was streaked with shame, self-doubt, but no intention of giving up.

The marathon seemed to get steeper by the day, as he lost still more weight, when one by one, little bits of advice from doctors and lactation nurses failed to pan out. People surrounding me didn't understand my raw determination. I wouldn't give up. All they saw was Bobby's stick arms and sunken, alien-like eyes that seemed to grow bigger as his body shrank down. His tiny diapers had to be folded down two times to stay on his skinny body. Deep down, I knew I had to conquer this feat—as a woman and a mother. I would fight with all that I had to make this dance flow naturally between us.

Most days I felt like a prisoner to the whirling breast pump. Because Bobby wouldn't latch on, feedings were physical feats of pumping to relieve my engorged breasts and then various ways to get that thick, white milk into his body. Doctors and nurses offered conflicting advice. Don't dare give him a bottle, or he'll never learn to nurse. Give him a bottle or he will get even skinnier. He cooed and cried like a normal baby. I sobbed and sniffled like a defeated new mother. We finally settled on the exhausting routine of feeding him bottles, followed by me pumping for another half-hour to maintain my milk supply.

The turning point came when he was close to three weeks old. I thought all the alternatives had been exhausted and I was close to running off of the path I had sweated and cried and huffed over. I huddled in the doctor's office on my weekly visit with the nurse, who decided to try a nipple shield, a soft piece of silicon that fit over my nipple. Bobby suddenly "got it" and latched on. He stayed on and chugged milk. The creamy liquid spilled out of his frantic mouth and the gulps beat in sync with my disbelieving heart. There would be no more marathon pumping sessions, no more tears as I had to give him yet another bottle, then continue to pump, only to start the process anew an hour later. Finally, I could see that gleaming finish line and knew that we had made it.

A few more weeks and he was weaned off of the shield and we were finally nursing as nature intended. Of course the unimaginable physical rigors weren't completely eliminated. He was still eating every two hours, for close to an hour at a time. His doctor called it playing catch-up on the weight gain. But I was finally free to rock or lay with my son without all of those medical gadgets interfering with what I had imagined would be the most natural dance in the world. And once we learned the intricate steps and dips and turns, it really was.

Breastfeeding was a practice of endurance for me—endurance of physical stamina, of commitment to my own beliefs of what I thought best for my son, of emotional upheaval, and of jagged bits of determination. It was a steep battle where I finally gave up explaining my beliefs and my deep-set emotional need to nourish my baby with my own body, just as I had when I contained him in the folds of my belly. When I envisioned breastfeeding, I saw a slow lazy waltz, with a few simple steps that anyone could master. Raise the shirt, flip open the bra, draw in his birdy mouth, and slip my nipple inside. What I learned was that it was more like a chaotic hip hop dance, foreign to me, with awkward steps that all have to master at their own pace. I had been the girl always out of tune with the music, shoved to the outskirts of this life-affirming dance. Until that one sweet day of victory, when our steps finally became synchronized.

Kelly Pollard is a freelance writer and stay at home mother of two boys in Livermore, California. She edits the Budget Living Department at www.mommiesmagazine.com.

LOVE ISN'T BLIND

Vanessa J. Kyles

I had been in the store only a few minutes when I happened upon the little girl. She looked about four years old, tiny, with soft blond hair. She was so adorable. She held her mom's hand and trailed along while her mom browsed through greeting cards.

The sound of a woman's voice laughing and talking rang out from a couple of aisles away. The little girl looked startled as she moved her head about, trying to determine the direction of the voice. I heard the unseen woman laugh again, then the little girl slipped her hand from her mom's and eagerly moved toward the sound. As she rushed into the adjoining aisle, which was wider, I followed, curious.

On the other side was a black woman in her thirties. She stood about ten feet away, smiling. She squatted to the floor and held both arms out to the little girl. "Krissy!"

The little girl jumped with excitement, and loped toward the lady like a toddler just learning to walk. Her mother walked fast behind her, a hand outstretched, to assure the child wouldn't hurt herself. I couldn't see Krissy's face, but I could hear her high voice. "Ms. Joyce, Ms. Joyce!" she said. She continued with fervent steps toward the woman, then stumbled.

The woman stood and rushed to meet her. She lifted the little girl from the floor and hugged her tightly. Krissy reached her little arms around the woman as tight as she could. Ms. Joyce kissed her on the cheek, the little girl kissed her back, and they hugged some more. The little girl talked fast with excitement. I couldn't quite understand what she was saying, but she was very happy. I could feel the love between them. I blinked the tears from my eyes and walked toward them.

The woman placed the little girl back on the floor, careful to pull her dress neatly back together. The girl held on tight. Her face snuggled against the woman's hips and her little arms around Ms. Joyce's legs. Krissy's long blond hair rested neatly against her pale blue dress, just above the huge bow that pulled the pleated dress together. As I got closer, she turned around with the cutest round face and full powdery pink cheeks and she smiled.

I said, "Hello!"

Her eyes wandered toward me and she said, "Hello."

I looked deep into her blue eyes and realized the little girl was blind. My heart felt like it would stop beating. I tried to hold back the tears as I looked up at her mom. I looked back at the little girl and then hugged her. She politely reciprocated. She then turned back to her friend, Ms. Joyce, and cupped both little hands around the woman's right hand.

I was curious about this bond and knew that I had witnessed something very special. I stood in the aisle and talked with Ms. Joyce and Krissy's mother. Ms. Joyce had been an employee at the store for more than 10 years. She would stop whatever she was doing to spend time with Krissy. She would take the girl around the store, playing and introducing her to everyone who worked there. Other employees paged or phoned her when they knew that Krissy and her mom were in the store. The little girl had been sick and had not been in the store for weeks.

After several minutes, the mother looked at her watch and told the little girl it was time to leave and to tell everyone goodbye. The little angel slowly turned about as if she was on a pageant runway, and smiled, waving goodbye. Then she said, "Bye-e-e-e-e," as if she never wanted that word to end. She obviously sensed others nearby.

I wondered what it all meant—what was the purpose of this experience? Why was it available to my eyes? Was there something missing in my life? Had I become weakened by life's triangles of ups and downs? Had I not loved unconditionally? Then it hit me. This had been an expression of the innocent love of a child. A love that has no barriers, no sight, and no fear. I'd just witnessed an unquestioning kind of love.

I wanted to learn to give—to carry that feeling inside me always.

The few shoppers left wandered away, leaving the little girl standing with her two favorite people. I drifted into an adjoining aisle of more greeting cards. The time seemed perfect to send a few "Just thinking of you" cards.

Ms. Kyles works for a large corporation, yet she finds time to enjoy her spirit of writing. Her work in progress includes a memoir, Mocha at Midnight. She resides in Baton Rouge, Louisiana. Visit her website at www.inkbutter.com or e-mail vjkyles@inkbutter.com.

It's My Job, Sink or Swim

By Kathryne Lee Tirrell

I live in the sink. My world is awash in dishes and bubbles that swirl around my rubber-gloved hands. My objective: Scrub those pots and pans! Take a bite out of grime! Make those glasses shine!

Outside, the spirited cries from the neighborhood boys playing basketball interrupt my thoughts. I crane my neck so I can see them through the kitchen window, out there having fun, getting some exercise, as free as a bunch of birds. I envy their freedom. How I would love to trade places. Hey—any of you guys wanna wash some dishes?

Back to the suds. Only ten more pots and pans left to scrub. My kids howl with laughter about something they're watching on television. I wonder what's so funny. Can't break away now or my task will never get done.

My mind begins to wander. Suds. Soap. Soap operas. I wonder why women on soap operas are never shown washing the dishes. Do they own dishes? From all appearances, they dine out for every meal. But since soap characters usually seem to have big bucks, I guess they probably can afford to.

If I were a rich girl . . . The Fiddler on the Roof song floats through my mind. Wouldn't have to work hard. Maybe not, but I'd probably get bored. Take away all of the dishwashing, bed-making, floor washing, clothes washing, oven cleaning, vacuuming, and kid wrangling, and what have you got left? Lots of free time! But how to fill it?

Sure, for a while I'd love the freedom from the drudgery of lowly housework. The maid would do all of my former chores while I played tennis, went shopping, took in some movies, visited friends, traveled the world and, of course, played with my kids. But sooner or later, I know I'd be looking for a pan to scrub.

Maybe there's something about daily rituals and routines that becomes ingrained in our personalities. Even though I hate housework, I'm used to it. My fingers need something to clean, something to iron, something to make right. And when I'm putting together a lunch for my 9-year-old, I'm putting some of myself into it. Here's a sandwich I've made for you. Here are some of your favorite cookies. I can just picture the happy look on his face as he's unwrapping these little tokens of love.

But I must admit I do find myself wondering how one measures the significance and worthiness of a life spent folding T-shirts, scrubbing stains, mixing recipes and mending boo-boos. Is this the job that God wants me to do? And how good a job am I actually doing?

The answers come to me from time to time in subtle ways to which I must try and pay attention. Like the unexpected pennies and dimes I find in the pockets of my apron, God has left me little clues sprinkled throughout my days.

It's the stranger who approaches me in a restaurant saying, "Your children are so well-behaved."

It's the satisfied look on my oldest son's face as he's finishing up his second helping of lasagna.

It's the beautiful birthday card, written and designed with love by my 12-year-old daughter.

It's the smiling face on my youngest child as he looks up and says, "I'm lucky to be in this family."

These are the clues, the answers to the mystery. I'm not rich in gold, but I'm rich in family. I've sacrificed an income and a career to be a role model for my children, to be their first teacher, their nurse, their nurturer, their attentive and loving mom.

There will be a time down the road for other things. I can put off my own dreams and aspirations for a while, but I can't freeze the fleeting milestones of these childhood days. Each moment in time is precious and will never be seen again.

So for now I'll wash these dishes and scrub these pans. And I'll smile, knowing it's the right thing to do. Knowing God is watching me and nodding His head. After all, it is my job, sink or swim!

Kathy Tirrell wrote this essay six years ago. She is now a freelancer who has sold hundreds of greeting card verses and whose writing has been published in Woman's World and Writer's Digest magazine.

WHAT THERE IS LEFT...

By Lisa Voiles

My family and I went through Hurricane Camille in Biloxi, and there truly are no words to describe the loss of hope, and what that loss, above all else, can do to damage a person. But words are powerful, and followed up with action, can create miracles in the darkest of hours.

You don't blithely tell someone who's lost everything that "there's always hope."

How many can truly say they understand what it means to lose everything?

Did you ever hear these words come from your spouse—"you can't hold me; let go and save the kids," and then live the rest of your life to hear them over and over again in your mind?

You don't reach and save a person's soul at that point by saying, "There's always hope."

Did you ever survive complete and utter destruction of every single thing around you that provided any measure of security—your home, your life partner, your job, all your family photos of the faces you loved, pictures showing that your being here mattered and that you were loved—then have the child you brought into this world hold your hand and ask, "Where will we sleep tonight, Mama? Will we be safe there?" and realize you have no answer to that question.

You don't calm a terrified child only by saying, "There's always hope."

Did you ever live in the wealthiest nation on the planet, but spend your entire life in spirit-crushing poverty, fighting for every break you ever got in a world where the odds were stacked impossibly against you from the beginning simply because of the economic class you happened to be born into? Where the pressure on your struggling family and community just to survive affected everything in your life from the food you eat to the clothes you wear, to the quality of the education you receive, and even the amount of time your parents can spare to nurture you or the amount of hope they can offer for a better future? Where the need for self-respect and dignity almost never wins the battle against the need to put food in your child's mouth. Did you ever live a lifetime like this, then watch helplessly as what little you'd managed to obtain is washed out from beneath you in a matter of hours? The odds that were always against you, however, not only remain solidly in place but are now a thousand-fold higher.

How convincing would the words "there's always hope" be to you in that moment?

If the words "there's always hope" aren't of use, then what is there left?

Love.

Love is the only thing left that is strong enough to defeat hopelessness. Love is the one and only certainty that man has ever been able to rely on, when all else fails.

It doesn't take much to show caring and concern. Yes, words of hope are necessary. But, in times of catastrophic pain, it takes those words offered also with minds and hearts open, and hands willing to reach out and lift up.

For those who sense the world growing colder and more isolated with each passing year, please look around you and see the enormous outpouring of love that is flowing to the ravaged coastline of the United States. Small children who are demanding not attention, but rather that they be allowed to help and insisting someone take their pennies and stuffed toys to the children affected by disaster; teenagers and young adults stepping up to raise money not for a new car or spring break in Cancun but for food and blankets for the hungry and cold. Doctors, construction workers, firemen, celebrities, and truck drivers alike—adults from every walk of life—pausing to step outside their own problems, gathering all their resources and rushing to help with whatever they have to offer. Your love is needed, too—much more than you might possibly understand. Please don't dismiss your importance in this moment. Be it food, water, clothes, shelter, money, or prayers, what you have to give is important and significant. Somebody wise once said, "There are no small kindnesses." It seems that never before have any words summed up so much.

What there is left is the need to recognize that in the long run, whatever it costs to reach out with compassion and love for those so displaced in this world will come back to you and make you richer in ways so much more important than money ever will.

There is always hope.

We who are among the standing know this. Those on their knees or lying face down in despair know anything but that at the moment. What there is left for them—after having lost everything else—that will give them the courage to reach out a hand for help and dare to hope another human being will be there to take it and lift them up, is love. Love each of us has inside us to give and love we can ill afford not to share in this moment.

Lisa Voiles is an active member of the Indiana chapter of Romance Writers of America. Unpublished as yet, she hopes to see her romance stories in print soon. When she was 13, her family lived in Biloxi, Mississippi and survived Hurricane Camille. She is grateful for the chance to offer words of support to those affected by other devastating storms.

RAFAEL'S GIFT

By Esther Avila

As a nursery Sunday school teacher, I have seen many children come and go through my class—some were so adorable that I knew I would never forget them. But no child ever touched me more than Rafael.

Born to a single mother, Rafael arrived ahead of schedule—two months early, weighing only two pounds and ten ounces. The tiny infant was born blind and with a heart murmur. He never saw any of us with his eyes, but he did see us with his heart—the same heart that ultimately failed and claimed his life at the tender age of 11.

When he was born, he was transferred to Children's Hospital Central California where his mother was told he was too weak, and surgery for his heart was too risky.

Rafael could not see. He would never talk and it was possible that he would never walk. Rafael was also born with an esophageal-reflex disorder. He had no sucking ability and could not be fed with a baby bottle. A grim picture was painted and his mother was told that there was a good chance that Rafael would not survive to see his first birthday.

But from the beginning, Rafael had plans of his own and he struggled to survive. He was a fighter and without knowing it, he was going to prove his doctors wrong.

When he finally left the hospital, he was so tiny he fit in a shoe box. My hand could cover his entire body.

The ladies at church helped his mother feed him with an eye dropper, a few drops at a time. He reminded us of a little bird that had fallen from his nest—innocent and helpless. But Rafael needed more nourishment than the eye dropper could provide, and a feeding tube was inserted. His heart would occasionally flutter out of control, and twice he was rushed back to Children's Hospital.

For a while, Rafael wore a small portable heart monitor in a pouch around his waist. Several wires attached to electrode patches on his chest, recording activity of his heart on a magnetic tape. It was used to identify abnormal heart rhythms, fatigue, dizziness, and shortness of breath during several 24-hour periods.

It was more work than his mother could handle, and Rafael was moved to a care home for developmentally-disabled children. It was one of the hardest things his mother ever had to do and she was assured that Rafael was—and always would be—hers.

His mother visited him almost daily and as Rafael grew stronger, she took him home on special occasions, holidays, and every weekend.

Every Sunday, I knew he would be in my class, smiling and waving his little arms every time he heard a voice speak his name. He formed special bonds with everyone he met.

No matter where he was, he made people fall in love with him. The older children and church youth begged his mother for the opportunity to hold him. And Rafael ate it all up. He loved to be hugged and would wrap his long legs and arms—like a monkey—around anyone who picked him up.

Rafael knew no fear, had no enemies, smiled often, and loved to laugh. He had his own personality. He was not supposed to live very long, but he did. He learned to walk and he could stand on his head better than any gymnast I've ever seen.

He was a pleasure to have around. He never complained about anything and as long as he had a baby rattle in his hand—or anything else that rattled—he was happy. But Rafael had his naughty side, too.

When he turned 11, we threw him a birthday party in the church fellowship hall, where he crawled around until he found a box of oranges. He picked one up, shook it, and when he discovered it did not rattle, he threw it hard. He picked up another orange and repeated the shake-and-throw action. When he reached for a third orange, the box was taken away.

He knew when he did something bad. I would tease him, "Rafael, shame on you," and he would laugh.

But even with his medical condition, it still shocked us all when his mother called to say that his little heart finally gave out. We expected to have him for many more years.

Rafael was a very special little boy who touched people during the short time he was here. He loved everyone to the end.

Losing Rafael was painful, but I agree with his mother—I would take the heart-breaking experience all over again if it meant having Rafael for just one more day. Would we be willing to give up the blessings of knowing Rafael in order to eliminate all of the disappointments that came with him? Absolutely not.

People may ask why something has happened—and there is not always an answer. Sometimes we don't understand why things happen. But we must learn to trust God in everything. The main thing to do is not to dwell on the disappointments or problems of life, but to look at the positive and the beauty of every situation.

Rafael's mother had been dis-fellowshiped by her own family—not only for having a child out of wedlock, but because she had turned to another denomination for spiritual growth. But all that changed after the family fell in love with the little boy.

Rafael may not have been what his mother planned for. He may not have been perfect, but he was a blessing, and he won his mother's and everyone's hearts forever. In his own innocent way, he reached out and brought family and friends together.

Esther Avila is a freelance writer with more than 1,000 articles and stories published. She has received an "Excellence in Journalism" award for one of her human-interest stories. She lives in Visalia, California with her family. Her website can be found at: www.estheravila.com.

THE STRENGTH OF WORDS

By Robert Villanueva

Myelodysplastic syndrome. Anemia. Hemogram.

A writer is supposed to love words. And I do. But not those words. Those words invaded my vocabulary in the last half of 2000, and I almost wish I'd never heard them.

Sure, I'm glad that my mother now knows what she has, after having been afflicted with a nameless condition since 1983. Sure, I realize that words are neither bad nor good. But, neutral or not, words have power. And intimidating words like "incurable," "spontaneous hemorrhaging," and "rare blood disorder" came along for the ride when I learned those other words.

Such words can be like leeches. They can attach themselves to people, draining them of life and hope.

Every other Monday—sometimes more often—I sit in the Cancer Care Center of an Elizabethtown, Kentucky hospital. There, my 76-year-old mother gets platelet infusions, sometimes blood. I sit with her, ever vigilant for those leeches.

Looking at her, I still see the woman who encouraged my childhood writing. I also see Mom when she was in her 30s, 40s, and 50s. I see the youthful laughter in her eyes from days past when she joked with friends at the dining room table playing dominoes. I see the smile she wore when she came home from a night out dancing.

I even see Mom as the woman she was before I was born, the woman from the stories she told about her life before and after leaving her hometown of Saltillo, Mexico. I see the woman who couldn't read English and used a "colored only" bathroom in the Deep South of the 50s because the concept of segregation was more foreign to her than she was to this country. I see the intelligent, resolute woman who taught herself English in part because she wanted to sing along to the radio with the likes of Patsy Cline. I see the woman whose beauty was so undeniable that it inspired a photographer to follow her around Saltillo, snapping picture after picture of her when she was a teenager.

Many years ago, Mom gave me a glass reproduction of one of those photos. It stands on a worn wooden base. In the photo, Mom leans against a waist-high stone wall, a tree with hanging branches like a willow behind her, the Saltillo sun splashing down on her like a spotlight. She exudes glamour. She looks like a movie star, an undiscovered Lana Turner or Rita Hayworth.

I love that photo. It shows everything about Mom at once: her beauty, her poise, her dignity, her self-confidence. Those traits still comprise her presence.

But I also see something else when I look at the photo, something I've always known but rarely acknowledged. I see how delicate it makes its subject look, how much it is like looking at a ghost of an image. And now, sometimes when I look at her, I see Mom as that photo. I see her as delicate, breakable, even a translucent version of herself. And I know that I am being assaulted by doubt. It is like making myself vulnerable to those same leeches that drift around the Cancer Care Center waiting for an opportunity to attach themselves.

While Mom draws on her inner strength to deal with her condition, I have had to take strength wherever I can find it. My family and loved ones are great sources for me, but I also find myself looking at the situation with a writer's eyes.

Maybe I see these things to write about them, to force them to make some sort of sense. Words have always sustained me.

When I was a child, my words assumed the form of bad poetry on home-made cards I gave to my mother. She still enjoys pulling those cards out and showing people, not as a means of embarrassment but as a source of pride.

Throughout my junior high school and high school years, my words formed short stories and more bad poetry. Later, after I graduated from college with a degree in journalism, my words took the form of news stories, features, and columns that I wrote as a staff writer or news editor for local newspapers.

Now, as a fiction writer and freelancer, I write a little bit of everything. And Mom is still as proud as she was when I wrote poems on homemade cards. She is still my Mom, and—at 45—I am still her little boy. Her pride in me cannot be shaken from her no matter our ages or personal trials.

I look back at myself as a child, and I realize that I wish I knew now what I knew then. And I mean that just as I wrote it. Back then, I knew days would always keep coming, Mom and Dad would always be there, and bad things were temporary.

Those days are gone, and somewhere along the way I had to find something I could use to reconcile the difference between childhood innocence and adult reality. We all have something that sustains us.

Despite the machines, the tests, and the infusions, Mom finds something to sustain her. She is first and foremost a parent, a strong, intelligent woman who does not yield to her hardships because to yield would mean to give up something that she could give to her children.

So I must use what I have always used to sustain me: words. Writing words usually helps me put things in perspective.

I have to write. I have to guard against the leeches and nurture the comforting words.

I have to believe words have power, that they can sustain me indefinitely.

I have to believe—no matter what else happens—words can be truth, and truth cannot die.

I have to believe writing some words gives them more substance, and those words become stronger. And I have to believe one of those words is "hope."

Hope.

Hope.

Robert Villanueva's short stories, essays, poems and articles have been published by AbsoluteWrite.com, C/Oasis, The Heartland Review, Writer's Digest magazine and other e-zines, newsletters, and magazines. Villanueva lives in Kentucky.

ADOPTING A NEW TRADITION

By Jeanie Kezo

Christmas will be different this year. For the first time, our family will scramble to put together a holiday meal that may equal the simple but tasty items that my stepfather, Julius, always brought to the table. Besides being my stepfather, he was also my mother's husband of 41 years, a father to my half-sister Kathy and my stepbrother Tony. He passed away in May, leaving a vacuum in the lives of his family and the extended family around him.

It's hard for me to admit, but I'll have to agree with my mother's repeated observation that "things just aren't the same anymore," even though I sometimes feel like walking out the door now if she says it even one more time. For quite a while after Julius's death, I used to think that Mom refused to even try to move forward with her life and focused only on the emptiness and sadness that her husband's passing left her with. Her tendency to look on the negative side of life sometimes even annoyed me. In a gentle tone, I reminded her, "Nothing stays the same forever, Mom." Despite her worried nature and selective memory, a part of me didn't want to admit that she may be right, on some level, and I may be wrong. It shamed me to think that I may not have realized how much she really depended on my stepfather.

The proof of this realization came to me as I waited for Kathy to hand down the beleaguered, artificial Christmas tree, the box of bulbs—their colors faded by time—and the strings of insulation-clad lights from the attic to me, instead of to Julius. Plugging my nose against the insulation, we carried the decorations into the living room where Mom sat, surveying the spectacle with a wistful look on her face. "I just know your dad is looking down from heaven right now," she said to us. "The tree doesn't look so bad, after all, and I'm glad I let you talk me into putting one up." I talked her into putting it up? I thought, poking the spindly branches into each color-coordinated hole. It looked as though Kathy and I were doing all the "putting up."

Years before this artificial tree assumed the focus of attention, a parade of fresh pines and spruce trees had taken its place, my stepfather dragging each one into the house and wrestling it into a stand. I always laughed at the determination on his face and the words that flew, as though this were the only way to tame a wild Christmas tree. Once he positioned it in the perfect spot, he returned to his favorite kitchen chair in front of the TV and surrendered the tree to the rest of us. He seemed more comfortable away from the hub of activity, content to play digital card games or watch old movies, while everyone else visited with each other.

On Christmas Eve, the tree would be lit and the decorations arranged with care, some of them holding special memories of his parents. When I walked in the door, he would usually be hovering over the stove, stirring gravy or tossing one of his signature lettuce salads with mayonnaise dressing. The mouthwatering aroma of roast beef with mashed potatoes and gravy or roast turkey with stuffing used to waft through the house. My mother always received the first plate of honor, hand-delivered by Julius and an unspoken signal for the rest of us to dig in. As each of us finished eating, he grabbed our plates and washed them, never allowing anyone to help with dishes.

Today, as I accepted the mini lights from Kathy, I remembered that stringing these lights used to be Julius's job, not mine. Now, it belongs to Kathy and me—a new and fragmented tradition that seems foreign to me; still, it's a tradition that I also know makes Mom happy. To hear the smile in her voice makes the task of slinging garland on the tree a memory laced with love for the parent who still remains and the other who is still in our hearts.

Jeanie Kezo is a freelance writer from Sturgeon Bay, Wisconsin who is a regular correspondent for The Door County Advocate and has had several fiction pieces published online.

There is Strength in All of Us

By Catherine A. Harris

There is strength in all of us.
Just a breath away from sorrow and powerlessness,
It stands quietly alongside vulnerability.
Sometimes, it roars to the surface, like anger,
But anger is a fuel that runs out.
The strength that perseveres is
The strength that tiptoes into our hearts,
Like a memory,
Reminding us of how good life can be.
This is the strength that pulls us out of bed each morning;
This is the strength
That allows us to keep loving each other
Through every loss and every betrayal.
What we have to remember is that
Strength is at its best
And its power most multiplied
When we share it with
The people we love and need;
When we share it with the people
Who love and need us.
For just as we cannot endure
Without our brothers and sisters,
Strength cannot endure
Without hope and faith—
Hope and faith,
Woven from those memories
That live inside our hearts.
When life seems unlivable
And our souls are wrought with despair,
The strength that is in all of us
Will rise up to carry us on its shoulder.
And together,
We will make the slow, healing journey
Home again.

Catherine has written numerous children's rhyming books for WJ Fantasy, Inc. She has also been published with Woman's World, Blue Mountain Arts, and Andrews McMeel. She lives in Connecticut.

COMMA EYES

By Sandra Coker

"She's no bigger than a pound of butter!" Dad exclaimed as he pushed his face against the window glass of the nursery.

My little girl was resting quietly, her tiny bird-like chest moving up and down with the machines in the "preemie nursery" at our local hospital. Pulled low over her brow was a little pink hat that my sister had crocheted for her. It looked like a doll's hat, for a head no bigger than an orange.

Patches and tubes were everywhere, monitoring her every heartbeat and movement. Paige was born in my fifth month of pregnancy. The doctors were less than optimistic about her prognosis. They—and I—were worried about her undeveloped lungs. Infection could occur so easily.

I was afraid to love this pint-sized harbinger of joy. I was so afraid that by the time I gave my heart, she would be gone. I tried to keep myself from caring. But how could I help getting attached to my little girl?

I went through the sterile, protective nursery doors to be closer. The air smelled clean and antiseptic. The machines beeped comfortingly. I was able to gently stroke her little arm; her skin was very soft.

"Hey, little angel, Momma's here," I whispered, leaning close. She opened her dark blue eyes and smiled at me, a smile like nothing I had ever seen before. Her eyes squinted into commas. My heart burst into a million tiny pieces. I felt joy careening through my spirit, connecting electrically through my hand to her. I was lost and so in love.

For a month I went to the nursery, taking turns with her daddy. We took care of her as much as the nurses would allow. I brushed her skin tenderly with a soft toothbrush to stimulate her circulation. I rocked her in the parent's rocking chair, crooning love songs and lullabies to her sweet ears. I could barely feel her weight, but there she was in my arms.

Paige started to decline at one month old. Her lungs were failing. I lived in the world of fear and worry, caught between earth and spirit. I prayed unceasingly. I constantly touched the rosary in my pocket, hoping for comfort. Sometimes a loving spirit was with me, holding me up and away from all the pain. When I did sleep, I dreamed of angels singing to me.

My daughter would not awaken. She kept coding and trying to leave this world, and the doctors kept bringing her back with their care and machines. Then came the night the doctor woke us from a deep sleep. We had to decide, he told us. Should the doctors continue their heroic efforts or should they end the fight? We knew we had to let her go.

Paige had suffered greatly trying to exist here on earth.

I hung up the phone and howled my misery to the dark night. Paige was gone. The little comma eyes would never squint again.

The same gentle spirit who had haunted my dreams led me through the next days. The days blurred into each other until finally I could smile again. Smile, and remember a tiny brave spirit who had been here on earth with me for a very brief time.

Sandra Coker is a painter and poet who is inspired daily by the Rocky Mountains she lives in. She is founder of a non-profit organization dedicated to promoting abstract art in her area: www.renegadeartistsgroup.org.

A COAT OF PAINT

By Maggie B Dickinson

When he was well, Jim and I shared a wonderful sense of fun and liked nothing better than to laugh until we cried.

Alzheimer's disease is a thief. Jim was still relatively young and working in a managerial position when it stole his sense of humor—along with other important faculties like his short-term memory, navigational skills, and word-finding ability.

What it didn't seem to suppress in the initial stages was his desire to paint surfaces with emulsion. He was in that painting mode for quite a while, and at times I got desperate to find new areas to hold his interest.

Our cottage, which is 250 years old, nestles in one of those villages of rural England where you expect The Squire to ride by on his horse and pause whilst you tug your forelock in deference. It has roses growing round the door, clumps of scented lavender basking under the windows, and lots of parsley, sage, rosemary, and thyme poking through the cobbles of the forecourt. It is also, predictably, painted white.

The autumn arrived. He'd done the wooden boundaries of the back garden in a handsome shade of chestnut and the outdoor furniture in Mediterranean blue and now he was getting restless.

Only the front elevation of the property remained untouched, so I invested in a large tin of white stone paint and he was happy as Larry as he made a start.

I went through to the back of the house and set about my chores, with a mind to check on Jim in a few minutes. The telephone rang and I got delayed, but part-way through the conversation I heard Gill, one of my neighbors, calling, "Outside. Quickly."

Jim wasn't painting our house at all: He was slapping the emulsion on next door instead, and he'd done a fair chunk in the space of around 15 minutes.

Fortunately the owner was away, but his property obviously hadn't seen a lick of paint in many a year, so Jim's handiwork was all too obvious. In a flash Gill had run into her home and returned with a couple of rags. "We'll scuff the edges so you won't be able to see the seams," she told me with real conviction.

By the time we got through the scuffing you could barely tell, except that an area of around 6' by 20' looked happier than the rest of the cottage.

"I hope you don't mind," said Gill's husband, emerging from their house with his face all blotchy and red, "but that's the best laugh I've had in years."

I didn't mind at all. And I knew that Jim wouldn't have minded either. By the time I realized I had lost him to Alzheimer's disease, it was too late to say goodbye or ask him whether he'd mind someone laughing at the crazy mistakes he would make.

One thing I know for certain, he'd have laughed louder than anyone else that day: a day that comes to mind frequently as I continue the long battle of waving goodbye in slow motion. It is from moments such as this, and other pleasant memories of our time together, that I draw in terms of strength and am thankful that my life has been enriched by all the good times.

For those of us whose personal journey goes through periods of tragedy, loss and utter grief there is a part of us that rallies, given time and patience. It is in our nature to survive and ride through to the other side, guided by an inner strength that we often didn't even know we possessed.

But it's there, just waiting to be called into play. Having found it, this strength is a tremendous force that takes us by the hand to a safer place where one day we can look back without the great pain we have suffered in the main event, and perhaps even smile at the memories.

Maggie considers her greatest literary achievement her original research and the arduous physical challenge for writing "Early Trackways," which prompted a major conservation programme of overgrown packhorse routes in the Pennine hills of northern England.

The Strength to Start Over

"Our real problem, then, is not our strength today; it is rather the vital necessity of action today to ensure our strength tomorrow."

~ President Dwight D. Eisenhower

SEARCHING FOR HOPE

By Judith Alice

Nothing
Nothing
Then something
A crust of hope
Thrown out, to keep you hanging on
To keep you going
To keep you trying

Falling
Falling
Giving up all hope
Then, hope's tattered rope dangles
Reach out
Grab hold
Hand over hand
Pull yourself up
Enough to carry you
just one more day

Sinking
Sinking
Further than the bottom
Only to pull from within

Rising
Rising
Touch the realm of possibility
Taste the desire
Fill your soul with

Hope
Hope

Judith Alice is a freelance writer who lives in Las Vegas, New Mexico. She is a published poet and writer with numerous articles to her credit. A mixture of observation, research and inner feelings gives each work depth, color and a unique texture.

HUMMINGBIRD SUMMER

By Anne Culbreath Watkins

Some of my favorite childhood memories center on my grandmother's yard, which was graced with two gigantic mimosa trees. In the summer, the trees, with their sweeping limbs and their fluffy, sweet-smelling pink flowers, were havens for hummingbirds. It seemed like thousands of the minute, fairy-like creatures filled the branches. It was a sight I never tired of, and I spent hours watching them. Fascinated by their whirring wings, I tried to get close enough to the little birds to study them. They would be too shy to let me get near, though, and I had to content myself with watching from a distance.

Then I grew up and moved away. Years passed and I saw fewer and fewer hummingbirds. Sometimes I would spot one while visiting friends who had flower gardens, but the sightings were few and far between. Then something happened to make me wonder if anything in my life would ever be as simple or as innocent as watching hummingbirds again.

My marriage, troubled from the beginning, had collapsed, and I barely escaped with my life. Bruised in body and spirit, I fled to a domestic violence shelter. I had always been a private person, and having to live in this new place, filled with other women trying to make sense of the same sorts of horrible things that had happened to me, was almost more than I could bear. My heart cried out for privacy, for time to heal, and for the assurance that things would be all right again. Though I was physically safe, I had doubts that my mind or my soul would ever heal. It was as though I had lost everything, even myself.

The shelter staff was compassionate and understanding. They assured me that I could stay as long as I needed. They even gave me a job, which in turn, helped reassure me that I hadn't lost everything; I could still type, file, and do any office work they needed. Each skill remembered was a tiny step forward.

My abuse had been so severe that the police felt it was better for me to stay in the shelter as long as possible. Threats had been made against my life and I would be safer there. But I began to feel stifled, and as I grew stronger, I needed a space of my own; I craved a place where I could begin to stand on my own two feet and regain my independence. That's when my family stepped in.

They moved an old mobile home to a spot near my dad's place and fixed it up for me. My father planted a pear tree and several strong, young oaks in the yard. My sister-in-law created a small flowerbed, and other family members pitched in to do some yard work and make minor repairs to the trailer. It was a cute little place, and I was happy to settle into it.

With family members living on each side of me, I had a secure, albeit very old, home. Still suffering nightmares and flashbacks of the abuse, my nerves were stretched wire-thin and every noise or sudden movement startled me. Warily, I set out on the journey to a new life.

One day my dad tapped on my door. I opened it to find him standing there, clutching several red and white plastic objects. "Here," he said, thrusting them into my hands. "I thought you might like these."

Surprised, I realized that the funny red and white things were Mom's old hummingbird feeders. They were dirty and scuffed up, but looked usable. A twinge of something nudged my heart. I found myself transported back through the years to my grandma's yard. Could some of those funny, swift-flying little birds still be around? A glimmer of excitement, of timid anticipation, took hold.

I cleaned the feeders with boiling water and a brush, then filled them with sugar water. Carefully, I hung them on a length of clothesline stretched between two porch supports.

Before very long, I was rewarded with the sight of a tiny, shimmering body buzzing around one of the feeders. It hovered there, sipped from one of the feeder ports, then zoomed away. Later, a couple more tiny diners paid my outdoor cafe a visit. A bit of warmth crept into the dark, cold recess that filled my heart. For the first time in a long while, I looked forward to something.

The summer wore on and eventually, I found myself growing stronger. It was an agonizingly slow process, and I had many setbacks. Sometimes it seemed for every step forward, I fell back two. Yet something inside, some stubborn part of myself that I'd thought buried, kept driving me to put one foot in front of the other, to take each day one difficult moment at a time.

On really bad days, I would sit quietly on my porch and watch the hummingbirds. While they appeared fragile, they were strong. Though they were tiny, nothing intimidated them. And they were incredibly active, yet took time to hover in place at the feeders and enjoy the nectar that nourished them. It occurred to me to try standing still, to hover in place, and to find nourishment in the simple passage of time.

I learned many lessons that summer. I learned that moving forward didn't come in giant leaps; rather, it took many tiny, tentative steps. I learned that healing could not be rushed and that there was more strength inside me than I ever realized. I learned that if I sat very still, I could hear a small voice inside telling me that I was worthwhile, that I was somebody, and that I would reclaim my life. I learned not to give up. And gradually, I learned the way back to myself.

Previously appeared in Chocolate for a Woman's Courage (Simon & Schuster, 2002).

Anne C. Watkins is the author of The Conure Handbook as well as hundreds of published articles and essays. She and her musician husband, Allen, live in a rural Alabama community where hummingbirds abound.

...FROM THE ASHES

By Christa Kolster

All right, Leonardo. Since you're ready for a walk, I guess I'm with you. You'll have to wait up a minute, though, so I can get my coat. It's starting to feel like our extended Indian summer may finally have passed.

Aren't you lucky, Leonardo da Vinci, to be blessed by nature to grow your own winter mantle? Just think, you could have been a short-haired Manx cat instead of a thick-furred German shepherd dog! The cold doesn't even faze you.

Christmas lights are blinking on and off up and down the street, yet I can't get warmed by their message of good cheer. I'm still cold. Maybe this past mild weather's spoiled me. Maybe that's why mustering up a mood festively ho-ho enough to endure putting seasonal lights up has been a real chore this year. Strangely, though, I sense the same lack of enthusiasm in others, although I'm not sure how reassuring it is to know it's not just my own peculiar brand of elusiveness tainting me.

There is something different in the air this Christmas. It's not that we're not going through the expected motions, or participating in the usual well-worn traditions, yet I sense a subtle underlying current amongst people. This year the holiday season seems connected to a gossamer thread of universal loss that is sifting like the season's first powdery snow over the spirit of mankind. Mankind, engulfed by masses of those who must suck it up, in order to endure their first Christmas without. Without a loved one.

I understand about firsts, Leonardo. My father died in the bittersweet month of September when summer was just beginning to wither into autumn. I was 16 that year, and I didn't think there would ever be another joyous celebration for me. But still, like a puppet on a string, or, like you, Leonardo, a dog on a leash, I moved myself through all the appropriate motions. And then all on its own accord, Christmas that first year was—well—Christmas, after all.

I think of all the families who will feel a collective tear at the empty place at the table this year. I think of all the mothers who will cringe at the refrain "peace on earth, goodwill toward men" as they weep silent prayers for those sons and daughters among the troops in a foreign land who grunt uphill on bellies, or remain far from loved ones while on duty somewhere on a lonely deck of a war ship.

In my mind, I hear Bing Crosby joyously addressing American soldiers after WWII in his well-known rendition of that all-time favorite carol, "I'll Be Home for Christmas." But for how many people today do those words evoke the now-familiar sting behind the eyes and the lump in the throat? How many mothers and fathers and sons and daughters will never again come home for Christmas?

Isn't it true that throughout history, firsts have stolen innocence and opened the grieving heart like a rite of passage? Like a birthing channel breaking down the defenses of blind ignorance and leading us onward to where greater awareness beckons like a promise.

"Christmas Eve will find me where the love light gleams..." Many have tried, Leonardo, but you and I know nobody can sing it like Bing. Or maybe his voice taps into the nostalgic repeating reminders of eras when hearts celebrated ends to wars and those sons who, although broken, would still come home.

I can't help but think of the many who would gladly return to the time before the first loss of innocence to regain the yesterdays that would have their loved ones home once more for Christmas—the many who now find the innocence of snow and mistletoe only in their dreams.

Burnishing lights in our windows, we still follow the age-old tradition of leaving a light burning through the darkest of nights so the Spirit of Christmas will find the way to the house. As we silhouette our lives behind the lights, we ache for the spirit to find our own species' well-trodden paths of endurance, recognizing as long as we cry out, we will continue to survive. Does the hope springing out of the season's promise of love become the mantra beneath our every action?

And do you know what I think, Leonardo? I think we all weep in the same language.

Grief doesn't differentiate between the loss of a firefighter daddy, an aged parent, or a community's own beloved son laid to rest in his country's uniform. It doesn't distinguish between tears shed at the end of an era of peace and love, and tears from baby-boomer parents whose troubled children, seeking ideology and spiritual solace, turn on paths of wild mass destruction.

A brisk winter's walk is a good thing, don't you think? It gets the blood flowing. Makes you warmer. The stars seem brighter on a winter's night. It looks like they glitter more without all that warm summery haze obstructing the sky. And the wintering trees, now bare and vulnerable, seem to be reaching their limbs to touch something just beyond their stretch.

Look, Leonardo, we're almost home. It's good to see the lit windows winking from afar, lighting the path, so once again, "Christmas Eve will find me where the love light gleams."

Christa Kolster is an award-winning writer, columnist, and author of Conversations with Leonardo (DeWitt Books, 2003), from which this essay is excerpted. She has written more than 1000 articles and stories, many of which have traveled globally on wire services. Her book is currently used in two literature curriculums at Manchester College, IN.

ROSES WILL BLOOM

By Connie Schlosberg

Grasshopper is hiding
Ghostly clouds hasten their way in
Saturday afternoon silence

My friend tells me that sun and rain
Come together to paint the rainbow's way

Grisly rain is pouring down
I don't feel dismay
Sun will follow with its shining beams

Have good cheer
Roses will bloom again

Everyone is at war
Yelling and screaming at one another
I am ready to explode

Make your amends
A new beginning will be here

My friend has convinced me
Everything is going to be
All right—All right I know

Roses will bloom

Connie Schlosberg is the owner of Integrity Creative Business Solutions. She is currently working on her bachelor's degree in journalism. She lives in Colorado Springs with her husband and 5-year-old daughter.

LIVING STRONG

By Sue Marquette Poremba

I wear a Livestrong bracelet.

I spent the dollar for the bracelet, knowing that in return for the yellow plastic I was giving money for cancer research. Moments after I got it, I slipped it on my wrist and unless it slipped down on my wrist, trapping my thumb, I mostly forgot about it.

Fast-forward a few months. I discovered that my job was losing its funding. If I wanted to stay within the company and not lose my seniority, I needed to find a new position within four months. Figuring I had plenty of time to find something new, I sent my résumé and a kick-butt cover letter for positions I really wanted. After a month of dead silence, I sent out my résumé to every position for which I was even remotely qualified. After two months and only one failed interview, I worried.

What was I going to do? I loved the company I worked for. Besides, after 14 years, I didn't want change. I liked how comfortable my life was. At nights, I'd stare into the darkness, wondering what was going to happen to me, to my family, if I couldn't find a new job.

One evening, only a few weeks before the end, I was at the gym for my nightly workout. I was on one of the leg machines, resting between sets. My yellow bracelet had wiggled its way down my wrist, trapping my thumb. I twisted it to get it back into place. The letters caught my eye. Livestrong.

Live. Strong.

What would really happen if I lost my job? Squeezing the weights between my thighs, I realized the worst thing about being unemployed would be losing my free Internet access. Losing my job wouldn't destroy my health or break up my marriage. It wasn't the end of the world.

In fact, it was the chance for a new beginning. It would give me the chance to live out my dream. I wanted to write full time. I'd been working on developing a freelance career for a couple of years, but my original plan was to continue working in a regular job while my kids were in school. Once they graduated, then I could do what I wanted, but that was a long-term goal.

Except now wasn't the right time. It came seven years too early. I balked at the idea that this wasn't part of my plan. I was scared to death of the uncertainty of an irregular paycheck and the loss of income.

Live. Strong.

I had the chance to do what I loved, and I was trying to find excuses not to do it. Was I nuts? The two simple words on the cheap plastic bracelet hit home. If I wanted to live strong, I had to conquer the fears, hurdle the obstacles, and be willing to give up something important to me. Living strong meant not being a chicken.

After I finished my work out, I met up with my husband at the hot tub. "I decided not to look for a job anymore," I said to him. "I'm going to write and see what happens."

I could see the concern in his face. I've been married to the guy long enough to know he was worried about money.

"You really think you can do this?" he asked, the uncertainty rising in his voice.

I twisted the yellow band on my left wrist. "Yes," I said.

"Well, then," he said. "Let's see what happens."

I sit at my computer now. The yellow bracelet has slipped down my arm, over my wrist, trapping my thumb. It is turned so I can only see the word "strong."

Strong.

That's how I live.

Sue Marquette Poremba is a freelance writer in central Pennsylvania and author of The Phillies Fan's Little Book of Wisdom.

FORGET ME NOT

By Rose Thomason

It wasn't real. It couldn't be. I felt like a victim trapped in time, unable to move. Frozen. My head was a mess of jumbled thoughts, words screaming out at me that didn't make any sense. My mind was trying to tell my body what to do. My body refused to listen. I shook my head. No, this wasn't happening. If I closed my eyes, it would all go away. It had to.

"Rose, do something!" my mom shouted, grabbing my shoulders, shaking me back to this nightmare of a reality. I knew she was right. I had to something.

My brother handed the telephone to me.

"Hello?" I asked as my voice quivered, even though I knew whom the voice on the other end belonged to.

"Rose. I need you to tell me what happened." The 9-1-1 dispatcher spoke in a perfectly calm yet reassuring voice.

My knuckles turned white from gripping the phone so tightly. "I was looking for her. My grandma. Her bedroom door was cracked. I opened it. That's when I saw her."

"Tell me what you see." I could tell the operator was trying to hurry me along in this emergency, but I couldn't seem to get the words out fast enough. It seemed as soon as I said the words aloud, that the situation would be entirely too true.

"She was . . . is laying here." I continued. "She's on the ground. I only see her legs. The bed is blocking me from seeing the rest of her."

"Is she breathing?"

"I do . . . don't . . . know," I stammered. "I can't see her chest." Didn't I already tell her that? Why was she asking so many questions? Why wasn't she sending for help?"

I felt myself start to give way to panic. My heart hammered in my ears. I could barely hear what the operator was saying, much less understand my next instructions.

I handed the phone over to my mom so I could attempt CPR. As I ran to her feet, intending to grab her legs and pull her towards me, my mom screamed.

"STOP!"

I froze in mid-step. My mom, waving her free hand frantically at me, yelled something into the phone. She had a horrified look on her face, more so than before. For a moment, our eyes connected and we both looked down in the same direction. Between my grandma's feet lay a gun.

Everything moved very quickly and became a blur after that. We moved out of our home and into another within days. We could not bear to walk down the same hallway each day, passing by Grandma's room. The last image I had of her was the most horrible, and hardest to escape.

Guilt weighing heavily upon all of our shoulders, we dealt with our feelings in different ways. Although we didn't discuss it for a while, we each believed we had, in some way, contributed to this tragedy.

My brother sought guidance from a counselor. He was home alone the day everything happened. Any noise he may have heard, he shrugged off as noise from outside, considering our neighborhood was very loud during the day.

My mom, I suppose, dealt with it the hardest. After all, it was her mother and she believed she should've recognized the signs to prevent such a thing from happening. Grandma had given away some of her belongings to us only days before. She made a remark once, "This will be my last year anyway." We would just laugh and tell her not to be silly. Mom would sometimes wake in the middle of the night to catch her staring at us while we slept. Every little detail seemed terribly significant now.

I felt indirectly responsible for her death. The week before, the three of us had a huge argument, which I was the cause of. It resulted in none of us speaking to one another, up until the day Grandma died. I couldn't help thinking that maybe, just maybe, if we hadn't fought, she would not have taken her life.

My mom and brother, although religious before, turned to prayer even more and held onto their faith to get them through such a hard time. They made peace, which enabled them to accept what happened, rather than having it consume them. They always said they knew Grandma was still with us. I could feel it, too.

My mom, though fighting a battle inside herself, would never let us see that. She was hurting, but she was strong. She always gave us a shoulder to lean on, although she probably needed it the most.

I was the opposite. I held my emotions in. The only time I cried was the day I found my grandma. Tears were a sign of weakness. I would not reveal how weak I was, how completely torn apart I had become. Nobody had to know that I secretly cried inside.

Holidays proved to be the worst. We didn't have any family other than ourselves, so it was very noticeable that the fourth chair at the table was always empty at dinner. There was now one less person sitting around the Christmas tree with us, one less person giving thanks at Thanksgiving. One less person.

We soon realized that talking to each other proved to be great therapy, when we finally shared our confessions of guilt. I suppose time played a main factor in helping us heal, to allow us to look at the situation realistically. Even if we changed every thing we felt guilty about, it may have prolonged the tragedy, but the ending would've eventually been the same.

The following year we welcomed a baby into the world. My son, Christian, who would've been her great-grandson. He was born on the day of her birthday. He brought the light back into our holidays, back into our lives, giving us a new reason to celebrate and experience happiness. He became our main focus and kept us living in the present rather than dwelling on the past. Each smile, each innocent laugh, showed us how precious life was and to cherish it for as long as you could.

October 19th was always a difficult day for us, as the memory of that tragic incident that sits in the back of our minds is pushed forward. Ten years later, it still is. On that day, especially, I make a point of reminding myself life is too short to be angry, hold grudges, and let the negatives weigh you down. I look at what I have rather than what I don't.

Every once in a while, I catch a glimpse of an older woman, curly gray hair and glasses, and think of Grandma. I'm not sad, nor am I angry with her for leaving us. I think of all the wonderful memories I have and that is what puts the smile on my face.

My son is proof that wonderful things can happen after facing a difficult time, a time when it seems things couldn't possibly get better. It gives me the strength to move on and look for the positive, even if it's deeply buried. My son is a remembrance of a life that was taken, but a constant reminder of life that was given.

Rose Thomason is a freelance writer from Sacramento, California. She especially enjoys writing nonfiction and children stories. You can learn more about her and her upcoming projects on her website, www.rosethomason.com.

ADDICTIONS CONQUERED

By Sharyn Bowman

Overcoming an addiction is not easy, and when you do treatment research on drug abusers, it's possible to lose hope. Effective treatments are few. Most of those who seek treatment keep the same group of friends who share the addiction and have multiple relapses.

I chose a career in substance abuse research because I believed my research might make a difference in people's lives. While researchers in this field are recognized in various ways by their colleagues, few experience the heartfelt gratitude of recovered addicts.

One sunny morning several years ago, I walked out the doors of Baltimore's Penn Station and hopped into the back seat of one of the taxicabs waiting at the curb. I slid my briefcase across the seat, sat down, and gave the driver the address of my destination but not the name of the building. I recited by rote the route I wanted him to take.

"Hey, you know a different way than most people use. Do you take the train here often?"

"Every day," I said. "I'm going to work. Other cab drivers taught me the route."

He smiled and pulled into traffic. I guessed he was in his early thirties. His brown hair was cut short. He wore jeans with a crisp shirt. A talk show played on NPR. We talked about the weather and other innocuous topics. He apologized as the cab bounced through the huge potholes that peppered the narrow streets of East Baltimore. We passed countless red brick row houses with white marble steps. These residential neighborhoods were sprinkled with a few bars that had been open since 7 a.m. After passing some warehouses, the cabbie drove under the Lombard Street Bridge and turned into the back entrance of the campus where I worked. I directed him through the series of streets that led to the building.

As he drove into the semicircular driveway in front of the building, I pulled a ten-dollar bill from my wallet and grabbed my briefcase. The cabbie stopped at the front door; his eyes riveted on the sign beside the main entrance. I reached forward and held the money at his side.

"National Institute on Drug Abuse," he read. "I've been to other buildings out here but I've never seen this place. Does it have something to do with drug addicts?"

"Yes, it does," I said. "We do drug abuse research."

He turned around and stared at me. "Are you a doctor?"

I tensed inside. Personal questions made me cautious. I wanted out of that cab. "Yes, I'm a Doctor of Science." I moved the bill toward him. He didn't take it.

"What kind of research do you do?"

"Drug abuse treatment research for people addicted to illegal drugs."

He looked at me for a few seconds. "Ma'am, I can't take your money."

I was confused. I didn't know what to say.

"Ma'am, I was a heroin addict. I went into treatment lots of times but couldn't stay off heroin. Finally, I got on methadone and stayed on it. I got a job and was earning money."

I told him about Vincent Dole, one of the physicians who did the research that proved methadone is an effective treatment for heroin addiction. Dole did some of his methadone research at this Institute in the 1960s when it was located in Lexington, Kentucky. It was a revolutionary discovery because no treatment existed for heroin addiction. No better treatment for heroin addiction has been found since.

His eyes widened. He shot an awestruck glance at the building. "Really? He worked here?" He turned back to me. "Do you know him?"

"No," I said. "I never met him."

"Methadone saved my life," he said. "But it's addicting, too. After I was on methadone for a couple years, I didn't want to take any addictive drug. So I went off it."

He impressed me. When people are addicted, they are psychologically and physiologically dependent on the drug. Their bodies need it to function. The body recoils when the drug is taken away. It struggles to function without the substance. This often produces pain and other uncomfortable symptoms. Heroin withdrawal is very painful, and addicts frequently become extremely ill while they withdraw. Methadone withdrawal is usually accompanied by excruciating pain. Many people who are successfully treated with methadone won't consider stopping it because they don't want to face that kind of pain.

"I thought I wouldn't live through methadone withdrawal," he said. "But I did it!" He sat up straighter and smiled.

"You have a lot to be proud of." We smiled at each other. "But you must let me pay you."

He shook his head. "I've been off all drugs for a couple years now. And you know what? Around a year ago I got this cab. It's all mine. I have my own business." He beamed.

I wished I could pay him but didn't want to insult him.

"I want you to keep your money," he said. "It's my way to say thank you and to ask you to keep doing research to help addicts like I was. We need people like you working for us."

The warmth and sincerity of his comments meant more to me than many types of professional recognition. After slipping the money into my pocket, I told him how much I appreciated what he had done. We said goodbye. I never saw him again.

People sometimes ask me if any of "those junkies" ever do anything good with their lives. I immediately brighten and tell them that getting off drugs is very hard but some people accomplish it. I tell them how heartwarming it is to know of the successes. Some are pleased by my response; others are skeptical.

I'd like to introduce the skeptics to a certain cabbie in Baltimore.

Sharyn Bowman is a public health researcher who published many articles on substance abuse in scholarly literature. She recently finished her first mystery novel, Hospital Homicide. She lives in the Washington, DC area.

NIGHT AND FOG ACTION

By Heide AW Kaminski

About ten years ago, I stood before my church congregation and made a plea for support for a local battered women's shelter. I began with a story about a young woman who fell in love with a man. They shared their dreams and visions of the future and talked of building a house in the country with cathedral ceilings and lots of skylights. They pictured a sunroom for her to write in, surrounded by beautiful gardens. To her, it felt like a match made in heaven.

After a whirlwind courtship, he moved in with her. One evening, he returned home from work with an odd expression on his face. Instead of his usual smile, an air of anger surrounded him. Without warning, he raised his hand and struck the woman. Instead of loving arms embracing her, a balled fist shot into her stomach like an unbridled canon ball. She ran into the bathroom and crouched behind the toilet in terror. He towered over her with fury, but she mustered courage. "Touch me again and I will call the police!" she screamed.

"Call the police and I will kill you," he responded.

At first she hoped that it would never happen again. After all, he apologized and promised her. He swore on his love for her, and she believed him. Why would he want to hurt her again? At times, when he wasn't angry, he seemed so sincere and full of love for her. But soon it became a daily fear, and she began to ask herself continually what she did wrong this time. A stranger smiled at her, a male co-worker called after work, a male cut her hair in a beauty salon, a friend of his commented on her pretty smile. After every beating, he broke into tears and begged for forgiveness.

She eventually stopped believing him. Fear, anger, and hatred replaced her love for him, overshadowing everything in their lives. No one knew what happened to her at home, but one day she found the courage to call the police and ask for help. Get a restraining order, they told her. She read about domestic violence and knew the path they were heading down, but she felt trapped; the restraining order may as well be a coffin, she thought.

She began sleeping with scissors under her pillow.

"If I kill him in self-defense, they can't put me in prison, can they?" she thought. "I'd rather be in prison than keep on living like this."

But another fear soon took root and she began to worry he'd find the scissors and use them on her. After almost a year, she tried to kill herself, feeling that was the only sure way to escape him. She swallowed 60 sleeping pills at work after everyone left and quietly awaited peaceful relief. Slowly, she staggered to the train station, thinking she'd fall asleep on the train. But the very person she'd been trying to escape met her at the train station unexpectedly. She tried to convince him she'd had too much to drink, but he soon realized alcohol was not the culprit.

"If you think for one second that I am going to save you, you are dead wrong!" he yelled. Then he called 9-1-1 and told the dispatcher what she'd done. When he hung up, he grabbed her and forced her to walk until the ambulance arrived. The lights and sirens of the ambulance amused her and made her laugh; it all reminded her of singing cherub angels. But then she found herself in an emergency room, tubes being forced down her throat and people yelling at her to stay with them.

Two days later, her boyfriend arrived at the hospital to pick her up—he hadn't visited since the ambulance took her away. On the way home, he announced he'd been with another woman while she was away, but that was over now that she was back.

When she returned to work, she finally found the strength to confide in her co-workers. That night a neighbor (who was also a policeman) invited her boyfriend in for a beer. While he was gone, she threw personal things into a grocery bag and planned her escape. In Germany, where she was living at the time, she began what Germans call a "Night and Fog Action."

Friends drove her to meet a representative from a local battered women's shelter. From there she took a cab to the train station. The cabbie, feeling her fear, walked her to the train and sat with her until it arrived.

She traveled 500 miles; sitting rigid and paralyzed by fright, she was sure he'd find her. She stayed with her sister for two days, never sleeping, her eyes glued to the windows, especially at night. Finally, she decided she needed to leave the country to find peace. Booking a flight to the U.S., she bid her family goodbye. As the plane doors closed, she finally let go of the fear she'd been holding onto, just like she'd let go of all of her possessions. She was lucky. Many battered women don't make it out alive.

As I finished telling my story to the people I love and care for at my church, I let the silence settle. Finally, I confessed that the woman in the story is no stranger. I am her, 20 years later and ever so grateful to be alive.

Surviving this hell not only taught me to love life for each and every moment. It also taught me to always watch for the light at the end of the tunnel, no matter how long or dark the tunnel may appear.

I still have scars in my heart; I still have fears. I've learned to put those feelings to work, helping other women in similar situations, be it domestic violence or feelings of despair and depression. I've found an inner strength that lights my way, and I now know I can survive anything.

Heide A W Kaminski is the single mother of three children and lives in Michigan. She is a freelance writer, published author and preschool art teacher. Visit her website at: www.thewriterslife.net/Kaminski.html.

CONTINUANCE

By Michael Hawkins

Picture a painting
Poised on a wall
The ancient descendant
Of one who stood tall

Clasped in his hand
The want of the one
Who gave to this man
A deed left undone

You must go forth
To realms of afar
Leap to the distance
Of the furthest star
Search ye forever
If forever you must
Look for a man
Who thinks and does just

Into the vigil
This man in print went
On to fulfill
The task he was sent

Early came spring
And the man was found
Digging his fingers
Into the ground

With his goal so near
On this certain day
Sad men saw no reason
And they took him away

And so came the legend
Of his infinite search
All now but forgotten
As he's bordered by birch

Alas! Something different
As I look once again
Nothing but wrinkles
In his now open hand

A look to his face
And a smile appears
Moist, relieved eyes
Slowly filling with tears

And as I look down
I can now understand
An unopened fist
Ends at my right hand

West to the sun
And north to the snow
Come early tomorrow
I know I must go

Mike is a singer/songwriter and corporate manager developing history-based action mysteries. He lives with his family in Florida.

PERSEVERANCE

By Joanne D. Kiggins

Just when my life had settled some, and I'd published the last issue of my newspaper and told my readers I was going to work on my book, I found myself lying on the kitchen floor, numb, unable to move or speak.

I know I was crying, but I couldn't feel the tears run down my cheeks as I watched paramedics attach medical equipment. I closed my eyes and tried to get a perspective of the scene taking place, but nothing would register. Fear washed into my throat as I faded into unconsciousness.

When I woke in the emergency room, doctors told me I'd had a stroke. I looked at them through wide, glassy eyes and shook my head "no."

"You're young, so after physical and speech therapy, you'll be almost as good as new," they said. It was the "almost" that made me cringe. I couldn't feel my limbs, but I could feel the chilling, unadulterated fear that flushed through my body. What was the "almost" I would be left without?

Those who didn't know me wouldn't notice the slight droop in the left side of my face. The slow, slurred speech and long spans of time between sentences, while I searched for words that wouldn't come, made me sound like a second grader trying to talk with a mouth full of cereal.

By the fourth day, I was walking with a limp and a cane, my left arm twitched and went wherever it wanted to go, and my smile faded. I was scheduled to see physical and speech therapists three times a week for rehabilitation. After one week I knew there wasn't anything that I was being shown I couldn't do every day at home. I insisted on going home where I could rehabilitate myself to gain those things I desperately needed most. And what I needed most was to write.

In front of my computer, in my home office, I sat staring at the blank screen. No words would come. I glanced up and scanned the diplomas, awards, and pictures of me and Senator John Glenn, Charlie Daniels, and Kenny Rogers.

Then, I cried. Long and hard.

I began my writing career in 1981 as a stringer for two major newspapers and two weeklies in Ohio. Since then, I have crafted and published more than 2,500 articles and two nonfiction regional books. I owned, operated and published my own newspaper. I wrote, copyrighted, and taught my Sell What You Write course, sponsored writing seminars, spoke at many conferences and writing groups, and won the 1990 Beaver County Times Woman of the Year Award for contributions to the community and excellence in journalism.

Eleven years ago, the reporter who wrote about my winning this award began her story with the sentence, "When there's time she sleeps." She then listed part of my daily routine in one long paragraph, asked the readers if they needed to take a breath yet, then continued, ". . . she returns to her personal computer where she seizes the late night and early morning hours to do what she enjoys immensely—write. She is as relentless as the pink Energizer-battery rabbit—steady, persistent and determined to succeed."

I received the award in October 1990. In December, at age 38, I had a stroke. My writing career died along with a part of me. My ability to remember what I had taken years to learn was destroyed. That award-winning writer no longer existed. I was once again a beginner.

PERSEVERANCE: TO PERSIST IN SPITE OF DIFFICULTIES.

Those words are posted in large, bold print and tacked to my bulletin board. When my feet hit the floor in the morning, I walked into my home office, read those words, turned on my computer, then hobbled to the kitchen to pour a cup of coffee.

I grabbed my writing course notes and my tape recorder and began pacing and reading my notes out loud. None of it sounded the least bit familiar. When I played the tape back it didn't take long to realize I never would be the same person I once was. All that I had learned to earn those diplomas and awards had vanished. Being an avid Stephen King fan, I often referred to it as the "dead zone."

I read magazines, newspapers, and books out loud into the tape recorder. All day, every day for the next month, I followed the same routine. I would turn on the tape recorder, read, and listen.

By the end of January, I began to sound somewhat like myself. But that wasn't good enough. I would pace, cane in hand, in front of the mirror, reciting parts of what I'd memorized and reading parts I'd forgotten. By the end of February, I had gained some coordination, some inflection, some pride.

When the envelope from Slippery Rock came with my spring semester course agreement, my hands shook when I opened it. It was my creative writing course. Every student who had taken the Sell What You Write course was on the roster, along with ten new students.

Standing in front of a mirror practicing my teaching skills was one thing, but I wasn't ready to face or speak to a classroom full of people. I set the envelope aside.

It took me six trips from the car, with one hand balancing a box on one hip, and a cane in the other hand, climbing two sets of 15 stairs each, to get all my course materials into the classroom. I wanted to bolt, but instead I smiled, walked behind the desk and said, "Welcome to my creative writing class." One former student glanced at my cane and said, "It's great to be here . . . what happened?" I took a deep breath, closed my eyes for a second, opened them, and said, "I'm here tonight to learn along with you." Those who had taken my other course looked at me questioningly. "Before I begin, I'd like to tell you that if, after you've finished this course, you're not satisfied with what you've learned, I will personally refund your money." The student who had asked what happened said, "Yeah, right, as if we wouldn't be satisfied. You're an excellent teacher and speaker. And what do you mean you're here to learn?"

I thanked him, smiled, and began to tell them what had happened since we had last met in this classroom. I told them that I had almost canceled the course because I didn't feel that I had a right to teach it, since I had just begun to learn what I would be teaching. After I told my story, I assured them that it wouldn't hurt my feelings if they chose to leave.

Not one of the students left the classroom. I paced in front of them, leaning on the cane, repeating everything I had memorized over the past three months. I used the gestures and inflections I had practiced. I tripped over the cane a few times. When they'd all jerked in their seats anticipating my fall, I smiled and said, "Just wanted to make sure you are paying attention." I was thankful that my sense of humor hadn't slipped into the dead zone. Then, after four hours of speaking, joking, and tripping, I passed out handouts, gave the assignment for the next class, and closed my briefcase.

As I began to pack my boxes to go home, I heard chairs sliding, papers jostling, and a loud thundering noise. When I looked up, each and every student was standing beside his desk, clapping and smiling at me. It wasn't until that moment that I felt success. My vision blurred from tears that I wouldn't let drop, but I didn't need clear vision to see that the months of pacing, reciting, and learning had paid off.

I use my cane every day now and keep telling myself I'm okay. The pictures, awards, degrees and all the published articles still carry a lot of meaning to me, but hold no validity now. I shake my head in awe of that person's ability to write and remind myself every day that I am a beginner.

My experience taught me that regardless of the detours my life had taken, I need to continue to set my goals and diligently work toward them. I follow the road to the goal I've always had. That goal is—and always will be—to be the best writer I can be.

Perseverance is to persist in spite of difficulties. It does pay off.

I love to write. Writing is all I ever wanted to do. I'm still here. I'm still okay. I'm still writing. I'm still learning. And I have persevered.

Joanne D. Kiggins has published more than 2,500 articles, essays and op-eds in newspapers and magazines. Kiggins can be contacted at joannedkiggins@comcast.net. Her work can be seen by visiting her website at http://home.comcast.net/~joannedkiggins.

BEHIND CLOSED DOORS

By Misti Sandefur

"I'm sorry. It won't happen again." His words played over and over in my head.

I believed him, but the beating continued no matter how much I begged and pleaded for him to stop. And there was a time in our relationship, I thought maybe if I fought back, he'd leave me alone. I painfully remember that day like it was yesterday . . .

Nervously walking into the living room to approach him, I felt my eyes sting with tears.

"What's wrong with you?" he asked me, halfway withdrawing his attention from the television.

"I just . . ." My voice shook. ". . . miscarried our baby."

He darted up from the couch. "Why didn't you tell me you were pregnant?"

Taking a step back from him, I feared his next move.

"I didn't know I was pregnant, not until I went to the bathroom."

He waited for me to continue, sternly scrunching up his face while placing his hands on his hips.

"I thought I was just on my period, until I saw something gray in my stool."

Because of my experience in the medical field, I knew that the gray matter I saw was a miscarriage. It also explained why my bleeding was heavier, and why I hurt more then usual. I tried to explain it all to him without emotion.

"It wasn't mine! Who have you been sleeping around with, bitch?"

"You know cheating isn't my style. Besides, you always make sure I'm in your sight." Fighting back my tears, I continued, "So how could I cheat?"

Like a flash of lightning, he was standing smack dab in front of my face. I knew right then, I had made a mistake.

"Never, and I mean, never, speak to me in that tone again!" he said as he shoved me down on the couch.

"I just lost a baby. I should see a doctor," I softly pleaded.

"You don't need a damn doctor! Go to bed and rest!"

Feeling the sting across my face, I tried to get up as one lonely tear ran down my left cheek, and then another down my right cheek. All I could manage to do—to try to keep him from hitting me—was to kick him between the legs. I only made my beating worse.

A few days later while my husband was at work, I saw a doctor, who confirmed that I'd had a miscarriage. He treated and released me, and I swallowed my heartbreak alone.

Over the years, I made it a point not to show my pain to others. There were many trips to the hospital emergency room, where I would tell doctors and nurses that I fell in the bathtub, or a litany of other excuses. I think they knew the truth, but they couldn't do anything unless I spoke up. Instead, I was given brochures and pamphlets that I would hide in my purse, and later throw away so he wouldn't see them. I thought it would only be worse if I told; sure, he'd go to jail for a day, but then what?

Many times I tried to leave, but each time he found me and begged for me to come back. He would always say, "I'm sorry. It won't happen again." Then he would tell me that no one would ever want me.

Through the stress and daily abuse, God was at my side. God and my three children—the only good that came out of my marriage. I call them my little angels, and they made me realize I didn't need anyone else. My children were all that mattered, and I knew they had been through enough. I finally got help from family, friends, and the local police, and I was able to leave.

Why did I stay in an abusive marriage for so long? I've been asked this question many times, and though I know I stayed too long, I stayed for the children. For a long time, I felt helpless when he would hit me in front of the children. And as they got older, they would run to their rooms and hide. I felt better when they were hiding—I didn't want them to see their daddy hitting their mommy.

It was lonely at first, starting over again on my own, but my children and I have found freedom, and we are now living a much better, more peaceful life. And later, after a five-year relationship, I remarried. Entering into a new relationship was scary at first, but as we came to know each other, I realized God had blessed me with a wonderful man.

I pray that all the victims of domestic violence find the strength to leave, no matter how hard it may seem. Your life and happiness are worth it.

Note from the author: This is dedicated to all the men and women who are, or have been victims of domestic violence. In addition, I would also like to dedicate my essay to those who have lost a loved one due to domestic violence. If you ever need to talk, or would like to know where you can find help in your area, don't hesitate to e-mail me (msks04@shawneelink.net). May God bless each and every one of you!

Misti Sandefur is a freelance writer and author currently living in southern Illinois. She has published two books, and her articles have appeared in many publications. You can find out more about Mrs. Sandefur at www.mistisandefur.com.

PINE SCRAPBOOK

By Robin Bayne

"I'm finally going to do it," I said, hugging the phone between my shoulder and ear. "I have to." Tapping a nail lightly with the back of a stapler, I prepared to hang my fresh pine wreath on my apartment door.

"You know your dad and I will stand behind you, no matter what you decide."

I sighed. It had taken more than two years to make the decision—but my husband was noticeably absent, making it all the more inevitable. "I have to get divorced. I can't take it anymore. I've given him so much time to come around, but he thinks I only want presents. He just doesn't get that it's his presence I need." I watched the jar candle's flame flicker on my glass coffee table, and smelled its holly berry fragrance.

"I know."

I stepped back to admire my handiwork, and blew my nose on a tissue. I'd sworn I'd never get divorced, that I'd stick to it and work it out. The priest's words "till death do us part" had meant something to me. The fact that my husband never so much as picked out a gift for me over the years was only a minor factor. I could live with that. I could live with the fact that he'd quit his job to go back to school without discussing it with me.

But his absence hadn't made my heart grow fonder.

"He's staying out all night now. Says he's working on side jobs."

"I'm sorry, sweetie. You're both so young . . ."

And that was all she said. My mom was the best listener in the world, never criticizing or offering unwanted advice, not even the occasional "I told you so." And she'd been doing it every week or so for the better part of two years—had been there, listening, being a shoulder to cry on, even over the phone.

"So you think I'm doing the right thing? Father Smith told me I could get an annulment, due to the circumstances."

This time Mom sighed. "I think so."

I blew my nose once more, and forced a smile I hoped she could hear. "Thanks, Mom. Hey, why don't you and Dad come over this weekend and see my tree? I'm putting it up after work tomorrow night. Janie's coming over to help."

* * *

This really wasn't my first Christmas alone, and Janie really wasn't coming over. I'd been putting up a tree by myself for years now, but I didn't need help making my place as festive as possible. To be honest, the first few years I'd had only a two-foot high table-top tree, which was easy to assemble. Now I had the six-foot tree my grandmother could no longer handle. It opened like an umbrella, and I just fit a few pieces together and wrapped fake pine around the trunk to make it look real. Someday, I figured, I'd have a big house and get a real tree that dripped sap everywhere and smelled like Christmas in a can.

With carols playing on my turntable, I tossed the light strands from one side to the other. I still had the LP albums from my youth, including an album our chorus had recorded in high school. The record was scratched and hard to hear, but I loved Handel's Messiah and it helped my mood.

Once the lights were on, attractively if not evenly, I strung sparkly silver garland to fill in the wider gaps between branches. The hand-me-down tree was so old it had the inconsistencies of a live tree. I took a break and sampled the sugar cookies I'd brought home from work—they were iced with pink frosting, and the sandy textured cookies melted in my mouth. They also tasted slightly like peppermint, reminding me of the time Mom and I had made candy-cane shaped cookies from a TV show recipe. I was really little, and can only vaguely recall that Mom hadn't liked the way they turned out, but I could still recall their flavor some 20 years later. And the fact that the "J" candy cane shape stood for Jesus. It definitely felt like Christmas now.

After sealing the few remaining cookies back in their tin, I uncovered my box of ornaments. Each year since I was small, Mom had made sure my sister and I had a special tree ornament dated for that particular year. They were the pride and joy of my tree, and I liked arranging them on the branches myself.

If my husband had ever shown interest, I would have welcomed his help, but it had become my own tradition to trim the tree with candles, music, and my own company. Some day I'd add a little dog to the mix, but for now, I'd made peace with myself. Although I didn't feel at peace with God, needing a divorce, I knew I'd been blessed in so many ways.

Finally I had just one ornament left. In the far corner of the crate sat a glass ball, with a snow scene and little red cardinals. It read "First Christmas Together." My gut clenched when I saw it, and I stood there, for long moments, allowing bad memories to scramble the good.

I turned the little box upside down, then shoved the crate under the dining room table. I only wanted to think about the good stuff.

* * *

"Your place looks great," Mom said, setting a covered dish on the table. "Great job on the tree." She moved to look at it closer, bending in to examine some of the smaller items it boasted. She pointed at a globe-type ornament that housed a little boy, tucked in his bed, staring at the night sky. "Christmas Eve Vigil," it was called. "Remember that year Mom-Mom slept in your room, and you kept her up all night saying you thought you heard Santa Claus?"

I nodded, smiling. She reminded me of that every year. The reminder itself had become a tradition.

Dad shook the tree a bit, proclaimed it stable enough, and took a seat on the floor, leaning his back against my couch. Mom circled the tree, pointing out memories here and there.

"It's almost like our trees are scrapbooks, like our lives," I said, following her. "Thanks for starting these collections for us, way back when."

"I bet some of those old ones are pretty valuable by now," Dad said.

"They are valuable," Mom agreed, meaning something entirely different.

We ordered pizza, and ate slices of greasy pepperoni at my dining room table.

"What's this?" Dad had kicked something, and now pushed my forgotten ornament crate out into view.

"Oh, I forgot to put that back in the closet."

Mom got up, immediately spied the lone ornament, and pulled it out. "Why isn't this on the tree?"

I shrugged. "Just because."

She looked closer, took Dad's reading glasses off his head and read the fine print. "Oh, honey, you should put this one up, too."

"Why? Why would I want that one on my otherwise cheerful tree?"

She gently took the ball and shined it against the bottom of her sweater. "Because it's a page from your scrapbook. It's part of your life you can't just wipe out. You were happy that year, weren't you?"

I nodded, unable to speak.

"Then let's hang it on the tree, maybe toward the back, facing the wall?"

I nodded again. My throat felt swollen and tight.

"C'mon, honey. I have another ornament for you this year. It's a lovely glass angel with a fresh new date."

Could I really have a fresh start? God said we could be forgiven, as long as we forgave others. It might take a while to forgive my ex, and myself, but I wanted that new start.

Mom was still talking. "It will be your newest, happiest memento. Years from now, you'll be so glad to have all of your ornaments. The happy memories, and the not-so-happy ones. That's how we realize how many blessings we have."

I reached for the angel, and the new page of my life.

Robin Bayne is the award-winning author of five novels and three novellas, and is a regular contributor for the "Spirit Led Writer" ezine. Visit her at www.robinbayne.com.

AFTER LIFE

By Carol Ann Lindsay

I remember the quiet times together most. I enjoyed long walks and bike rides on the beach or across the desert with my best friend, my husband and soul mate. I felt free to say whatever was on my mind, to feel him, touch him and know him. As we walked, his long, thin, fingers wrapped around my short, stubby ones, we learned more about what bound us together. During day hikes in the mountains, he loved to stop and look at a rock or rattlesnake. I was amazed by what he knew. I admired him.

We sometimes laughed about the way we'd met. He'd walked into my office, asking for my predecessor just so he could introduce himself. We hit it off immediately, marrying a year later. After that, he made me laugh with jokes or his famous one-liners. His passion for life sustained us both, creating a physical connection between us that transformed our bond to a spiritual level.

I was filled with our lives until, at 47, his death nearly destroyed me. Until then, the future existed with my best friend. A few short months before I lost him, two sons married (one moved halfway across the country), our 11-year-old was in boarding school a thousand miles from home, and I was left with nothing but loneliness and the most difficult financial situation I've ever had to confront.

Not even my work as a writer mattered much without the daily feedback from my best supporter and critic. I realized I couldn't just give up, so I decided to pursue activities I've always dreamed of doing. I traveled out of state, and when I was home, I learned how to play hand bells, joining a bell choir. I took line-dancing lessons, stepping on the crowded floor of the local western pub to dance.

I was indeed distracted.

But suddenly all of our friends, an entire world of people who had been part of our lives disappeared from my life. The sense of abandonment worsened when I called people we had known and the calls weren't returned. It was as if I didn't exist because my husband didn't, as though being half of a couple was improper. Did they think I was a threat now that I no longer had my partner beside me?

I took myself to the beach every Saturday and Sunday. I explored areas we'd never shared, hoping that new places would fill me. Often I thought of how much he would have loved my discoveries, especially a beach I stumbled on that could be accessed only during low tide. During the week, I rode my bike, thinking about how much joy this had been with him at my side. I would stop and gaze at the ocean, wishing he were there, tears streaming down my cheeks. If he'd been there, he would have known something about the geological structure, told me a joke, or pointed out a cave for a romantic tryst.

Though he couldn't hold a tune, his deep voice would have laughed as he told me more of his shenanigans in the desert when he was a Caltech student. Or he would have told me (again) about the mini explosion he created in Dr. Pauling's chemistry class. A year before his death he wanted to stop at Dr. Pauling's house to apologize, but we didn't have time then. Would we have made time if we'd known?

I spotted bike trails we had never traveled and knew how much he would have enjoyed the scenes along a canyon I came across or one of the few reservoir lakes in San Diego County he'd missed.

My lonely nights were consumed with poetry writing. I wrote so many widow poems, I don't care if I never see another widow poem as long as I live. Some were love poems, some attempted to define him, and some described loneliness. It was a therapeutic exercise, especially when publication came.

I began to look outside my world and developed relationships with people fighting the education bureaucracy, even running for school board along with 16 other candidates. I didn't care whether I won, but I wanted my voice to be heard. It worked and I have a book of press clippings to prove I was a rebel with a cause that resulted in police officers ousting me from a teacher training seminar.

Finally, though, I realized that all the assiduity with exploits away from home was merely an escape from a reality I had not faced. I was alone. I once made a vow that I would always remember his idiosyncrasies so I wouldn't put him on a pedestal that no other man could match. And I promised never to forget how irritating his stubborn streak could be, but the men I dated didn't fill my need for a lover who is also a best friend. No man I knew could understand my thoughts and feelings the way my husband had. And the trouble is, all of our joyful times eclipsed the difficult ones. The pedestal is growing higher.

Today is the third anniversary of his death.

To look beyond the shadow of death, I need to take a turn. I need to see that in spite of everything, my husband will always be here in spirit. Today I will step forward and remember yesterday was fun, but tomorrow deserves to be embraced with as much excitement and joy. In this life, my after-life, there is still time to smell a flower or visit a lonely person. Time is a gift, and I will not waste one precious second.

Carol Ann Lindsay's poetry has appeared in numerous literary and commercial publications as well as juried art/poetry exhibitions. She was host of KDCI TV programs, featured poet on local CNN headline news and she authored four books. She is a letters member of NLAPW, member of the Academy of American Poets and the Carlsbad Oceanside Art League.

FEBRUARY'S ASHES

By Kira Connally

I remember feeling snow so cold it burned the soles of my feet. So many people think they would save prized possessions or expensive stereos if their house were on fire. I ran back in for shoes. After 11 years have passed, I still have those shoes.

I also have the necklace I was wearing that morning, and the unofficial family title of "Girl Who Burned Down Grandma's House."

It was an accident, and the results were unstoppable. I fell asleep while a candle still burned. I was 16, and Grandpa had just paid off the mortgage.

My mother, hair wet from her shower, shook me awake at just after 7:00 that February morning. She had the dog leashes in one hand and was wearing only a robe and slippers.

"Get up—the house is on fire." She said it so matter-of-factly it didn't seem urgent. She'd already called 9-1-1, and I saw Grandpa stumble down the hall toward the front door. His suspenders were loose, his shirt open.

We stood in the front yard, ankle-deep in snow. Mom had remembered her slippers. Grandpa's work boots were unlaced. The smoke blended into the gray sky until I couldn't tell where one ended and the other began.

Then Mom remembered the dog leashes in her hand. Flames snicked out of the basement windows, and she sent me back in for Beauty and Sam, a black Lab and a cocker spaniel. The snow on the bushes flanking the front door was melting; the cement slab stoop was warm.

Once inside, I saw the dogs run out the open back door. My feet should have been numb, but I could feel the heat from the floor. That's when I grabbed my shoes. They were in the bedroom, and I could see smoke coming up from the wooden floor, the walls, an orange cast to the windows. The air was a dense fog, and it crackled.

More than the visible flames and dense smoke, it was the crackling sound that made disaster suddenly real. I ran for the front door.

They told me that I screamed for Grandma hysterically when I came out. I believed them only because my throat was so sore.

I remember watching the roof rattle as the gas furnace exploded. I remember a fireman asking me if everything was okay, and how the absurdity of the question hit me like a blow to the chest.

"The roof exploded!" I screamed at him. He just shrugged and walked away. I sat down in the snow and watched the house burn.

I can't recall the moment when everything was okay again. There must have been some singular hour when the fire stopped dominating my world. It might have been an algebra test, or the first time I realized how ridiculous it was for Grandma to bring home grocery bags of smoky, ruined wreckage every day. Those brown bags quickly filled every nook of the hotel room we now lived in, paper mountains of a lost way of life.

It wasn't the day a woman from church brought a frozen turkey to the hotel room. It was useless—you can't thaw a turkey in a hotel sink, and you can't cook it on a hot plate. Her well-meant charity doused us in more gloom.

It wasn't the day, nine months later, when we moved out of the hotel. Somewhere between then and now, I've come to realize that nothing was the same after that February morning in Connecticut. But it's okay.

Since then, I've learned to use the good china whenever I can find an excuse. Nice winter coats don't hang, unused but admired, in the closet. I've learned that security can't be measured on a tangible scale. I am not what I own or where I live. I am a collection of experiences I've chosen to hang on to, and I don't need physical representations to remind me.

I learned that life goes on without hairspray and bracelets and kitchen gadgets. I kept waking up even though the only pair of shoes I owned sported soles seared by fire and frozen mid-melt in the snow. The odd pattern left behind became interesting after a while. It became part of me, a reminder that even though it felt like it, the world didn't end.

Maybe today is the day that everything's okay again. Grandma still has those brown bags of ruin in her garage, proof of what she once was. But Mom and I don't hang onto what we don't need—there are only so many uses for frozen turkey.

Kira Connally is a writer living in Weatherford, Texas. She's currently at work on a supernatural novel and a nonfiction book concerning ghosts. She can be reached at kira-connally@yahoo.com.

STRENGTH IN FICTION

"Fiction is like a spider's web, attached ever so lightly perhaps,
but still attached to life at all four corners."

~Virginia Woolf (*A Room Of One's Own*)

THE BEST DAY

By Orson Scott Card

Once there was a woman who had five children that she loved with all her heart, and a husband who was kind and strong. Every day her husband would go out and work in the fields, and then he'd come home and cut wood or repair harness or fix the leaky places in the roof. Every day the children would work and play so hard they wore paths in the weeds from running, and they knew every hiding place in two miles square. And that woman began to be afraid that they were too happy, that it would all come to an end. And so she prayed, Please send us eternal happiness, let this joy last forever. Well, the next day along came a mean-faced peddler, and he spread his wares and they were very plain—rough wool clothing, sturdy pots and pans, all as ugly and practical as old shoes. The woman bought a dress from him because it was cheap and it would last forever, and he was about to go, when suddenly she saw maybe a fire in his eyes, suddenly flashing bright as a star, and she remembered her prayer the night before, and she said, "Sir, you don't have anything to do with—happiness, do you?"

And the peddler turned and glowered and said, "I can give it to you, if you want it. But let me tell you what it is. It's your kids growing up and talking sassy, and then moving on out and marrying other children who don't like you all that much, at least at first. It's your husband's strength giving out, and watching the farm go to seed before your eyes, and maybe having to sell it and move into your daughter-in-law's house because you can't support yourselves no more. It's feeling your own legs go stiff, and your fingers not able to tat or knit or even grip the butter churn. And finally it's dying, lying there feeling your body drop off you, wishing you could just go back and be young with your children small, just for a day. And then—"

"Enough!" cried the woman.

"But there's more," said the peddler.

"I've heard all I mean to hear," and she hurried him out of the house.

The next day, along comes a man in a bright-painted wagon, with a horse named Carpy Deem that he shouted at all the time. A medicine man from the East, with potions for this and pills for that, and silks and scarves to sell, too, so bright they hurt your eyes just to look at them. Everybody was healthy, so the woman didn't buy any medicine. All she bought was a silk, even though the price was too high, because it looked so blue in her golden hair. And she said to him, "Sir, do you have anything to do with happiness?"

"Do you have to ask?" he said. "Right here, in this jar, is the elixir of happiness—one swallow, and the best day of your life is with you forever."

"How much does it cost?" she asked, trembling.

"I only sell it to them as have such a day worth keeping, and then I sell it cheap. One lock of your golden hair, that's all. I give it to your Master, so he'll know you when the time comes."

She plucked the hair from her head, and gave it to the peddler, and he poured from the bottle into a little tin cup. When he was gone, she lifted it up, and thought of the happiest day of her life, which was only two days before, the day she prayed. And she drank one swallow.

Well, her husband came home as it was getting dark, and the children came to him all worried. "Something's wrong with Mother," they said. "She ain't making no sense." The man walked into the house, and tried to talk to his wife, but she gave no answer. Then, suddenly, she said something, speaking to empty air. She was cutting carrots, but there were no carrots; she was cooking a stew, but there was no fire laid. Finally her husband realized that word for word, she was saying what she said only two days ago, when they last had stew, and if he said to her the words he had said then, why, the conversation at least made some sense.

And every day it was the same. They either said that same day's words over and over again, or they ignored their mother, and let her go on as she did and paid her no mind. The kids got sick of it after a time, and got married and went away, and she never knew it. Her husband stayed with her, and more and more he got caught up in her dream, so that every day he got up and said the same words till they meant nothing and he couldn't remember what he was living for, and so he died. The neighbors found him two days later, and buried him, and the woman never knew.

Her daughters and daughters-in-law tried to care for her, but if they took her to their homes, she'd just walk around as if she were still in her own little cottage, bumping into walls, cutting those infernal carrots, saying those words till they were all out of their minds. Finally they took her back to her own home and paid a woman to cook and clean for her, and she went on that way, all alone in that cabin, happy as a duck in a puddle until at last the floor of her cabin caved in and she fell in and broke her hip. They figure she never even felt the pain, and when she died she was still laughing and smiling and saying idiotic things, and never even saw one of her grandchildren, never even wept at her husband's grave, and some folks said she was probably happier, but not a one said they were eager to change places with her. And it happened that a mean-looking old peddler came by and watched as they let her into her grave, and up rode a medicine man yelling at his horse, and he pulled up next to the peddler.

"So she bought from you," the peddler said.

And the medicine man said, "If you'd just paint things up a little, add a bit of color here and there, you'd sell more, friend."

But the peddler only shook his head. "If they'd ever let me finish telling them, they'd not be taken by you, old liar. But they always send me packing before I'm through. I never get to tell them."

"If you'd begin with the pleasant things, they'd listen."

"But if I began with the pleasant things, it wouldn't be true."

"Fine with me. You keep me in business." And the medicine man patted a trunk filled with gold and silver and bronze and iron hairs. It was the wealth of all the world, and the medicine man rode off with it, to go back home and count it all, so fine and cold.

And the peddler, he just rode home to his family, his great-great-great-grandchildren, his gray-haired wife who nagged, the children who complained about the way he was always off on business when he should be home, and always hanging about the house when he ought to be away; he rode home to the leaves that turned every year, and the rats that ate the apples in the cellar, and the folks that kept dying on him, and the little ones that kept on being born.

Orson Scott Card is the author of the novels Ender's Game, Ender's Shadow, and Speaker for the Dead, which are widely read by adults and younger readers, and are increasingly used in schools. Besides these and other science fiction novels, Card writes contemporary fantasy (Magic Street, Enchantment, Lost Boys), biblical novels (Stone Tables, Rachel and Leah), the American frontier fantasy series The Tales of Alvin Maker (beginning with Seventh Son), poetry (An Open Book), and many plays and scripts. Visit his website at www.hatrack.com.

THE HUCKLEBERRY PATCH

By Robin Lee Hatcher

Aunt Dodie—Dorothy Mae Collins to those outside our extended family—was an original. God broke the mold after making her, and that's for certain.

For her entire adult life, Aunt Dodie had lived in the central Idaho mountains in a cabin overlooking Payette Lake. She never married, never had kids of her own. But there wasn't a one of us—in any Collins generation—who didn't know where to turn when we needed help or advice or a bit of loving concern.

I suppose if she'd been born a southerner, they'd have called Aunt Dodie a "steel magnolia," for she was as strong as she was beautiful. However, we don't have a comparable description in our Idaho vernacular—unless you count "tough old bird." And that doesn't fit Aunt Dodie.

I was 32 the year I experienced my greatest need for a dose of Aunt Dodie's wisdom. I'd broken up with Barry, my fiancé of three years, after catching him in a, shall we say, questionable situation with my best friend. So much for being a keen judge of character. Then the firm I'd worked for longer than I cared to admit—in a rather boring position, to boot—decided to close their Boise office and relocate to Spokane, Washington. I had no desire to go with them, not for the salary I earned. Of course, they didn't offer me a job there either, so that was a moot point.

The final blow came when I learned the apartment complex where I lived was to be torn down to make room for a grocery superstore. Life was the pits—and it had nothing to do with cherries.

Aunt Dodie to the rescue.

"You come stay with me for the rest of the summer, hon. We'll have us a good time while you wait to see what it is the Lord has in store for you."

That was another thing about Aunt Dodie. Nobody had more faith than she did. She looked for—and found—God in everything around her. Maybe that's because she was a painter and sculptor and had a special way of seeing the world with those artist's eyes of hers. But I believe it's because she looked at everything through the Artist's eyes rather than through her own.

It was a clear, hot, August afternoon when I drove my 15-year-old Ford up the dusty, bumpy driveway to Aunt Dodie's home. She must have been watching for me. The door opened and out she came onto the deck, her face wreathed in a smile of welcome.

Aunt Dodie was in her seventies, thin as a model, with hair as black as pitch. "Thanks to Lady Clairol," she would announce to anyone who commented on her lack of gray. She didn't make excuses. You always knew where you stood with Aunt Dodie.

That's what I desperately needed right then—to know where I stood. Not with Aunt Dodie. With my Creator. It sure seemed to me that I'd been sent to the woodshed without being told the reason why. Worse, I felt abandoned, rejected, alone.

That evening, while we sat at the table, eating a supper of fried chicken with mashed potatoes and gravy and fresh cut green beans, Aunt Dodie let me pour out my confusion and heartache and anger. She listened attentively while I whined and railed. I complained about Barry. I complained about my former boss. I complained about the superstore mentality that had swept across America, wiping out all the little guys in the name of big bucks and big business. And finally, long after the food on the table had grown cold, I complained about God.

"What did I do wrong to deserve all this, Aunt Dodie? Why is everything going wrong? I've prayed and asked, but He doesn't answer me."

"Doesn't He?" She lifted one of her finely arched eyebrows. "Perhaps you simply aren't listening."

Ah, something new to complain about. Now I could complain about Aunt Dodie!

"God never promised us a rose garden, hon."

I sank into a mire of my own misery.

Aunt Dodie rose from her chair and began to clear the table. "We'll go huckleberry picking tomorrow. About six."

"In the morning?"

She laughed, and that was answer enough. I groaned.

"My dear," she said, leaning toward me, "you might be surprised at the many ways God can speak to you in a huckleberry patch."

* * *

The forest was hushed, almost reverent, at six in the morning. A light breeze whispered through the tops of the lodgepole and ponderosa pines. Dew sparkled on the underbrush. Dried leaves and needles crunched underfoot, and the air smelled of rich soil and wood smoke. I followed Aunt Dodie up the trail, climbing ever higher on the mountainside. Her stride was surprisingly long and sure for a woman her age.

I, on the other hand, had a hard time keeping up while carrying two large plastic buckets, one in each hand. I was panting from the exertion by the time we stopped.

Aunt Dodie glanced over her shoulder. "We're here."

Golden sunlight filtered through trees that surrounded a small clearing, gilding the bushes, warming the dark brown earth.

"Some years, there's a bumper crop." Aunt Dodie took one of the buckets from me. "And some years you have to look hard to find even a few. Let's see what sort of crop we have this year."

I stood there, feeling tired and cranky.

She leaned over and plucked a purple huckleberry from beneath a leaf. She held it out toward me. "The berries are tiny and the bushes they grow on seem so scraggly and worthless, it's easy to overlook them." She popped the huckleberry into my mouth, then added, "But they're wonderfully sweet to the taste."

She was right about that. The burst of flavor on my tongue left me wanting more.

"When I was a girl, back in the 'forties, my father used to bring the family to McCall in his Studebaker. Your grandfather loved huckleberry season, loved his huckleberry pancakes with huckleberry syrup. So up we came, every August." She set to work then, bending over the nearest bush.

"It took much longer than two hours for the drive back then. But oh, the view from the mountaintops. It always made the journey worthwhile."

I began to pick, too.

We worked in silence for a long spell, moving through the brush, leaning over to pluck berries, one at a time, from their hiding places. My back started to ache, and I worried about the size of my bucket. At this rate, I would never fill it.

This wasn't why I'd come to be with Aunt Dodie, I grumbled silently. I could have stayed in Boise and been miserable. One more lousy thing happening to me in a string of lousy things. But while I silently bemoaned the condition of my life—poor me, poor me, poor me—Aunt Dodie sang. It took time for me to really hear her voice through the cacophony of my complaints. It took even longer to recognize the words. They were from the Psalms. She wasn't singing them to herself or for my benefit. She was singing them to the Lord, singing words of praise for His faithfulness, words of trust in His love.

And somehow, in a way I can't describe, her song, her words, touched a place in my wounded heart and soul. Like waking from a deep sleep, I suddenly remembered that God was loving and just, that He had promised to walk with me in the valleys of my life, that I needed only seek Him and I would find Him.

How had I allowed myself to forget all that for even a little while?

"Look," Aunt Dodie whispered.

I blinked away the tears that momentarily had blinded me, then lifted my gaze. There, at the far end of the clearing, I saw a small doe and her fawn staring back at us. I held my breath, struck by the wild, delicate beauty before me. A few heartbeats later, the deer and fawn bounded away, hopping over fallen trees and underbrush until they'd disappeared from view.

"So many wonderful things of God to see," Aunt Dodie said, "if we just remember to look up every once in a while."

I turned toward her.

"God's blessings are all around us, hon, but sometimes we get so focused on our lives, we miss the beauty of the journey. All the steps aren't easy, and sometimes the climb is hard, but the journey is still beautiful because He's with us."

Last night Aunt Dodie had said that I might be surprised at the many ways God could speak to me in a huckleberry patch.

So what have I learned today? I wondered. What have You said to me? I pondered all the things Aunt Dodie had shown me, all the things she'd told me as we'd shared these morning hours. I pondered the golden sunlight and the scrawny-looking huckleberry bushes that produced a surprisingly sweet crop. I pondered the whisper of God's voice, carried on a mountain breeze into a woman's broken heart.

Then I smiled. For you see, I'd learned I couldn't find the huckleberries until I leaned over and searched for them. Many of God's blessings were like that, tiny and hidden from easy view. But not recognizing them—the huckleberries or the blessings—didn't make them any less there, any less bountiful, nor any less sweet.

Strange. Knowing that didn't change the circumstances of my life. Barry still had a new girlfriend, and I was still jobless and without a home to call my own. Yet knowing it seemed to change everything. Aunt Dodie was right. God hadn't promised me a rose garden.

But I think He might have promised me a huckleberry patch.

A native Idahoan, Robin Lee Hatcher has spent many a summer day plucking huckleberries in the forest that surrounds Payette Lake. She is the RITA Award winning author of over 45 historical and contemporary novels.

ATLAS SLOUCHED

By Richard Cobbett

There was something unsettling about the boy who held up the sky.

He was seven years old, and that was all most people knew about him. His name never stuck in anybody's mind for long—one of those kids who left school at the end of the day and returned the next, and may as well have disappeared from the face of the Earth in the middle. He rarely spoke. He never played sports. As far as Miss Briars' class was concerned, he barely existed—not interesting enough to either bully or befriend, or even notice outside of class.

Until Thursday.

On Thursday, when the school broke for lunch, the boy was already there on the school field. He stood on the highest hill, and he held his arms up as high as they could stretch—reaching until they quivered with the strain and the heat.

"What're you doing?" the other kids asked, one after the other, and in various ways.

"Holding up the sky," he said, as if it couldn't have been more obvious.

"Why?" asked another child, and he thought about it carefully. "Because it's my turn," he replied eventually, shifting his grip and leaving it at that. One by one, the other kids asked, and he told them—always the same story, always the same reason.

"My dad says the sky's just air," said one child, watching suspiciously. "Air don't need to be held, 'cause there's nothing really there, really. That's what gravity's for, he says."

"That's not gravity. Gravity's when you drop some apple on a guy while he's asleep." The other child nodded knowledgably. "An' then he hits you, 'cause you broke Newton's Law."

And one by one, they laughed, and one by one, they left to play games on the field and only occasionally looked back to see him standing there, arms still up in the clouds.

The boy who held up the sky ignored them. Half an hour later, he still hadn't moved. Children sat around the hill, eating their sandwiches and watching intensely, trying to spot the joke. Soon, five became eight, eight became 20, and then the whole class, watching with increasing unease. A small stone bounced off his chest, but he didn't flinch or waver. He ignored the jibes from the crowd and the aching of his arms—eyes fixed upwards and shoulders bursting under the weight.

"Um . . ." A nervous little girl in the front row stood, twirling a long blonde pigtail in one hand. She had to lift her voice just to be heard, and her face glowed bright red under the sudden attention. "What happens if you stop holding up the sky?"

The boy thought about it for a while. "Dunno," he decided. "Don't think anyone's ever let it happen. Not since the Dark Ages."

"Let's see it then!" came a new voice, jeering and hostile. The school bully strode through the watching children; a lifetime of malevolence already wrapped in a tower of muscle and blubber. He jabbed the boy in the chest. "What's wrong?" he demanded, poking him again. "No sky's falling here, dummy."

"Maybe it's on skyhooks," shouted a voice from the crowd—the little girl with pig-tails, as surprised as anyone to hear her voice. "What?" snapped the bully. He was a year older than everyone else here, so of course he knew everything.

"Skyhooks," said the knowledgeable child. "Everyone knows that. Maybe they broke. Like a curtain, only it's not a curtain, it's the sky, and that's why it's so hard to hold up, 'cause otherwise they just flop down and you need a ladder to put 'em back."

"Don't be dense," interjected another. "There's some giant who does it, over in Greece."

"Right, only he's prob'ly lost his ladder, so he needs help while he looks in the shed. That's common sense."

The bully ignored them, grabbing the arms of the boy who held up the sky, trying to pull them back down, only to be mobbed by the desperate crowd and pulled down to the ground. There was something in the boy's face, in the way he stood. He had a purpose beyond his years, and 45 minutes into lunch, they were ready to believe. They sat quietly in the circle around him, watching with horror as his arms began to shake and quiver. His breath turned into hisses, short, sharp and painful, and they cheered him on throughout.

"Idiots," muttered the bully. He'd been grumbling for the last five minutes, but this time, everyone noticed. The boy's wristwatch bleeped, and the playing field fell silent as he opened his eyes and fixed the bully with a piercing glare. Slowly, surely, the boy who held up the sky lowered his hands and folded them over his chest.

The world turned dark.

Every child looked up in horror, but the sun was black and the sky pressed down like never before. All eyes turned, anger fixed at the bully and the thick wet patch where his bravado had been. He shouted out in pain as the crowd turned on him, kicking and punching and pulling his hair.

"I'm sorry, okay?" he shouted, pleading. "C'mon! You can push it back, right?"

The boy who had stopped holding up the sky shrugged, sticking his hands in his pockets and shuffling back towards the dark school. "Too heavy now," he said, picking his nose. "Lower it gets, tougher it is, y'know? Need some giant or something to get it back up."

He watched as the bully flailed his hands into the air, joined by a few furtive prods from the rest of the crowd. Hand followed hand, every kid there pushing up against the darkness for all they were worth.

The boy's wristwatch beeped again, and he joined the crowd as well—all grunting with exertion as they pushed the sky back into place.

Slowly, light crept back across the world. The sun shone down, fixed in place as the kids cheered and clapped and dared to breathe out again. The sun hung there, where it was meant to be, no further pushing needed. "It's back on its hooks!" said the little girl, triumphantly.

And then the boy who had held up the sky left. They all left. The lunch bell was ringing, and Miss Briars was way too strict to accept saving the world as an excuse for lateness.

Nobody said a word as she taught math. They'd never been quieter during history. It wasn't until geography that a finger prodded the boy in the ribs, after the collective sigh of relief as she asked if anyone had seen anything interesting over lunch, and promptly stole another piece of magic from the world with her explanation.

The boy reached back; feeling the note press down into his hand from the next desk along. He unfolded it under the desk, reading the scribbled words next to the big cartoon grin and catching the shy wave from the little girl with pigtails.

"Will you be holding up the sky again tomorrow?"

The boy grinned. His pen scratched with practiced nonchalance against the paper, his hand slipping it back as soon as the teacher's back was turned.

"Nah. Someone else's turn now."

Richard Cobbett is a writer and journalist from the murky depths of Old England. He likes cats, hates spiders, and occasionally talks in the third person. His website can be found at ww.richardcobbett.co.uk.

No Way, eBay

By Alyson Mead

Description: Arithmetic Pez dispenser. This is a VERY RARE dispenser! EX-CELLENT CONDITION! Tight springs. No chips, no cracks, no melt marks. (small white plastic spot on stem (see pic). The inside number sticker on the stem is MINT. The two small stickers that go on the outside are missing. High bidder prepays high bid amount plus $10.00 for insurance/shipping/handling (higher outside the U.S.) PayPal preferred and receives immediate Priority Mail shipment. (Personal checks accepted but shipment will be delayed 14 days) BIDS FROM BIDDERS WITH NEGATIVE RATINGS WILL BE RE-JECTED! Please e-mail me if you have any questions. Have fun bidding and Good Luck! I will be on vacation from July 15 - July 29th and unable to answer questions or contact high bidder until July 29th. Minimum bid: $575.00.

Date: July 29, 2005
To: momopez302@yahoo.com
From: jerzy@aol.com
Re: Arithmetic Pez dispenser

Dear E-Auctioneer:

I feel like I should call you that because we don't know one another yet. I stress the "yet" in the previous sentence because I do believe that we can get to know each other better, and perhaps even develop a friendship that could prove mutually beneficial for both of us, if you know what I mean. I am in a position to facilitate the purchase of this rare Pez dispenser as well as any others that might be in your possession. My position as the head of a multinational corporation offers me access to one of the most important things money can buy, which is more money.

I notice that the bidding has been fast and furious in the last few hours, and in the case of a tie, I wanted to write and state my case right up front. You see, I have an ailing mother. She's been in the hospital for the past two years, threatening to die every hour, on the hour, and most people think she's just faking. But I know her better. My mother came over from Austria during World War II and operated a small bakery in Jackson Heights, so I come from good peasant stock. And before I was 14, I developed the formula for Bake-Ease. Mother's savings made it possible for me to get the patent on the formula and, if you read the newspapers, I'm sure you're aware that it's made me a very comfortable living ever since. So if my sick mother needs anything, I provide it.

Having lots of money gives me time I don't know what to do with, so I collect things. One of my favorite toys as a child was my cowboy Pez dispenser, and my mother and I shared a passion not just for rugala but for those delightfully fruity candies inside the chamber. You could say that your product helped to bring my family together, even during the Vietnam War, when most people were just hell-bent on being divisive, and my half-brother grew his hair long just to be contrary.

Collecting has become one of my greatest joys since my son, who's 12, has turned out to be a mama's boy of the highest order. He defines the term disappointment—no sports, no trophies, no bright-eyed little girls running around, nothing. Just sullen looks and video games and a hand out for more allowance. Bah. I could blame the whole thing on my wife (and probably will—ha, ha) but I haven't seen her in three months, since she lives at the other end of our flat now. Can't stand the sight of me, apparently, although I must admit I haven't been lacking for company, if you know what I mean. Anyway, I'm sure you have other things to attend to, like selling that voluptuous Wonder Woman Pez dispenser to some impressionable boy who's going to wonder what's between her silken thighs until he finds out, which by then will be too late, unless he wants to pay alimony through the nose, and child support for a brat who doesn't do much to improve the family name.

If you could see it in your heart, I could really use a hand. If there is anything at all I can do in return for your delivering this rare Pez dispenser into my hands, please just name it. Price is no object. Bidding, I'm afraid, does tend to eat into my schedule, and I am currently without servants since Johannes left last month with no notice, saying he needed to nurture his inner grappler, and joined the WWF. I mean, if one were to sit in front of the computer all day, pressing the "fifty cents more" button every few seconds, that could become tedious, as I'm sure you're aware. So, dear E-Auctioneer, please take pity on an old, rich man who would like to draw closer to his mother before her untimely demise.

My esteem for you is already immeasurable, and will be forever stamped across my memoirs if you do the right thing.

Sincerely yours,
Jerzy H. Goldman

Date:	July 29, 2005
To:	momopez302@yahoo.com
From:	eudora66@mindspring.com
Re:	Your Adorable Pez Dispenser

Dear Seller:

I wanted to write earlier, but noticed you were going to be on vacation until today. How nice for you! I suppose most people wouldn't do this, because there seems to be such an aversion to polite conversation these days, but where did you go? What did you do there? Forgive me for being nosy, but I am naturally curious about people and the things they do. I am also naturally concerned about people, even people I don't know, unlike my husband, who barricades himself in his room and doesn't care about me or his only son. I mean, what kind of man ignores his family so he can spend all his time online, figuring out new ways to spend money? Can you tell me that? All I ever did was try to make a nice home for him to come home to. I mean, with the help of the servants, of course. And I gave him a beautiful son, which is more than a lot of women can do, let me tell you. Now it's all the bastard can do to come out of the room every once in a while to track up the carpets or make a scandal bringing in call girls at every hour of the night, as if the doormen don't have eyes. Me? I haven't seen him in months. He's too busy playing hide the kielbasa with the hookers.

But back to my letter and your adorable Pez dispenser.

Surely you have other things to worry about than a woman who's trying to suffer through what's left of this life and maybe try to find herself amidst the fragments of her fractured family. Last fall, I was going to take a pottery class, because it seemed like such a solid, earthy thing to do, but I kept getting drawn toward plastics, like that character in The Graduate. Can you believe that was Dustin Hoffman? It's hard to believe so much time has passed. At one time, people said I looked like Katherine Ross, but with a bigger nose.

Anyway, I remember collecting Pez dispensers since I was a child, living in the Bronx and making my plan to get out of there. We mostly bought them out of vending machines then, or won them at carnivals. I have some amazing ones that actually survived my brother's firecracker period. Maybe I could leave my collection to my son when I pass away or, if he doesn't want it because all he cares about is Digimon and his violent video friends, perhaps I could leave it to the Brooklyn Children's Museum, which is where I used to take Jason every day in the afternoons, hoping he'd grow up to have culture or at least the sense that there was a world outside of the four very expensive and solidly-constructed walls of our apartment. So, if you could see it in your heart to sell your Pez dispenser to me, I promise I could give it a good home, since mine's been in Architectural Digest three times. I know the perfect place to display it—the glass case

I had Lucretia bring back from Italy last time. Or, if you're in the neighborhood and feel like experiencing the finest in New York cuisine, I could have the cook whip you up some lox and eggs or something. I always like to offer. People are starving everywhere, some of them even in Manhattan, so it's a good thing to get out every once in a while. I hope your vacation made you appreciate where you live. Did you get tan? I hope you used plenty of sunblock. You know what they say about melanoma.

Yours truly,
Celina Goldman

Date: July 29, 2005
To: momopez302@yahoo.com
From: mackin12@earthlink.net
Re: Pez Dispenser

Dear Seller:
Not that you care or anything, but I was wondering if I could ask a question about your very expensive but cool Pez dispenser. I guess I could pretend and fake you out that I'm all old and stuff, like I did with that guy in the Brunch Buddies chat room one time, but this is serious and I really want to make myself heard here, so I won't lie. I'm 12 and live on the Upper East Side of Manhattan. Next year I guess they'll make me do the Bar Mitzvah thing, which is good for money, I guess. My parents have loads of money, but they say I can't have any until I turn 21, which is way too far away for my taste.

Anyway, I don't know what I'm going on about. This really isn't about money or inheritances or anything. It's about the Pez dispenser you have for sale. I mean, I would really love to buy it for my Mom and Dad, because they both love Pez dispensers and their wedding anniversary is coming up, which they've probably both forgotten because they don't get along anymore. They just stay in their little parts of the apartment and I'm in the middle, just trying to live my life, which is somewhere to the left of painful on the boredom scale. They're practically divorced, or probably will do it soon enough, even though I wish they wouldn't. I mean, like, no way, eBay. There's, like, such an infinitesimal possibility that you can bring my family back together again that I don't even know why I'm writing this, but I wouldn't mind spending time with my mom and dad sometime.

I remember once in the wintertime like two years ago, my Dad was feeling all parental or whatever and he took us for this hansom cab ride in Central Park. Usually, this would have made me harsh with laughter, because only tourists do this sort of thing, but that day was great. We were cold and wearing our big ugly jackets, smashed in the cab of this horse-drawn thing, trotting through Central Park. It even started snowing, which it hardly ever does in New York, so it was fun. My dad had even taken us shopping and said we could buy whatever we wanted, which is pretty rare for my father, whose wallet is almost as tight as his fist, let me tell you. My parents were holding hands and laughing because everything was just perfect and fun at that moment in time. It was easily one of the happiest moments of my life.

Anyway, I'm sorry for rambling here, and taking up a lot of your no doubt valuable time. But if you could see it in your heart to sell me your very cool Pez dispenser, I would give it to my parents for their twentieth wedding anniversary and hope that maybe it would maybe save their marriage. I guess it couldn't hurt. And you never know until you try, right? At least that's what grown-ups are always telling me.

Peace out,
Jason Goldman

Alyson Mead's fiction, essays and articles have appeared in over 25 publications, including Salon, In These Times, Bitch, BUST, Whole Life Times, Punk Planet, MSN, The Sun, AOL, Rockpile, and the New York Daily News.

THE SACRIFICE

By Gabriele Campbell

Silence wavered around the fire; the men did not speak. Long ago they ceased to hand around tankards of ale; their bearded faces were haggard. King Brude could breathe the hopelessness radiating from the men, and it suffocated him.

The shine of the fire did not reach the wattle and daub huts where the king's warriors lived; they stood as black shapes against a starless sky. But none of those around the fire wanted to go back to a sleep filled with nightmares.

"Something strange is in the air," a man said and glared at the king.

"Columba says they don't use magic, and I believe him." Brude stirred the fire with a branch. "I want to believe him." He cast the branch aside and drew his fur-lined cloak close. The wind blew cold from the sea, the wooden palisade of the hill fort unable to keep it out. Then he heard the sound, faint, a strange harmony. The king heard words of the song over the wind, "God is our hope and strength."

"You hear it?"

Brude nodded. "There is power in their song." He leaned back against the carved stone that marked the royal seat.

A gust howled and drew sparks from the fire. King Brude flinched as one hit the snake tattooed on his wrist. Words fluttered in the air: ". . .Therefore we will not fear. . ." The king pulled his knees up, wrapping his arms around them.

The wind increased and its wailing drowned the echoes of the strange hymn. Snowflakes floated lazily down, soon becoming a dense swirl.

"Where is Broichan, the druid?" one of the men muttered. "He could tell us whether this storm forebodes a frozen lake, so we'll have to go without fish as well; the grain is already short and no game in the woods."

Another man lifted his head, staring at Brude. "Those strangers should never have been allowed to settle so near." Further words remained unspoken: The king is weak.

"Loch Ness never freezes," King Brude clenched his hands around his knees; the men's eyes, aglow in the shine of the fire, haunted him. He rose and walked away from the fire, head bowed against the wind.

In his hut, he sank upon the furs and hides covering the bed, and deliberately undid the eagle-shaped silver fibula holding his cloak, the heavy silver chain, the amber-inlaid bracelets: a king who lay aside the ornaments of his regal position for the last time. I will be strong. He drew his sword.

"There will be no need to lay down your life in sacrifice," a voice came from the door, and with it a gust of icy wind.

The king looked up. "Broichan?"

The druid entered the room, his imposing stature filling it. The tattoos on his bare arms gleamed with wetness, and water running from his deerskin coat formed a puddle on the clay floor. "I will challenge this Columba."

"But it is I who have failed. I should have refused Columba and the other monks a place on my land, no matter that Columba is a descendant of two powerful Irish families."

Broichan nodded. "The villagers are fearful of the strangers. They think the monks' singing evokes evil spirits that brought this cold upon us, and the dreams."

"I do not think Columba and his monks are hostile. They too suffer from the cold and lack of food. But something goes on here I cannot fathom."

"It's that Christian magic." Broichan spat on the floor to avert evil. "We'll make Columba and his monks leave."

Would Columba's withdrawal give my people food and restore their trust in me? Brude wondered. Aloud he said, "Columba would refuse to fight me. I believe his religion forbids the use of the sword."

"They have other means," Broichan growled, "but it will be to no avail. This Columba calls himself priest of the King of Heaven, and it falls upon me, the druid of the High King of the Picts, to fight him."

King Brude ran his thumb along the fuller of the sword. "It should be I who fights him," he murmured, "Even if it means my death."

"Victory, not sacrifice and death, is what you should seek." Broichan turned and stepped out into the blast.

Brude let the sword sink, the point touching the floor.

* * *

The morning dawned clear, and an icy salt wind blew from the sea. The men rode down a grassy slope, huddled in their woolen cloaks, chilled fingers grasping stiff leather reins, breath forming clouds. Shock struck them as they beheld the motionless surface of Loch Ness reflecting the light in a way dark water never did.

"Ice," a man whispered.

King Brude blinked back a tear the wind had driven forth, and with one hand, clasped the cold silver insignia of his position. He spurred his horse, and they rode on.

A few villagers watched them pass, faces gaunt with deep-sunk eyes. An old man murmured a curse. The king reined his horse and looked at the man, who held his gaze. You are weak. You have failed us.

Broichan guided his pony to the king's side and glared at the man, who took a step back.

Brude lifted his hand. "Not by fear does the king rule," he said to the druid, his voice stern. He put his hand on the hilt of his sword. I am still strong enough to die for the land.

The man's eyes widened in understanding.

They rode past more villagers staring at them, passed the rickety palisade that encircled the settlement, and trotted towards the church. A bell tolled, echoing in the clear air.

Columba met them in front of the wooden door, carved with crude images of figures wearing long mantles, and in the center, a naked man nailed to a cross.

Broichan dismounted and spoke to Columba. "You have put evil magic upon the country."

"It is not I; it is God who is great above all, and who has deemed it fit to send bad weather to remind us of our sins—you and me, and both our people." Columba's voice was soft and clear, but it resounded with a hidden power that made it carry far into the mountains.

King Brude clenched the reins of his prancing horse, his hands wet with sweat.

"I challenge you and your god," Broichan said. His voice sounded uncouth after Columba's gentle speech.

"I am a servant of the One Who Is Above Us, and it is by His grace I live and die." Columba turned to Brude. "Do you agree to this?"

The king dismounted. "Yes. Our gods have abandoned us, and my people suffer." He petted the neck of his pony, trying to get rid of the layer of cold sweat on his hands.

"I understand." Columba ordered two monks to build a large fire in the place in front of the church.

Broichan stared at the king. "Our gods have not turned away; they will lend me strength," he hissed.

"Drive the cold away and give my people food is all I ask." Brude avoided the druid's gaze and instead watched as the men in their coarse brown habits hurried to and fro, while other monks stood near the door, murmuring prayers in an unknown language. He remembered the songs of last night, their secret power. He should have stepped forth and taken the task upon himself, giving his life for his people by entering the sacred pyre. But something held him back.

When the fire burned brightly in the cold morning air, Broichan cast his coat off and stepped into the blaze with his tattooed chest bare, while the bard played the harp he had brought with him, the music subdued.

After a short moment, the druid jumped out of the pyre, mouth agape, but no scream came forth. He threw himself onto the ground, rolling around in an attempt to quench the flames. Brude ran towards him, but Columba's arm, strong as a warrior, intercepted him. "Wait."

The sound of the harp died, vibrating in the silence.

Columba ascended the pyre, and the prayers of the monks became louder, an intricate song of intertwining voices, with Columba's melodious voice dominating them.

"God is our hope and strength, a very present help in trouble. Therefore we will not fear, though the earth be moved."

A wail cut the air. It took Brude a moment to realize it came from Broichan. His men stood huddled together near the druid, but none dared approach him. The king remained on the other side of the pyre, spellbound by Columba's song.

"And though the hills be carried into the midst of the sea. The Lord of hosts is with us, the God of Jacob is our refuge."

Columba stood in the midst of soaring flames, unharmed.

King Brude threw his cloak back, unsheathed his sword, and sank to one knee close to the fire. He offered it to Columba on both hands, inhaling sharply as his bare arms met with the flames, but there was no pain. "If my death pleases your god, take my life." He felt calm, serene.

Columba took the sword and stepped out of the fire. When Brude withdrew his arms, he stared at them: the skin was pure and unblemished, the tattooes gone.

"It is a sign," Columba said.

"But why has Broichan been burnt, and I purified?" Brude said, astonished and awed.

"Because Broichan acted from ambition, and you from the desire to save your people. God knows the mind of men. But there is no need to sacrifice your life like your people have done before. Jesus has already died for all of us." Columba handed the sword back to Brude. "Rise, you are High King of the Picts. I am no more than a humble monk."

"You are more. You are a great mage and druid."

"No," Columba said with a gentle smile, "I am but a servant. And what was at work here was no magic, but a miracle."

"I don't understand."

"You will, within time."

King Brude rose and walked to Broichan, who still writhed in the mud in agony, his skin blistered and oozing fluid. Brude knelt down and, caressing Broichan's forehead, looked up at Columba. "He has served me well for so long a time. Can't you heal him?"

Columba took a plain iron cross off his neck and handed it to Brude. "You can do it yourself."

"But I don't know your . . . miracles."

Again, Columba gave him that gentle smile and said, "Act upon what your heart tells you."

The king grasped the cross. It felt heavy and warm in his hand. He laid it upon Broichan's chest and murmured a line of the song he remembered without understanding. "God is our hope and strength, a very present help in trouble."

The druid's skin healed, the blisters closed. He gazed at his king, confused. "What happened?"

"You have lost the challenge." Brude would explain later. There was more to it than a lost challenge; it might well be the end of the time they knew. And he felt both afraid and hopeful.

He turned to Columba. "Will you and your brothers accept the hospitality of my seat and tell me about your god?"

Columba inclined his head. "We will be honored."

When they passed through Inbhir Nis, the warriors leading their ponies to keep step with the monks, the wind grew warmer and the ice on the lake began to creak. Brude caught the glance of the old man. *I was wrong; you are a strong king after all.*

Columba began to sing. Brude hummed a few tones he heard the night before, "Therefore we will not fear . . ."

Gabriele Campbell is an aspiring writer of historical fiction novels living in Germany, a literary science academic, avid reader, opera enthusiast, rider, and traveler.

MOTHERHOOD

By Amey S Tippett

Somehow, my life has gotten out of control, I thought. I didn't want any of this. This morning, I found myself standing in the middle of the supermarket checkout, surrounded by other women's wailing children, and wondering what happened to my career.

How had I gotten there? It seemed like just yesterday I was managing accounts and dealing with clients. I loved the high-pressure world of advertising, and I was pretty good at it, if I do say so myself. Then, one slip and I was on my way to single motherhood.

I had debated my options—abortion, adoption, marriage—and none of them seemed right. I hadn't wanted to be forced into a decision of that magnitude. So I moved in with Danny and hoped everything would work out.

My belly and my despair had grown larger on a daily basis. Babies are fragile creatures, easily broken. I couldn't be a mother! I didn't know how! What if I did something wrong and seriously hurt my child? What if I couldn't love it enough?

As much as he'd been against commitment and children when I met him, I knew that Danny was going to be a wonderful father. At least the child had that going for it.

It still makes me smile to think of Danny lying beside me talking to my stomach. Sophie was so much more active when he was around. You could actually see my stomach jump when she kicked. It was almost as if she had always known that he would be the better parent.

As much I had detested pregnancy, the fear of labor was even worse. Why is it that every woman wants to tell her birthing story to the pregnant lady? Don't they know that we're scared enough to begin with? Don't tell me that you were in excruciating pain for 35 hours before you finally had a C-section! I honestly did not want to think about how this child was going to get out of me.

The day finally arrived. It was the event that everyone, except me, had been waiting for. The back pain made it impossible to sleep that night. What could possibly be wrong with me? I wondered. It had to be gas. I was so huge and uncomfortable all the time anyway. What was a little more back pain?

When my water broke at 5:00 that morning, I finally figured it out. I was going to have a baby. Oh no! I was going to have a baby! What was I thinking? There was no way I could go through with this.

But, as Danny said, it was too late to put the baby back by then. I was going to have to go through with this. I really didn't want to. Couldn't he trade places with me and do this himself? After all, he was the one who was so enamored with the idea of parenthood.

The rest of it is a blur of drugs and pain. I know that the labor was short, but I don't remember anything until they put Sophie on my chest. People talk about the rush of love that you feel for your children the first time you see them. It wasn't like that for me. Instead, I felt like I was greeting an old friend. A wrinkled, red, howling old friend.

Sophie's wails jarred me back into the reality of the checkout line. This is not my life! I wanted to scream as I jiggled the cart to keep her content. I just wanted to walk away from the load of anti-leak, elastic waist necessities that were eating through my savings.

Of course, I didn't do that. Mommies can't do that. I waited in line, paid for my items, and wheeled my child to the car. And I wished the whole time that I knew how to be a mother.

Other women seem to do it, I thought. They can juggle four, sometimes five, children and still manage to be executives in their spare time. Not me. I implode at the idea of getting dressed in the morning, and I have only one tiny little girl. Let me amend that—one tiny little girl with one amazing set of lungs.

And although my bundle of joy is beautiful, the only time she is ever quiet is when she is asleep or with her father. When I have her, she is a whole other story. I love her. Really, I do. But I'd really just like a modest amount of time to myself. A small section of time when I'm Kate again instead of Sophie's mommy.

It shouldn't matter that she cries all the time. Or that she fusses uncontrollably. Not when I can watch her sleep peacefully and wonder how something so perfect was created inside of me. What a miracle. And I had something to do with that.

And, in the morning, when she first wakes up, I know that she'll be smiling. She always giggles for me as I dress her, allows me to hug her and be awed by the tiny person that she's already become.

I should love this. Should want to be her mommy and nothing else. But I don't. I want to be me! And I've forgotten who that is.

I'm just tired. So, so tired. Tired of running and of anger, but most of all, I am tired of fear. The fear that has made me the frazzled blob of emotions who isn't sure how she managed to get the applesauce put away.

This is what I think of as I sit at the bottom of the stairs, fighting tears. Danny comes into the room and helps me to my feet, wiping the tears from my eyes. "Kate, do you need a break?"

I nod silently, and he hugs me. What a great man you are. I think the words that I cannot say. He wouldn't believe me if I could.

Sophie whines softly from the living room. I ignore Danny's protests that he will watch her, and I walk over to where she sits in the swing. What am I doing here? How can I wallow in my own self-pity like this? I'm a mother.

I'm a mother.

I touch my child's downy head in wonder. She's so soft, so fragile. Almost perfect. A tiny little person with every opportunity ahead of her. I see it. Finally, I understand.

My daughter quiets. She looks up at me with a toothless grin that says she has always understood, always known, that motherhood is not about what I've lost. In fact, it's not about me at all. Love crashes around me; it washes away my fragments of self-doubt.

Giving the swing a crank, I see Sophie's fists begin to pound out her happiness. Danny comes up behind me and touches my shoulder, letting me know that he will take over now. I hug him again, grateful for this gift he has given me.

She really is a beautiful little girl. For once, perhaps I really have done something right.

Amey S Tippett is the author of Alison's Journey and Spilled Ink. She currently resides in New Albany, Ohio with her cats, Gryphon and Sabine. To learn more, visit www.ameytippett.com.

THE BOY WITH THE GOLDEN HANDS

By Sharon Maas

(Nat returns to his native village after many years of fun and freedom in London.)

Rain fell in one solid sheet. Madras was under water, and Nat and Henry had to wade through knee-high, black, stinking water to get to their bus. They had bought umbrellas and raincoats and plastic sheets; they had wrapped their luggage in plastic. Traffic was reduced to a trickle; it had seemed a miracle even to find a rickshaw.

They hauled themselves into the 122 bus. It was already full, but the Indians on the back seat pressed themselves together to make room for them and they squeezed in. Soon after that the bus rolled off.

"This is bad. Really bad," said Henry. His brow was wrinkled, anxiety written into every line. "The village will be under water. Those poor people!"

Nat rubbed the mole on the back of his neck. He was thinking less of the poor people, more of his own poor self; because, obviously, if the village was under water, there might be some difficulties escaping into Town to find a bus to Bangalore. And by the look of things he'd want to leave as soon as possible because obviously his father's house was no holiday resort in this weather. He fleetingly thought of defecting here and now, while he still had a chance: excusing himself, jumping down into the black water, getting the boy to retrieve his suitcase from the bus's roof, taking a rickshaw or a taxi to the airport and the next plane to buzzing Bangalore.

However, he stayed put. Maybe it was an innate laziness, a disinclination to plunge back into the deluge after having found a temporary dry haven. Maybe it was cowardice; he didn't relish Henry's barely concealed disapproval. Irresolute, Henry would call him. Weak, wet and watery.

Perhaps, though, it was something else. Whatever it was; he stayed put.

That "something else" in Nat began to stir, like the tiniest seedling nudging itself through the earth, as the bus plunged through the countryside, through sheets of water falling from above and sheets of water rising from below, water as far as the eye could see. The bus lurched through an endless lake, for no road was visible, no roadside; only water.

By some sixth sense their driver wove his way though abandoned water-logged ruins of buildings, homes, shops, businesses, by some miracle keeping to the invisible road, by some miracle keeping his ark afloat.

Where are the people? Nat cried, and inside him he felt a constriction, tightness in his chest—he could hardly breathe.

Where are the people? Where are they?

He closed his eyes so as not to see and not to know, but his heart knew and sent tears out from beneath his eyelids, and he opened his eyes and he saw people.

A small family, beneath a tree, doing nothing, waiting. A woman with a baby in her arms, a man, two small children, knee-deep in water, under their tree. The man held a piece of cardboard over the woman's head. The rain fell on the tree and its leaves bounced in an almost merry rhythm, while the family just stood there in the wetness, waiting.

Nat knew what this deluge meant for the people of his village, and of all the villages around. Not only were their huts built on ground level; they had no floors, and no furniture. People slept not on beds, but on the bare earth, simply spreading one thin cloth to lie on and covering themselves with another. They cooked on the ground, using dried cow-dung or twigs as fuel. They had no sanitation: They went out in the fields to relieve themselves. They could not afford raincoats or umbrellas; they had only one change of clothing, which when washed was laid on the ground or over a bush to dry.

What happens, he asked himself, when all their clothes are wet, and there's no sun to dry them? When there is no dry cow-dung or twigs to cook with; when the earth on which they sleep and cook is no longer earth, but a sheet of water? When the dried mud with which their homes are built grows soggy and starts to dissolve, and their thatched roofs first leak and then cave in, and the rain won't stop? And the water keeps rising?

Six hours of water. Collapsed mud huts, collapsed roofs, a world collapsed and abandoned. Nat was speechless.

* * *

Long before dawn Nat was awake again, wide awake. A word, a name, had called to him through sleep.

Gauri Ma.

Where was Gauri Ma?

"Dad?" he whispered. The Doctor lay next to him, fast asleep, and no answer came. He felt for his torch, under the balled up lungi that served as a pillow, looked at his watch. Twenty past three.

He had to go. He couldn't sleep again anyway, and he'd be back by five. If Gauri Ma was safe, then no harm done. If she wasn't . . . he'd cross that bridge later.

He listened. The stillness outside seemed to speak to him. It seemed to tell him something important, something that he'd missed in his concern for Gauri Ma, and suddenly he knew, what it was: it was simply too still. The drumming of the rain on the rooftop had stopped, as had the splatter of rain on the floods outside. The rain had stopped! A good omen.

He got up and stepped gingerly between the sleeping men, following the ray of light his torch cut through the blackness, and left the schoolhouse. Outside all was dark. He made his way towards the gate and out into the village road, led only by the narrow ray of light and his own instinct. The night sky was still hung with clouds; no moon, no stars, nothing to be seen; no buildings, trees or bushes, no rock or temple, and not even the crouching shadow of the Holy Hill in the background. Nothing to tell where he was going; he could not even tell if he was still on the road or heading straight into the depths of the Ganesh tank. The whole world was a shining black lake, and all he could see of it was the circle of ripples moving forward around his feet, and all that he could hear was their gentle splashing as he made his way forward.

It was as if the water had swallowed up all sound. Not a frog croaked, not a cricket chirped. Silence surrounded him. It was a walk into nothingness.

It seemed as if an eternity had passed, and the world had become minutely lighter. He now could make out the shapes of houses he recognized, and the Durga Temple, and he knew he was right on course. Around him he saw the grey shadows of collapsed huts; their roofs, once neatly woven from coconut branches, broken through the spine as if a by a giant's blow.

Gauri Ma's hut must be about a hundred meters further on. He walked on. In the distance he heard a new sound, growing louder as he walked.

It was a gentle whimpering, like the whining of a puppy. Probably it was a puppy, left behind by a family that had flown in haste. Any other time, he'd have rescued it; perhaps he'd come back for it later. Right now there was only Gauri Ma.

As he approached the place where her hut had stood the whimpering grew louder; for indeed, there was no hut. What had been her home was nothing but a pile of mud, covered by the remains of the roof. Realization came to him; how stupid to have come this far, and in the night. She must have fled, while there was still time; the Doctor would have helped her, surely. Of course she was safe. Wherever everyone else had gone, there she must be, too.

The puppy's whimpering was louder now; very loud, in fact. It seemed to come from the branches of a mango tree; heaven only knew how it had managed to climb up there. Since Gauri Ma did not need saving he might as well save the dog. He shone his torch up into the branches of the tree, from whence the whining came; and to comfort the puppy he spoke in the voice reserved for young things.

The answer came immediately; not whining, but a torrent of words, Tamil words, words tumbling over each other, rapid and sometimes screeching; and Nat searched the branches with his light and saw her—Gauri Ma.

She was up in the tree, a stick-figure of a Gauri Ma, wrapped in a ragged old sari tied not only around her body but the branch against which she leaned, and it was she who whimpered and cried, and whose words rattled down to him so quickly he could hardly make out a single one.

"Gauri Ma!" Nat cried, and stepped towards the tree; but his foot slipped against a lump of something, something big and slimy; perhaps a fallen log, except that it was too soft for a log; and he shone his torch down to it, and it was a body, a swollen black body.

Appalled, Nat cried out and stepped back. Gauri Ma babbled louder; and at last the Tamil words began to make sense and Nat understood her litany of woe. It was her husband, Biku the leper, who had bound her to the tree as the waters began to rise; they feared she would fall off the branch in sleep. He had tried to tie himself, too, but couldn't; he had slipped and fallen from the tree, and could not hold himself as his hands were only stumps; and maybe he hit his head on the way down as he never again stood up; she had called but he had not answered. Three days she'd been in the tree. Biku had hung a pot of iddlies on a branch and she had lived from that, and water; but there were no more iddlies and she was hungry and ill; and Biku was dead, and she was dying too. She had called for help, but nobody had come.

"But now I have come, Ma!" said Nat. "It's me, your Tamby, your little boy! Remember me? Or have you forgotten? I came to get you, Ma, and now you're safe. You're not dying, Ma; I'm here."

So he spoke to her as he climbed the tree, and sat beside her; and she stopped her prattling and listened, and put the stumps of her hands on his cheeks, crying silently. He bit into the sari that held her to the trunk, and ripped it, and she was free. Then he laid her across his shoulder—she was as small and thin as a 12-year-old boy—and climbed back down and into the water.

He carried her home through the flood, to the village where dawn was breaking and people were emerging from their huts and rubbing their eyes, and pointing to the patch of blue in the sky where the clouds had drawn back; and when they saw Nat coming with Gauri Ma in his arms they cried out in amazement, and, pointing and calling each other, they ran to greet him, cheering; for it seemed that Nat had stopped the rain and brought back the sunshine, and luck.

Nat, they remembered now, was the Boy with the Golden Hands.

(Excerpted and adapted from Of Marriageable Age, HarperCollins, 1999.)

Sharon Maas is from Guyana, South America. She presently lives in England and is the author of three novels. www.sharonmaas.com

WADDLING FREE

By Cynthia Balog

Ugly . . .

Cucumber slices don't reduce puffiness, that's for sure. Even though the mirror's veiled in post-shower steam, I can see enough luggage under my eyes for a trip to Japan. As I'm waddling down the stairs in my bathrobe, I make a mental note to thank Oprah for that truly wonderful bit of advice, and to save the rest of the veggies in the fridge for dinner.

Guy is sitting at the kitchen table, nose buried in Computer User magazine. Not that he can tell RAM from a raisin, but he's always trying to "better himself," so that for once he won't have to come home smelling like whatever was being delivered to the Save-All that day. He looks up only when I set my waffles down beside him, but he seems more interested in my breakfast than anything else.

"You got any more of those?"

"In the freezer. Want me to make you some?"

"Nah, forget it." He inspects me like I'm an unlabelled bottle of pills found in the back of his medicine cabinet. "Whoa, Laney, is that normal for you to be gaining in your hips?"

I sit down at the table to shield him from the view. "Uh, well, I guess."

Or maybe not.

Ugly . . . Fat . . .

Of course, the three waffles on my plate suddenly become of even more interest to Guy. The second he gets that twinkle in his eye, I know what he's going to say. "Sure you should be having three of those?"

Up until a minute ago, I was. "Want one?"

He reaches over, stabs one with his fork, and releases it on a coffee-stained napkin beside his trusty magazine.

"Must have been a lot of deliveries last night," I say casually.

"I told you. I was with Charlene."

I have a bit of waffle in my mouth, and suddenly, swallowing seems impossible. I spit it into my napkin and say, "Oh."

Finally, he loses interest in my breakfast, and I get some real eye contact. It's the kind of look that would give penguins the chills. "Laney, how many times do I have to explain this? We're not together."

I'm aware of the drip of the kitchen faucet, the whirring of our neighbor's leaf-blower, the ticking of the cat-shaped clock with the roaming eyes. If only those sounds could drown out Guy's babbling. I've heard the lecture so many times, I begin to lip-sync it as he speaks. When he pauses, I say, "I know, but . . ."

"But nothing. I told you when you moved in. You're welcome to live here, but . . ." He buries his nose into the magazine again and sighs. "It just didn't work out, Laney."

I'm not exactly sure what "It didn't work out" means. Because whenever I ask for an explanation, I get a description of the current love of his life, Charlene Dumont. Torture. I bite my tongue and think of Charlene, who happens to have the lofty position of chicken cleaner at the Save-All. I've never met her, but from what I've heard from Guy, mutilating poultry isn't her only talent. Guy never fails to let me know how I can't compete. The telephone book in the hallway is constantly open to the Florists page, taunting me, and when he buys her a gift, he always has to parade it in front of me. He says he just wants my opinion, but it doesn't take a genius to figure out what he's really doing.

"You didn't give it a chance," I say into my chest, staring at my belly, which has swelled almost to the point where I can't stand to look at it anymore.

Ugly. . . Fat . . . Pregnant . . .

He winces. "You know that's not true. I gave it every chance. I want what's best for that baby, but you and I . . . together, as a couple . . . it's explosive. You know that. You have to know that."

A few fireworks, here and there. That's a good thing, according to Sally Jessy Raphael. As I'm about to point this out, he holds up a finger.

"Don't even mention fireworks, Laney. For the last time, I don't care what you've learned from your damn talk shows. You want to have this baby, even though you have no family, no job, no money, no place to live. I've told you how crazy I think you are, but I can't make you do anything. I will help you take care of it. That's more than a lot of guys would do. Got it?"

He's giving me that look, brows arched, pupils like pinpoints, mouth a thin, perfectly straight line. People would say he's handsome, almost too movie-star perfect to be found lugging crates in the back of a Save-All. I'd have to agree; after all, all my time in summer school was earned because I'd spent a little too much time drooling over the "unreachable" Guy McCormick instead of study-ing. I had enough romantic fantasies of him to last several lifetimes, so when we finally did get together, I thought it would be forever.

Ugly . . . Fat . . . Pregnant . . . Stupid . . .

"You look sick. Have you been outside lately?"

"Not for a while."

"That can't be good for the baby."

I shrug. I don't know, since I missed the last doctor's appointment. Maybe the one before it, too. For some reason, Montel's offerings always seemed much more exciting. If Guy was so interested in the baby's welfare, he could have taken me to the doctor's office. Something tells me that his idea of "being there" for the baby isn't going to win him "Father of the Year."

His idea of a real relationship, too, is pretty distorted. He made the mistake of telling me the one thing he really loved about Charlene. He said that one night, after they'd finished making love, she whispered in his ear, "Honey, do you ever think about how many other couples on Earth were making love at the same time we were?" He said that she always has thoughts like that. Really deep thoughts. As if he expects me to make dinner conversation like, "Do you ever think about how many people on Earth were eating corn on the cob at the same time we were?" Please.

There's a screeching from outside, almost like fingernails trailing across a blackboard. A garbage truck. I'm counting back to the last day I checked the calendar when Guy speaks my thoughts. "It's Garbage Day, isn't it?"

Tuesday. It's Tuesday. Great. Garbage Day.

Before I can pull my stomach out from under the kitchen table, he says, "You forgot again?"

As fast as I can, though I'm not about to break any records, I wrestle together the top of Hefty bag that's overflowing with remnants of last night's lasagna. Struggling with the twist-tie, I drag it outside, down the steps, which are covered with the leaves and morning dew of autumn. My slippers have no traction, but I manage to waddle fast enough, and wave my arms furiously enough, to catch the eye of one scruffy, white-haired trash collector.

He takes the bag from me and winks. "What's a sweet thing like you doing alone on this fine morning?"

I smile at him, wondering which supermodel might be standing nearby. He jogs off, leaving me standing in a halo of sunlight, cast down past the bare branches of the trees. Instead of hurrying back into the house, afraid of which neighbors might behold the pregnant, homely neighbor in the ratty bathrobe, I gather the courage to scan up and down the street. It's empty. Once the truck pulls around the corner, this perfect silence cushions my ears, and the sunlight embraces me. For a moment, I don't even think of Sally, or Montel, or Oprah, and I don't even care what topic they'll be discussing today. For once, there is nobody else. All that exists is this stillness, this perfect stillness . . . strangely frightening and thrilling, all at once.

Ugly . . . Fat . . . Pregnant . . . Stupid . . . Alone?

Alone. I say the word aloud, savoring the taste of it.

Alone. But no longer lonely.

The screen door creaks open, and Guy's voice shatters the silence. "Hey, what's up? You forget your way back?"

I don't bother to answer because I'm caught up in some really deep thoughts. Like where, in Guy's disaster of a basement, I might be able to find my suitcase.

Cynthia Balog has been writing fiction for most of her life and is currently seeking publication for several novels. She lives in Bucks County, Pennsylvania with her husband, Brian, and dog, Rosco.

MISS LILIA

By Sharon Cullars

"So, your Mama explain to you why I asked you over?"

Miss Lilia's slight rasp was courtesy of a three-pack-a-day habit she had held on to for years, or so Stevie had been told.

"Naw, she just said there's something you wanted to tell me."

Dim, sad brown eyes peered at Stevie, their depths shadows of the ghosts of Miss Lilia's life, ghosts that Stevie had heard about in snatches of gossip and dinnertime murmurings. Rheumatic, back bent from years of handling other folks' washing, Miss Lilia seemed a woman broken by a life that had never truly begun and now was almost finished.

Stevie shifted uncomfortably in the rattan chair in the neat little living room in the neat little bungalow. Jesus stared down from one wall while Martin Luther King peered from another, their eyes fixated on the two women.

A broken rattan scratched one of Stevie's bare thighs that were barely covered by her khaki shorts. The old woman sat across from her on a couch covered with a blue afghan dotted with white lilies. Lilia, lilies. Lilies in ceramic vases on either side tables, lilies on the blue wallpaper. Stevie reached for the sweating glass of iced tea the woman had brought from the kitchen earlier.

"Is it sweet enough?"

Stevie nodded. As a matter of fact, the cool liquid was sweeter than she was used to. But it was good on this hot, thirsty Auburn, Alabama morning. Despite the refreshing drink and the cooling breeze from the ceiling fan above, Stevie wished the woman would just hurry up. She wanted to meet up with Gwen at Wal-Mart. She needed to get a couple of skirts.

"Well, it's like this. I been knowing you since you were born, watched you grow up to be the lovely young lady you are now. And I am just so proud that you're going off to Spelman."

Stevie gave the woman an obligatory smile. Most of the neighbors had given her the same fawning congratulations. Most had never dreamed of going past high school; some hadn't even made it past grade school because they had to go to work early in their lives to help out family. And many of their grandchildren wouldn't see inside an academic hall either, because they hadn't thought past getting a job in the local post office or joining the army. Or hanging on the corner, doing only God knows what.

"Thanks, Miss Lilia," she said dutifully. Stevie expected her neighbor to say her peace and let her go. But then the woman reached inside her housecoat pocket and pulled out an envelope.

"I've saved up some money. It's not much, just a little something. Never really spent much on myself. This house was all I needed. Never saw any sense in taking vacations either. Too expensive. Besides, there weren't really no reason to go away. No family to visit. Just me, you know. So, I thought I'd give you a little something to take away with you when you head off to Atlanta."

Stevie's smile was genuine now as she took the envelope. Even a little something was better than nothing. Still, it was sweet of her elderly neighbor to think of her. Especially since Stevie had decided a long time ago that she didn't like Miss Lilia. The woman was always working, hardly speaking, and never taking time to do much else except attend church. And even then, she often sat in the back, removed from the congregation. Which inspired tales.

"Thank you so much, Miss Lilia. I can sure use the money."

"I know. I spoke with your ma and she told me you were taking a job to get you some books. Sugar, I don't want you to have to just make do. I've been making do all my life and let me tell you, it ain't nothing to crow about. So, I thought this little bit might help."

Stevie opened the bulging envelope and pulled out a greeting card with a young woman in a graduation cap on the cover. The words "You're on Your Way Now" ran across the top.

"Didn't get a chance to make it to your graduation."

Stevie hadn't known that the woman was invited. "That's all right."

She opened the card and a number of bills fell out. Actually, quite a few bills. Stevie bent over expecting to see ones, maybe tens. Instead, there were several fifties and more than a few hundreds. When she had the bills all gathered in her hand, she counted them up. There was exactly $2,500. Stevie swallowed in surprise.

"I believe that'll be enough to get you some books, don't you think?"

Stevie nodded silently before she remembered her manners. "Oh, Miss Lilia, I don't know what to say."

"I think 'thank you' might do."

"Thank you. Thank you so much." And even as she thanked her, Stevie felt a pang of guilt. All she had thought about in the last 20 minutes was getting out of here and all Miss Lilia wanted to do was give her money, money she had earned washing people's clothes. A thankless job that had left her bent over, almost crippled. Stevie stood up and crossed the distance. She hugged Miss Lilia; the woman smelled of peppermint and eucalyptus. Stevie remained over her benefactor. Saw through the wrinkles that Miss Lilia had been beautiful once. The elderly woman blinked back tears.

"I might have had a granddaughter like you had my baby lived long enough to get married. But Janice died when she was only 17. Meningitis got her just after graduation. She would've gone to Spelman that fall, you see. She was so bright, had so many big dreams. My baby didn't get a chance to live any of them."

Stevie hadn't known Miss Lilia had had a daughter. The whispers and rumors had said something about a man, but never anything about a child.

"At first, I was so bitter, I did some things I ain't proud of. But the anger died a natural death, and I figured I could do for someone else's child, help them along. So each summer I give a little something to the young folk going away to school. It's just a little something from my savings. But hopefully, it'll make do."

"Miss Lilia, this will definitely make do. Thank you so much again." Stevie thought about Gwen waiting at the mall, thought how many things she could buy now with this money. Instead, she walked back to the old rattan chair and sat down. "Tell me about her, Miss Lilia. About Janice. I want to know." Stevie wanted to know about those ghosts in Miss Lilia's life. About the ghost behind those dim, sad eyes.

Miss Lilia smiled. "Well, she was something like you, always with a smile . . ."

And for the rest of the afternoon, Stevie listened to one of the more important lessons she would learn that year.

Sharon Cullars lives in Chicago, where she works as a research analyst for a professional association. She has written several short stories, one of which will be featured in Masques V, *an anthology of horror literature (2006) edited by J. N. Williamson. Her novel,* Again, *a paranormal romance, will be in stores May, 2006. In addition to writing, she hosts the Short Stories section of Bella Online, a comprehensive site for women.*

THE OLD MAN OF FUNDY

By Adam Heskett

Perhaps it was will alone that saved Cairn Bishop's life. Perhaps it was his fear of never seeing Clare, his fiancée, that gave him the strength to leech onto that dead tree on the side of the rocky cliff as wave after wave tried to pry him off. That's his story. Perhaps it was his buoyant red hiking pack that kept him afloat and alive as the Bay of Fundy's relentless tides tossed him against New Brunswick's southern shore. That was what the news would like us to believe. But I was there. I know what really happened. Though I can't dismiss what kind of dark horror passed through his mind that long grey afternoon, I can relate what I saw.

Cairn and I go way back. From elementary school chums sharing gummy worms to, ahem, mature twenty-somethings on his last weekend of bachelorhood. He didn't want a party or a stripper. All Cairn wanted was one last hike down Dobson Trail before he and Clare traveled overseas helping bring technology to developing countries. He didn't know when he'd be back here. So we hiked.

We plotted our route along the Dobson from Riverview to the Fundy coast through Fundy National Park, home of the world's highest tides, and into Alma, or as we had marked on our map, 'Destination: Sticky Buns.' The bakery in Alma sold the best warm cinnamon sticky buns anywhere in Atlantic Canada. Sold and wrapped in a brown paper bag, it became our cinnamon and sugary Grail.

We exited the woods near a majestic rural cliff west of Fundy Park. One of many that provided an excellent view of the bay and Nova Scotia on its far side. Yet, on this unfortunate day, most of it was veiled in fog and mist.

Cairn sulked.

"Maybe you could postpone leaving," I said, "Or bring Clare along sometime."

"She'd never make it," he said, "Her idea of roughing it is forgetting her Visa at home. Plus there's no time before the wedding and even less afterwards."

I stared out into the grey fog that hung about a kilometer off the coast. Maybe I'd come back myself and take a picture for him.

"Hey," Cairn said pointing down the cliff. A large glinting object sat upon the rocky shore below. Foamy brown waves crashed. "I'm going down."

"Cairn, the tide . . ."

"I can be down and back before you know it."

"At least leave your pack."

"Need something to carry it up."

In a fall of crumbling sandstone, he was gone. And, as he predicted, before I knew it he was there.

Cairn didn't say a word at first. Then, "It looks like a giant emerald." The emerald was Clare's birthstone. It would've made a perfect wedding gift. Cairn knelt beside it as the water licked its edge.

"He shouldn'ta touch that," a rustic voice said behind me, "That be the Devil's Stone."

My heart jumped into my throat.

A ragged, skinny old man stood before me. A pewter cross earring hung from one ear. A gap-toothed smile.

Now, the connection of the Devil to the Bay of Fundy is mythic. Fundy National Park is even home of a short hiking loop called The Devil's Half Acre where it was rumored that Satan left his mark upon its shattered coastal crevices. Until now that was only speculation. There was no proof. There is even a story about an emerald that loosed from Lucifer's crown as he was banished from heaven.

"I'd fetch yer friend before . . ."

A scream.

". . . it be too late." The ragged man puckered.

The tide slammed Cairn to the cliff wall and retreated. Another wave flung him back against the stone. The tides of Fundy have been known to take lives in this manner. The brown silt water too violent for him to scream again. The emerald lost below the waves.

"Y'ev been warned," said the man and walked away.

"Let him free," I shouted.

"Even if I could, why should I?"

Cairn tossed in the rising froth, his red pack his only life preserver. The ragged man harrumphed, rubbed his cross earring, and disappeared into the woods.

I let him go. I wasn't about to leave my friend. I crouched at the precipice. Cairn struggled to stay afloat above the raging surf. Somehow he managed to seize on to a small pine tree growing out of the side of the cliff.

"Hold on," I said. "I'm coming down."

I threw off my pack and lowered myself over. My left foot slipped. I dug my fingers into the loose pebbled soil at the top.

"Y'fool."

Thin arms pulled me back up. The ragged man stooped beside me holding a length of rope and a wooden plank tied like a swing at one end.

"I can't pull him up alone," he said.

We winched the rope around a sturdy tree and lowered the plank to Cairn. The wood clanked at the mercy of the swell. Cairn lunged for it and missed. He was again free-floating in thunder.

"I'm going down," the man said.

"Why you?"

The man flexed a withered muscle, "Wait for my tug." And he scaled over the edge.

I waited. A minute, an hour, an eternity. Time had no reference as I held a rope while my friend died below. Trust placed in a strange hermit I had no reason to trust.

The tug.

I pulled the weight until my lungs burned. My hands bled. Cairn's red pack catapulted to the top. His head and arms followed. Another pull. We both collapsed to the ground head to head.

"Where's the old man?"

"What man?" Cairn said after a moment.

We rested there that day. Cairn shivered and dozed through most of it. More than once I walked up to the edge looking for a sign of the ragged man. The sun broke through late afternoon. Cairn paled. We had to make it to Alma.

"C'mon, Cairn, time for some warm sticky buns."

I bore Cairn's weight on my side as we trudged along the coast. Clare may have been his motivation. Those scrumptious buns were mine.

We got to Fundy National Park a couple hours later. A park ranger picked us up and couriered us to the Alma Medical Clinic. An ambulance drove us back to Moncton to treat Cairn's hypothermia.

Cairn never went back for the emerald. I didn't blame him.

"It disappeared with the first wave."

I got Cairn a brown paper bag of sticky buns as a going away present when he left for overseas. That was a few days ago.

I don't know what happened to that ragged man. Guardian angels come in all forms. Perhaps he was guarding foolish mortals from the Devil's Stone. Or maybe he was just a figment. Perhaps he fell into the bay. Maybe he was a ghost. There are numerous such ghost stories of lost hikers haunting in the back woods of New Brunswick. Perhaps in times of great peril the mind creates what it needs to survive. For Cairn it was Clare. For me it was this man. I don't know.

All I know is what I saw and, as I hold in the palm of my hand the tarnished pewter cross earring that I discovered in my pocket later that day, that is the truth.

Adam Heskett is a part-time writer, part-time dreamer living in Halifax, Nova Scotia. He has published a couple short stories and poems, an online column, and is working on his first novel.

WHO WANTS A HERO?

By Jenny Schwartz

"Merde!" cried the Wicked Witch on seeing Rapunzel's white and gold Mohawk, a gilt-edged security against princes and other heroes. "After all I've done. Towers aren't cheap, you know. And keeping your hair tidy and growing all these years nearly drove me up the wall."

"Mother," protested Rap.

"Look at you! What self-respecting, handsome prince would rescue you now?"

The Mohawk was only the beginning. Rap was dressed in combat boots and army fatigues in green and fawn and black paw print, a khaki T-shirt and a gray, unraveling sweater to camouflage her curves.

Rap stuck her pretty nose in the air. "I'm a modern girl, Mother. I don't need a handsome prince or a Mr. Right. I can look after myself."

"Hmph," said the Wicked Witch. "So prove it."

The tower disappeared and Rap found herself lying in a comfortable bed in a cozy cottage.

"Who is sleeping in my bed?" growled a voice from the doorway. An unshaven, sleep-rumpled, drop-dead gorgeous man glared across the room.

"Your bed?" Rap scrambled out.

"Yes, my bed. I bought the cottage from the three bears and had the locks changed and the windows secured. So how did you get in here, Goldilocks?"

"It was my mother." Rap smelled coffee brewing and edged in the direction of the heavenly scent. "I'm Rapunzel—minus the long hair, obviously. I had to cut it. Mom wasn't listening. She expected me to stay in the tower forever, waiting for a hero. As if rescuing people is any basis for a mature relationship. I read . . ."

"Hold it," growled Rap's audience. He smothered a yawn. "Who's your mom?"

"The Wicked Witch of the Wild Woods."

"The Wicked Witch!" The man gaped mid-yawn.

Rap put her hands on her hips and leaned forward. "You got a problem with that?"

The stranger, very large and masculine, was close now, blocking the doorway and her access to coffee.

"My mother's a strong woman with strong powers. She lives life on her terms; that's why they call her wicked."

"And you want to be just like her?"

Rap blinked. She had never thought of her bid for independence that way, but "Yes."

"Well, far be it from me to get in the middle of a mother-daughter spat. Would breakfast compromise your independence?"

Rap considered this for a moment. "Not if there's coffee."

"I'm George Knight, an engineer. I moved to the Wild Woods to build a bridge over the Troubled Chasm." Rap's host poured the coffee.

"Wow. That's a huge job." So George wasn't just a handsome face, and he had a real job—no empty hero nonsense in his life. Rap smiled.

"Yeah. The job's not made any easier by the dragon that keeps eating our construction materials. None of the guards will stay because they keep getting their butts burnt."

Rap swallowed coffee and laughter, and hiccoughed.

"I thought I'd fix the problem this morning," George continued. "Do you want to come with me and see the Troubled Chasm?"

"Sure."

The Troubled Chasm was deep and terrifying. White water crashed over jagged rocks, the spray lighting rainbows in the sunlight. The thunder of the cataracts woke echoes as if storm clouds had found a voice.

"Uh-oh." Rap sat down abruptly on the grass, her knees voting for cowardice.

The deeper roar wasn't white water, but the challenge of an immense silver dragon.

"Stay back from the edge, Rap." George strolled toward the dragon, a sword held loosely in his right hand. Where had that come from?

A stream of fire flashed towards George. He murmured a word and the flames froze. The dragon blinked. George ducked and rolled under the fire. He emerged behind the dragon and plunged his sword into the dragon's tail, pinning the monster to the earth.

"Yoww!" The flames unfroze and scorched the earth. The dragon spun around. The sword held, and the dragon cursed.

George eyed the dragon coolly. "We need to talk. Why are you eating the steel girders?"

The dragon snorted, nostrils the size of size of dinner plates flaring red.

"How would you like people traipsing through your front yard, scurrying and gossiping?"

"I wouldn't," George admitted.

"Well, that's what you're doing to me. There'll be litter and noise, and the next thing you know there'll be tourists wanting to take my picture."

"I noticed your home was just below the chasm edge." George rubbed his bristly chin. "I'm afraid I can't move the bridge. This is the shortest span across the Troubled Chasm."

The dragon steamed, his long neck turning the incandescent orange of glowing coals.

"George," said Rap, tentatively.

The dragon's obsidian eyes narrowed. "George? As in George Knight, dragon slayer?"

"Oh!" Rap gasped. Her knees strengthened in outrage and she stalked forward. This was her mother's interference. Since Rap wouldn't wait for a hero, her mom had sent her to one. Well, Rap would show her! She'd show all of them.

"Shut up," yelled Rap. Man and dragon stared at her, their jaws dropping comically.

"No more fighting. No more steel girder indigestion. Compromise."

"And what do you suggest?" asked George.

"I assume you really are a construction engineer as well as a hero?"

George nodded.

"Then the solution is easy. You build the dragon a new home further along the Chasm, out of reach of the bridge traffic."

"I don't want a new home," rumbled the dragon. "I like fine the one I've got."

"George can make the new one exactly like the old, or you can suggest improvements. Maybe a wider landing ledge, a small cavern for cold storage, a strong treasure house door."

The dragon looked thoughtful. "You know a lot about dragons."

"All part of my damsel in distress education. I also know healing, diplomacy . . ."

George snorted.

Rap ignored him. ". . . etiquette, cosmetics, and seven languages."

"A sound education," the dragon said, nodding his approval. "And you're a smart girl. Pity about your looks." He gave Rap's Mohawk and punk costume a disapproving sniff.

A dimple quivered in George's lean cheek as he bit back a smile. Rap's pique at the draconian criticism suggested the punk look wasn't her.

"Okay," George addressed the dragon. "Think about what you want in your new home and we'll discuss it tomorrow. We'll need to scout for a suitable site."

The dragon unfurled huge, leather wings. "No time like the present."

George yanked his sword out of the ground and the dragon flipped out into the immense space of the Chasm.

The Chasm edge echoed with silence after the dragon's departure. George cleared his throat.

"You interfered to give advice, now I'm going to return the favor. Why do you think your mom wants to marry you off to a hero?"

Rap shrugged. "Storybook ending." She had been so busy resisting her mother's pressure, she had never questioned its cause.

"Uh huh. Because she loves you. In every life there is danger and heartache. Heroes, by definition, are people who can cope with that. Your mum wants a hero for you because she loves you and wants to protect you."

Rap avoided George's intense, blue gaze. She studied the ground, kicking at an inoffensive clump of grass. A spider scurried away.

"Okay," sighed George. "I've had my say. Do you have enough money to get home, or wherever it is you're going?"

Rap wiped away a tear. "I don't really need rescuing, do I?"

"No," George wrapped his arms around Rap and tucked her close. Rap wiped a second tear away against the linen of George's shirt.

"Everyone needs rescuing sometime. You rescued the dragon and me from a pointless, dangerous fight. I'm no more a hero than you are, Rap. Hero is just a label for caring enough about someone or something to be brave." George cleared his throat. "Have you ever thought of starting your own business?"

Surprise stopped Rap's slow leak of tears. "No," she faltered, looking up at George. "What could I do?"

"Well, according to you, you had a first class, damsel in distress education. Why not set yourself up as a healer? I'd like to think we'll build the bridge without accidents, but the reality is people will be hurt. And the town's growing. There's a genuine need for a healer."

"Hmm," Rap smoothed George's linen shirt, feeling the hardness of muscle and the steady beat of his heart. "It's a good idea, but I'd need somewhere to stay."

George cleared his throat. "You could stay with me."

"Oh, George," Rap said with a smile. "You're my hero."

He kissed her soundly.

And far away, in the Wild Woods Tower, the Wicked Witch punched the air and shouted, "Yes!"

Jenny Schwartz is an Australian writer. She prefers dogs to cats, beaches to snow fields, and humor to wallowing in gloom.

THE LIGHT

By Christine Norris

Sarah called out, like she had a hundred times before. Her voice was hoarse, her throat on fire. No one answered. And why would they? She and Jeffrey had been alone when they went into the cave. No one knew where they had gone, only that the couple had gone to National Park for a week of spelunking and rock climbing. They were alone. She was alone. Jeffrey lay back there, at the other end of the cave-in, his body broken and bloody. He'd been breathing when she left his side to find help, but she didn't know how much longer he had left. Crawling in the dark toward what she hoped was the cave entrance, she had lost all track of time. Her watch was useless, the face cracked and dark. Lifetime guarantee, my ass, she thought.

Sarah took a shallow, ragged breath, then coughed out a mouthful of dust. Looking up, she focused her mind as she pushed her way past the enormous rock that had fallen in on her and Jeffrey. It was an immobile wall; the only way she could move forward was to find pockets of space between them and squeeze her body into those crevices one at a time. She hadn't had time to panic, not yet, but now it started to creep in around the edges of her consciousness. The air was running out, Jeffrey was slowly dying, and they were completely alone. She concentrated on her task, trying bravely to keep the fear at bay.

Up ahead, there was a light. Just a tiny pinprick, but to her it looked like the blazing beacon of salvation. Sarah's arms trembled; her nails were cracked, her lip bled from where she had cut it on a sharp rock. Sweat and dirt ran from beneath her helmet and into her eyes. She silently cursed the rope that had helped them to rappel down here; it had broken when the cave collapsed. She pushed herself up as hard as she could, and made it a mere few inches. The light seemed to move shrink and move further away.

Sarah reached for the next space, and rock came away in her hand. Oh, crap. A shower of dirt and pebbles fell on her head and bounced off her helmet in time with her racing heartbeat. She held her breath as the seconds stretched out. The whole pile of rock could shift at any moment, she knew, and crush her.

No more rock moved, and she exhaled carefully. Then her fear broke through, and tears coursed down her face. How can I possibly get out of here? Jeffrey and I are going to die, here in the rubble and the dirt and the dark. At least Jeffrey's unconscious. He doesn't realize what's happening. Her shoulders sagged against the rock, and her tears became sobs that wrenched her whole body. Maybe it would be better if it did crush me. I can't do this. I might as well die right here. It's hopeless.

"There is always hope."

She lifted her head. Where had that voice come from? It was as clear as if the speaker stood next to her. It sounded familiar. She called out, "Help me!"

"Sarah."

Now it came from above her. The pinpoint of light flared to sudden brilliance, and Sarah shielded her eyes. Peering between her fingers, she saw her mother's smiling face, the light catching the red-gold highlights in her hair, the smoothness of her skin. She was so beautiful.

"Keep going, Sarah. Don't stop. You can do anything you put your mind to, no matter how hard it seems to be."

Sarah's pounded on the rock next to her. Some things are too big to overcome. You couldn't overcome the cancer. And I can't get out of here. Crying silent tears, she thought, Death comes to us all.

"No. Not today, my darling. You are tougher than this! You fight. Fight for you and for Jeffrey. This you can beat. Now, go!"

Her mother's face pulled away, rippled like water in a pond, and was gone. The light was itself again—small and so very far away. The voice of her past pushed the fear aside, and the love Sarah and her mother shared washed over her. She wiped her tears with the back of her hand, squared her shoulders, then reached out and pulled herself upward once more. Sarah fought for every inch, but her arms no longer shook; her heartbeat was steady and strong.

"You can do it, I know you can."

Her mother's voice was now in her head. Sarah ignored her screaming arms and legs, scratches, bruises, the blood crusted on her lip. The only thing that mattered was the light. She must get to the light. She would get to the light.

It was so close now, only a little farther to go. It brightened again, but not as much as before. It swung to the right, then the left, like the beam of a . . .

Flashlight! Sarah pulled her voice from the bottom of her soul and yelled, "Help! Please help us!"

The light pulled back, and was again replaced by a face, but this one was of a man Sarah didn't know.

"God! Someone's down there. Hold on, help's coming!"

This voice was not in her head. He disappeared, and Sarah heard him talking to someone. "That's a 10-4. I have someone trapped in the cave in the Northeast quadrant. Send me a chopper, and medics, ASAP."

Sarah cried again as a hand came through the rock and reached out for hers. This time they were tears of joy.

Christine Norris is a lifelong resident of South Jersey. Her first novel, a middle grade fantasy titled Talisman of Zandria, is due out in November 2005 from LBF books.

BREAKING THE ICE

By C. Montgomery Stuart

My best friend Darin had guts galore, at least from the perspective of us 9-year-olds who hung around with him back then. I, on the other hand, had none. I think Darin got my share when they were handing them out. There was a comedian back in the twentieth century who once said that when something scares us, we humans have a tendency to turn and run away, but our heads can't help looking back at whatever it was that spooked us. Well, I never looked back, but my pal Darin never ran away.

My father said that made him careless, an accident waiting to happen, but I didn't agree. Darin was my hero. Why? For one, he was the only kid I knew who ever dared ride his skateboard while hanging onto the back bumper of our school bus. Mind you, he only tried it once. I thought old man Miller was going to bust a blood vessel when Darin fell off going over the railroad tracks and started yelping. Good thing old Bert always kept his window open in case one of us was late and had to yell for him to hold up, or he might not have known Darin wasn't in his seat until he stopped at his house to let him off.

For as long as my young mind could remember, it had never been cold enough around our place for the rivers and lakes to freeze, even in the middle of winter. Which is why I forgot all about school that morning when Darin's folks dropped him off at the end of our lane where we always waited for the bus. As soon as their car disappeared over the hump in the road, he told me the pond out behind their place had turned hard overnight.

"Hurry up, Chet!"

"I'm coming," I panted. Darin could outrun me without even trying, and today he was. The frost-coated grass under my feet crunched as I clomped along after him in my over-sized boots. Mom said I'd grow into them, but that didn't help me much right now. The trail we'd cut over the years with our boots and bikes weaved through the copse of trees between our places and I lost sight of him by the second turn. When I came out the other side next to their pond two minutes later, he was already a good ten or 15 feet out onto the ice.

"Welcome to Canada!" he shouted. "Let's play hockey."

"Canada's a billion miles away," I said when I'd caught my breath. Darin slid around the ice, pretending to skate, getting further from shore with each skidding step. "Are you sure you should be doing that? What if it melts?"

"It takes time to melt, you yellow-bellied sapsucker!" he shouted, now nearly thirty feet away, and jumped up in the air.

The crack the ice made when he went through could probably be heard all the way back at our place, but there was nobody to hear. My folks had gone into town a few minutes before Darin had been dropped off.

I could clearly see the look of surprise in his eyes as he went under.

I stood at the shore, as frozen as the ice between me and the hole Darin had left behind. He popped up after a few seconds and began to flail about. Every slap of his arms only made the hole bigger. His shouts were even louder than the crack.

"Hang on!" I managed to yell. I turned and started for Darin's house, but stopped when I realized their car was gone. His folks had gone to work. We were supposed to be in school. Nobody would be looking for us out here. Not yet, anyway. Not in time, that was for sure.

When I turned back to the pond, Darin had gone under again. His mitts were waving just above the water, then his head came up again. The sound he made chilled me far more than the cold air blowing across the pond. I had never heard Darin cry before. I knew he was beginning to panic. So was I. I still couldn't move, until I remembered something Dad told me when he was arguing with me about Darin.

'Not being afraid isn't brave, son, it's foolish. If you're scared and find the strength to stand up to it, that's brave.'

Stand up to it! I told myself. I took a deep breath, but it didn't help. My heart was still pounding as I looked around Darin's yard. I spotted a rake leaning against the side of their house and made myself move. As I sprinted for it, Darin's sobs stopped and I knew he'd gone under again. I didn't look back. But this time, I wouldn't keep running.

I grabbed the rake and ran back the way I'd come. Sure enough, Darin was under water again. All I could see was one mitt holding on to the jagged edge of the ice. I reached the edge of the pond and laid flat on my belly like I'd seen in those safety movies they showed at school. I always thought it was dumb showing us how to crawl across thin ice when we never got any, but now I knew it wasn't dumb at all. I pushed the rake ahead of me and squirmed like those army guys crawling under barbed wire in the war movies Dad likes to watch. I was more than three-quarters of the way out to the hole before the tines of the rake got anywhere near Darin's hand. I kept pushing until it touched his mitt . . . he must have felt it because he grabbed for it and snagged it on the first try.

My initial jubilation faded when I tried to pull him up. My feet kept slipping on the ice. It took me a few long seconds to move backwards enough to get Darin's head up. He coughed and spit up water. His face was nearly blue and he didn't seem to be able to open his eyes.

"Hang on, Darin," I shouted at the top of my lungs, even though he was only a few feet away. I don't know why, maybe I thought his ears were frozen. "I got you! Don't let go!"

He didn't say anything, but he hung on to that rake for all he was worth. I knew I had to get him out of there, now. His lips were a sickening shade of purple, and they were vibrating in time with the chattering of his teeth. I pulled myself forward along the rake until I was able to reach his hand. That's when the ice started to crack beneath me. I think I peed my pants right then, but I was so cold, I couldn't be sure. I started to cry, I couldn't help it. I hooked my fingers around his wrist and pulled with everything I had in me . . . and he came up out of the water as far as his chest. The ice made popping sounds as I kept pulling at Darin until he was out up to his waist. The ice below us was starting to sink and water was coming towards me, first to my arms and then my chest . . .

That's when I felt a strong hand close around my ankle and a man's voice said, "Hold tight, boys. I've got you."

* * *

Every year on the anniversary of Darin's close escape, we get together and toast old man Miller's memory. He wasn't all that old at the time, just in his fifties, but to the eyes of the young boys we were back then, he seemed ancient. Burt Miller kept driving the school bus on our route for at least another five years, and our parents made sure we brought him a little something on every holiday and his birthday. After all, if it wasn't for him and his habit of driving his bus with the window cracked open, he never would have heard me bellowing at Darin. There's no way I would have been able to get Darin to the hospital by myself, even if I had been able to pull him all the way out of the pond. Old Burt always denied doing anything special.

'You're the one who kept him from goin' under for the last time, Chet. Darin would be dead if it weren't for the guts you showed that day.' Nothing anybody said before or since made me swell with pride in quite the same way.

When Burt Miller finally retired and then passed away a few years later, we knew the world had moved on. Nowadays, the whole area where our acreages were is a typical suburban subdivision like you'd find anywhere. Darin's old pond looks more like a big fountain now, surrounded by fancy bricks shaped to look like rocks. It sits right smack in the middle of the parking lot belonging to a two-level shopping center with more stores in it than our whole town had on Main Street when we were growing up. Yet every time I happen to drop by on a morning after one of those rare winter frosts has put a sheen on that water, I can't help getting out of the car to stand next to it and remember the day the ice broke and I finally found the strength to turn back.

C. Montgomery Stuart lives in the Rocky Mountains of western Canada with his wife and two Sabre-toothed Carpet Cougars, better known as their tabby cats Casey and Finnigan. He writes a weekly movie review column for his local newspapers and is currently putting the finishing touches on a science fiction novel and writing the sequel.

TORNADO LUCK

By Andrea Allison

Every summer since I was 12, Mom and Dad sent me to Grandma Jones's house out in the country. Things that I'd considered cool at 12 were boring at 17. We spent most afternoons sitting on the loveseat, making quilts. Not exactly my idea of fun. When I mentioned this to my parents during our weekly phone call, Mom said that it was important to spend time with Grandma. Privately, I thought they sent me because no one else visited Grandma anymore. Uncle Tom said he had better things to do. Mom and Dad were always working. And no one talked to Uncle John for reasons that I didn't know. That left me.

"Christina, honey, hand me those squares, please," Grandma said, pointing at the pile of fabric.

"Here you go, Grandma." I handed a few to her, then selected one for myself and began stitching it onto the quilt.

"I want to tell you something that my grandmother told me when I was about your age."

"What?" I stared at her as she shuffled through the fabric, her wrinkled hands shaking vigorously. "There's not some kind of disease that runs in our family, is there?"

"Oh no, nothing like that." She paused to take a sip of her iced tea. "Sometimes life puts obstacles in our lives. At first they seem unimportant, but they can become disastrous. These obstacles occur when you least expect them. My grandmother called it Tornado Luck."

"Tornado Luck?" I repeated, wondering if she was starting to lose it. "Is this a joke?"

"It's no joke. It has afflicted everyone in this family, and it will happen to you, too." Grandma stopped sewing and looked deep into my eyes. "This is a very serious matter, Christina. You won't know when, or where, but it will happen to you. You can do everything right, but it will still happen. I know—I'm making it sound like it's a terrible thing. But it doesn't have to be."

How could I not know anything about this? "It sounds like some kind of plague!"

"I'm sorry if I'm scaring you. Just because something terrible occurs doesn't mean a good thing can't develop out of it." She slid closer to me. "Listen, I just need you to understand this so you will be prepared when the time comes."

"I understand, Grandma." The words left my lips without any confidence. I didn't really understand, but it seemed very important to her that I did.

Grandma smiled. "I think we should take a break. How about some milk and cookies?"

After our snack, we put the final touches on the quilt, sharing unsettling glances while sewing the last few stitches. Neither of us said a word. Tornado Luck wasn't brought up again.

Later that night, I began packing my suitcases. I'm sooo happy to be leaving this place. If I never see another quilt again, I'll die a happy girl. A warm breeze rushed past me from the open window. I staggered over the piles of clothes on the floor to close it, but instead I found myself admiring the nighttime sky's beauty. A few flashes of lightning momentarily brightened the darkness and with it came a feeling deep inside that something was wrong.

The sound of dishes breaking interrupted my thoughts. I scrambled out of the room toward the source of the commotion. In the kitchen, I got my first bitter taste of Tornado Luck.

I called 9-1-1, then Mom and Dad. They met me at the hospital, and talked to the doctors while I sat in the waiting room, staring at the walls. Mom came in a few minutes later and told me the news about Grandma. I felt so guilty. I didn't know why, but I did.

Mom notified friends and family that the funeral would be Friday. That is, she contacted everyone except Uncle John. She made Dad call him.

A lot of people showed up that rainy Friday. Most of them I didn't know. After the funeral, some people came to Grandma's house to eat and talk. I sat on the loveseat next to my Great Uncle Sam; at least, I thought that's who he was. He talked endlessly about Grandma from when they were kids. I smiled and nodded a lot, not really paying attention. After noticing my mom and uncles going into the kitchen, I excused myself to get something to eat. I actually meant to do a little eavesdropping. With Mom and Uncle John in the same room, nothing good was going to happen.

"Mama left everything to the three of us," I heard Mom say. "We're supposed to split it evenly between us. Who said you get to dictate over what we can or can't have, John?"

"I'm the oldest. It's pretty obvious I would be in charge."

"So what? We aren't children anymore," Uncle Tom said. "I say we make a list of the stuff we want and meet back here on Sunday."

Mom said, "And what if we all want the same thing? Or what about the things none of us want? This house has to be cleaned out by next week so the Realtors can put it on the market."

"We'll put our names in a hat," Uncle Tom said, "and the stuff we don't want, we can sell or donate. Satisfied?"

"Sounds fair to me. What about you, John?" The conversation fell silent, with only the sound of rain in the background.

Uncle John finally said, "Okay. Sure. Under one condition. I'm in charge of Mama's finances."

"Are you crazy?!" Mom spluttered.

Uncle Tom said, "Caroline—"

"You know I'm right, Tom," Mom said, cutting him off. "When we were growing up, all John ever did was steal money from Mama. And for what? To pay off gambling debts, alcohol, and cigarettes. Now that she's dead, he's still trying to do it." I could hear the years of anger and resentment in her voice. She stopped talking, maybe to turn to Uncle John, because she said, "David was named executor of her will. You will get your share of the estate. After that, I never want to see you again."

I couldn't take the arguing anymore . . . I had to get out of there. I dashed out the front door onto the porch. Rain pounded steadily on the house, and thunder echoed in the sky. I peered up at the angry sky—and what I saw made me shiver.

I bellowed, "Mom! Dad! Get out here—quick!"

My folks rushed outside to see what the emergency was. When Dad saw the active clouds swirling in a circular motion, he grabbed me and Mom, then raced us to the storm cellar, yelling, "Tornado's coming!" The rest of the family followed close behind. We crammed into the underground cement room, shutting the steel door behind us. Dad nearly tripped over an old lantern as we made room for everyone. Then he pulled a box of matches from his pocket and struck one, using it to light the lantern. Soon, the rain halted, and everything grew calm.

A slight rumble like a distant train filled the silence. The sound seemed to roll forward, approaching rapidly. The shelves vibrated, and I squeezed between my parents as we huddled in the back corner.

The sound swelled, becoming deafening. The shelves continued to jolt, canned food and other supplies dancing on them. I cringed against my parents when I saw how wildly the door shuddered. I prayed it wouldn't fly off its hinges.

As the rumbling subsided, everyone relaxed, except for me. With my arms still clenched tightly around Mom, I shivered uncontrollably. She held me and gently ran her fingers through my hair as she repeated, "It's all right."

Ten minutes later, we came out of hiding. I blinked as we exited the storm cellar, trying to get my eyes to adjust to the light shining down. Everyone stayed pretty close to one another as they examined the damage in disbelief.

The house was gone. The one thing left untouched was the foundation. Shattered glass covered the unrecognizable debris.

At least now no one would argue over Grandma's stuff. Just like her, it was no longer there.

Emergency vehicles soon arrived, and officers escorted us to the town shelter. Like us, other people were first showing up. Volunteers set up cots and arranged tables to hold donated food. Pain and heartache surrounded me; I just wanted to go home and forget about all of it.

"I know what Grandma meant now," I whispered, sitting next to Mom.

Her face stained with tears, she looked up from her coffee cup and asked me, "What's that?"

"The day she died, Grandma told me about Tornado Luck. I didn't really understand what she meant until now."

At first, she only stared into her coffee cup. Then she replied, "Your grandmother always meant well, but there were times she would over-exaggerate things . . . Tornado Luck being one of them."

After all the times Mom high-praised her, now Mom was telling me that Grandma was crazy. What is wrong with this family? "How would you know if she was off her rocker or not? When was the last time you visited Grandma?" I felt anger building up inside, and I let it get the best of me. I shouted, "You made me visit her every summer for years. You told me to get to know her, that she was this incredible person. Now you're saying she was crazy? Look around, Mom. Of all things, it was a tornado that did this. Maybe she wasn't as crazy as you think!"

"Young lady," Mom said, her voice grief-stricken, "don't you ever speak to me like that again. You're my child—but she was my mother."

We stayed for five hours—the longest five hours of my life. When the police finally let us leave, we all checked into a nearby hotel. That night, I didn't get any sleep. Why didn't Grandma tell me about Tornado Luck sooner? Was Tornado Luck the reason why our family was so screwed up? Why did Mom suddenly label Grandma as a crazy person? I had so many questions, and no one to answer them.

The next morning, we took cabs back to what remained of the house. The roads had been cleared, and servicemen were working vigorously to get the town back up and running. When we got to the site, the men began hauling debris to a single pile. The rest of us gathered what could be salvaged and separated them in boxes.

When my uncles removed a large piece of wood, I noticed an undamaged package. I picked it up and spotted my name written on it. I tore open the paper and found a quilt. Unfolding it, I saw it wasn't the one Grandma and I had made together. This one was white with a navy blue trim. Embroidered in the center was Home Is Where the Heart Is. My name was stitched beneath it.

It wasn't original, but I liked it.

We spent several weekends clearing out all the junk. A unanimous decision was made to use Grandma Jones's money to rebuild the house. It was the first thing Mom and her brothers had agreed on in years. The new house was used for special occasions. Family reunions were added to the list of family holidays. Uncle John was even invited after a few mediated conversations.

It turned out that Grandma had been right about Tornado Luck. I may have lost her, but I regained my family.

Andrea Allison grew up in a small town in Texas but is currently living in Tulsa, Oklahoma. She has been published at Runesmag.com and won several writing contests. You can view her website at http://andreaallison.bravehost.com.

WHERE THE SHREWSBURY MEETS
THE ATLANTIC

By Sara Spock

It's a sort of pilgrimage now, this threshold where the river meets the ocean. I was 12 then; they were 10 and 8, my brothers. We went fishing every Saturday, out in our little boat. It was little by ocean standards, at least. We weren't fishing in a little hole near our house or even in a pond a few miles' hike from the neighborhood. We were real fishermen on Saturdays when my father shared with us a trip to where the Shrewsbury meets the Atlantic.

He knew how to fish and how to teach boys how to fish. We learned fast and well. As good as we were, though, we were also little boys, humbled by the nature of the great Atlantic, by the nature of the Shrewsbury. This was no normal meeting of river and ocean. This was tumult, mayhem, tempest, commotion on its grandest scale. She would eat you alive, she would rend you from your bones, she would churn you to oblivion should you fall in. We respected her. We did not fall in.

With our boat, we brought our gear. Our tackle was strong and seaworthy, heavy grade for a heavy ocean, a heavy fish. Our gauge was thick, our poles sturdy; we were prepared for the storm, prepared for the ocean. There in the maelstrom we caught striped bass, a massive fish that came to feed where she churned up the food, where the Shrewsbury poured out. We grappled for fish heavier than ourselves, fought them, defeated them. My father helped—he was a giant, at least to us. He gave help only when we needed it the most, when we had fought to our end and had no more to give. He graced us with these trips, with the fishing, bonding over rails, over reels. There were no other young boys to be seen in these waters.

It was there that we saw him. The man was easily 60 years old, in a flannel shirt and cotton blue pants that old men wear. He wore a fishing hat, of course, with lures hanging from it; the hat was tan like the old man's face. He had a boat, smaller than our own, and on it he was alone in his loafers, his old man loafers. How would this old man fish? Not just fish, for he could do that very easily a little further up the river, but how could a feeble old man catch a bass bigger than us boys? You should have seen him, you should have seen his tackle. We actually laughed, my brothers, my father, and me. It was light, river fishing gear. He must not know, we reasoned, about the big fish that were caught here, about the unrelenting nature of Mother Ocean and the Shrewsbury. He drifted too far down the river and found himself here, we thought, amongst the real anglers, as if we three small boys were real fishermen.

And then he began to fish.

We did not laugh after that. We did not bow down to him, although we probably should have. He was worthy of at least that. He, with his deteriorating gear, fought the colossal striped bass. We watched him for the first time in awe. He cast his line, secured his reel and began to draw it in . . . a bite! He reeled, turned his wrist. The fish turned; he parried, he reeled. He was patient, he was strong; it went on like this for an hour. The man and the fish would do battle there, where the Shrewsbury met the Atlantic. In the end, the man would win; the fish would tire out and he would reel them in, slowly now, slow enough to keep the line from breaking. He was caught; it was over. The man reached down and grabbed the fish by the gills, never using a net or a gaff. We all used nets, but he was raw, he was Neptune, he stuck to line. Week after week, month after month, we came to the Shrewsbury, ostensibly to fish, but really to watch the man. How he could increase in greatness in our eyes was unknown. But then he did.

The fish were his as they always were. The fights were long, the fish weary. The morning was ending; it was his last catch. We'd watched him now for most of the summer, faithful followers studying his routine. This catch would end his morning, and with it, our fascination. The fish was at the side of the boat in less time than usual. Our hero was reaching down to grab the bass with his weathered hands and his glasses fell off, into the oblivion. Down they went, into the chaos, into the swirl and he was blind. This would be the fall, the dethronement of our hero, we were thinking. But his hands moved faster than our minds. The fish was set free, the pole placed firmly on the deck, his clothes, shoes stripped off in one solid blur of motion and he was in the water before my father could shout a warning. He dove fearlessly beneath the churning waves and I imagined he was a pirate with a knife between his teeth, diving deep for lost treasure. I imagined that he would not come back up. He did, gulped for air, and dove again, more determined than before, or so I thought from my vantage point 50 yards away. It seemed like eternity, there on the deck with my brothers and my father. It wasn't even long enough for anyone to react, Father would later say, not even long enough to dive in after him for an ocean rescue. I turned to my father and he looked like he was resigning himself to a jump as well, but what happened then cemented it.

He emerged, climbed aboard his little boat, dressed, wiped his lenses off, and cast again.

I cannot say that I am a man of God; I do not worship in a church. But every spring, when the rivers and lakes teem with fish, when I take my little boat out on the waters, whichever waters they may be, I am in a reverential state of mind. I recall the man, the larger than life man, battling the mighty waters that day, where the Shrewsbury meets the Atlantic. His name, I do not know. His ancestry, unfamiliar. His end, mysterious. But whoever, wherever, and however, I bow down to him now in tribute. He is my God.

Sara Spock is a freelance writer and poet, studying Comparative Literature and Archaeology at Penn State University. She is currently working on her first novel. Visit her site at www.saraspock.com.

MY BIG BROTHER BEN

By Robert Rohloff

On October 6, 1967, a procession on the street corner of Haight-Ashbury in San Francisco proclaimed The Death of the Hippies. I remember watching on TV the longhaired flower children in their tie-dye wear carrying the coffin down the street. I was looking for my older brother Ben, who had left for California six months earlier. Ben dropped out of high school when Principal Myers told him he had to get a crew cut or leave. My brother left, and he left home, too. Mother cried. Father got angry and told him to never come back. Me, I just stared out the window of our house with a tear running down my face as he walked down the road with his packsack on his back. Ben wrote a few times to Mother, telling her that he was doing fine. He was living in something they called a commune in San Francisco and working as a waiter in a teahouse. After a while, my brother stopped writing altogether.

In 1972, I graduated from high school with honors. I got a job in a lumber-yard where Father had worked for the last 25 years. Mother and I talked a lot about Ben, but we had to do it behind Father's back. Father said Ben was a no-good kid who had gone wrong, that he'd lost his way with God, and that he was no longer his son. I could never understand what Father meant by that.

In the year I spent in the lumberyard, I saved up as much money as I could—enough to buy an old 1962 white and lime green Volkswagen van— and on July 4th, Independence Day 1973, I packed my belongings into that old van and set out to San Francisco to find my brother.

When I arrived, there were no more hippies with flowers in their hair and beads around their necks. Sure, there were still a few around, but they were old and burned out, as if they'd taken one too many bad trips back in the heyday of the hippie movement. I had the return address from my brother's letters, so I headed over there with hope in my heart that he was still living there.

The house was old and run down. There were all kinds of junk piled up on the front porch from old bikes to beer cans. The screen on the front door had a big hole in it, and behind the hole on the inside door was a sign that read, "Watch Out for the Old Hippie, He Bites."

When I moved closer to the house, I could hear a song by the Grateful Dead playing inside. I knocked on the door, and waited several minutes for a re-sponse. The old man who finally opened the door was in his sixties with long white hair and a white beard. He gazed at me while I explained why I was there, and then he flashed me a yellow-toothed grin and asked me in.

The inside of the house was as much a junkyard as the porch. I seated myself in an old, gray leather chair that had been ripped in many places and was mended with duct tape. He said he remembered my brother, a good boy, never any problem, always willing to help someone in trouble. I asked him if he knew where he was. That's when I got the shock of my life.

Ben had been drafted into the Army and left for Vietnam in 1969. He was killed in action, and his body was never found. Ben told the authorities that he had no family and that the only one he considered family was the old man. That's who they contacted when Ben was killed in action.

In the ensuing days, it took all my strength to carry on. I had no will to live. The idea that I would see my brother again was the fuel that drove me for the last six years. I reached deep into my faith and asked God for help.

One week later, I left San Francisco with a heavy heart and a heavier burden upon my shoulders. I was going to have to go back home and tell Mother of my discovery. I was going to have to tell her that her firstborn was killed in some Godforsaken jungle somewhere over in Vietnam. Worst of all, I was going to have to tell her that they never found Ben's body.

Three of us sat in the living room of the big house back home where once there was a happy family of four. Mother and Father sat on the couch, holding hands. I told them about the old man and how he had said that Ben was a good, loving boy who would never hurt a fly, and that he knew that when Ben had met his maker that he was sure that he was welcomed into the kingdom of God with open arms.

I held Mother in my arms and we cried. Father left the room quickly and went into Ben's room. When I opened the door, Father was sitting on the bed with Ben's picture in his hands. He was sobbing, and looked up when I entered the room. "You know something, son? I never stopped loving him," he whispered.

Robert comes from a small town and a family of 11, and he draws a lot of his material from both. As a young man, he hitchhiked across Canada and most of the United States, and credits that experience to his knowledge of human nature. Robert is a collector of exotic daggers, and dream catchers. Visit his website at www.yonisha.com/rohloff.html.

REDHILL'S GHOSTS

By Robin Bridges

Beth dreamed about having a baby last night. She remembered looking at herself in the bathroom mirror and feeling her uterus contract. She tried to find the hospital where she worked, but ended up having the baby on the avocado green carpet in her old bedroom at Grandma's house. It was a girl who looked just liked Beth's baby pictures.

As she was getting ready for work that morning, she told Mark about her dream. "It comes from working too many 12-hour shifts in a row," he told her. "You work with babies all day. Of course you see them in your sleep."

"Maybe. I think I'll sleep at my place tonight. Okay?"

He came up behind her and massaged her shoulders. "Yeah, you do need some rest. Think you'll be too busy for lunch today?"

"Probably. But call anyway if you get a chance." She kissed him on the cheek before she left. She wanted her dream to mean something more.

The east wall of NICU glowed blue from the bilirubin light pointed at Baby Boy Edwards. Another cocaine baby who'd end up in a foster home. Beth took his vitals and had to blink when she turned away from the blue light to chart them.

"Beth? Phone call," Lisa yelled from across the unit.

"Hello?" She cradled the receiver on her shoulder while she opened a bottle of formula.

"Ms. Madison? Hi, this is Hazel, from Coast Realty? I looked at your grandmother's property yesterday. It's beautiful."

"Thank you. How much do you think I can get for it?"

"Well, it's beachfront, and buyers are crazy for waterfront property right now. But if you fixed it up, you know, repaint the outside, trim back that huge oak tree in the front, you could get a lot more."

"That sounds good. I'll be over there this weekend, packing up some of the last things, so I'll get back to you next week, okay?"

Beth hung up the phone and unplugged the monitors on her patient so she could feed him. His head was shaved where they had put an IV in his scalp vein. "Okay, Mister." She sat down with him in a rocking chair. "Breakfast time."

Lisa was wiping down an empty isolette with disinfectant. "We're planning on Chinese for lunch. Do you want to order with us or are you eating with Mark?"

"No, Chinese sounds good." The baby held her finger. His eyes followed her face as she rocked back and forth.

Before lunchtime, Beth called Mark in the Information Systems department. "My trip to Pass Christian may take longer than I planned. The Realtor suggested I fix the house up before she brings anyone to see it."

"Want me to come with you? The doctor said you weren't supposed to be doing any heavy lifting."

"No, I'll be fine." She heard a sigh on the other end.

"All right. Be careful."

* * *

The last time Beth visited her grandmother's home had been the Fourth of July. Once she crossed the Bay St. Louis bridge, she could see and hear the fireworks going off up and down the beach. Bottle rockets screeched across the sky overhead. The air smelled like sulfur, and Beth had been certain she was driving through hell with the windows down.

Today, the drive was more like a trip through purgatory. Fog was coming in rapidly on an October afternoon, pushed across the highway by a frantic wind. It slipped through the oak trees, like lost souls escaping a demon's claws.

Beth's gray Nissan pulled into the acorn-covered driveway at Redhill, her grandmother's home. The house sat empty since her grandmother's funeral three months earlier.

The oaks seemed to reach out for her as she walked up the drive, acorns crunching under her shoes. The largest oak in the front yard had gnarled branches that dragged in the dirt. Long ago, Beth climbed those branches and played hide-and-seek with her cat, Sunny. She had not gone near it since the hurricane more than 20 years ago. It made her nervous. She hurried past it and up the porch steps.

Beth shuddered as a gust of wind rustled the big oak. It shook its branches at her. "Momma." She sighed and leaned against the porch column. "You should be here instead of me."

The baby she miscarried had been an accident. She and Mark had only been dating for three months. But now she wanted a baby, and she was lying to Mark about taking the Pill.

The wind was kicking up. The old house settled, sounding like a person swallowing or gulping nervously. She would be free of Redhill soon. A young doctor and his wife were interested and were coming to look at it next week.

Beth stared at the harvest gold and brown wallpaper over the kitchen sink. The kitchen would look so much brighter painted white. With new white appliances to replace the brown ones. She imagined the doctor's wife replacing the wallpaper with ceramic tiles, and refinishing the pine floors. She'd probably weed the old flowerbed in the front and plant impatiens and roses. They would exorcise the house of all traces of Grandma and her family. Refilling the spaces with their own things, their own lives.

Beth did have some happy memories of Redhill, but they were all from before the hurricane when Momma died. Momma had given Beth the tortoise-shell cat that played with her in the hydrangeas. They spent summer evenings chasing toads out of Sunny's food bowl.

Momma would come out to the garden and scoop Beth up for dinner. Beth could smell Windsong cologne on her mother's neck. Inside, she smelled the corn muffins Momma was baking.

"Didn't I teach you how to make cornbread from scratch?" Grandma said, that night before the storm. Her arms were crossed as she leaned against the kitchen counter.

"Yes, but a mix is a lot faster," Momma said, licking the batter off her finger. "Besides, Beth likes the mix. It's sweeter than homemade."

Grandma sighed. "You'll have that child spoilt on sweet things, Emily." Then she clicked her tongue in disapproval. Momma had given Beth the spoon to lick.

Beth stared out the kitchen window at the overgrown hydrangeas. She wanted her children to grow up with those flowers, breathing the same beach air, hearing the same house sounds.

If the doctor and his wife could do it, so could she. She'd rid the house of all of Grandma's things and totally redecorate. She'd bring her furniture and her plants from New Orleans and she'd make Redhill her home again. She'd start in the kitchen, getting rid of Grandma's depressing golds and browns. No. She grabbed a steak knife out of the kitchen drawer. She'd start by getting rid of the avocado green carpet in the living room and hallway.

The smell of the carpet sickened her. It wasn't an identifiable smell, like cigarette smoke or pet odors, but an old, bitter smell. Beth used the knife to pry up a corner of the carpet. When she had enough to hold onto, she put the knife down and pulled hard. It came up easily in the hallway, but Beth had to tug when she got to the doorway of the living room.

It took her all afternoon. With a sense of accomplishment, she sat down on the pine floor and looked around the empty room. She could imagine a baby girl in a red walker smiling as bare toes pushed her across a polished floor. Beth realized why Grandma had covered up the floors with the ugly carpet. The floorboards were warped and covered with large water stains. Beth remembered when the carpet was installed after Momma's funeral. And then she remembered how she'd let the cat out of the house the night the hurricane hit Pass Christian.

Beth ran around the back of the house, where the leaves and branches were breaking off the magnolia and flying across the yard. Oak branches tossed wildly, leaves hissing as the wind beat against them. The plastic cat dish rolled across the backyard. "Sunny!" she shouted into the wind. She ran after the dish and caught it, clinging to it tightly. The rain started to pour down and Beth, with hair and clothes soaked, ran around to the front yard where her mother was.

Momma was soaked too, but was trying to shield Beth from the rain. She set her on the porch, saying, "Stay right here. I'll be right back." She tucked a strand of wet hair behind Beth's ear and kissed her forehead. "He's probably on the beach looking for dead fish." Momma ran across the highway down to the beach.

Grandma came out onto the porch, shouting after Momma, but the wind blew her voice back in her face. Beth cried, as she hung on the porch railing and peered out at the waves. Grayish, yellow foam pounded on the beach, reaching closer and closer to the seawall. Neither Grandma nor Beth could see Momma through the rain. But Grandma could see the storm surge, a 20-foot wall of water pushing towards the shore. She screamed "Emily!" over and over, but at the last minute, she had to grab Beth and run inside.

Behind the boarded up windows and latched doors, they listened to the water swirl over the house, dragging tree limbs and other debris across the roof. Beth cried for her mother. Grandma held her, singing, "Hush Little Baby" and "What a Friend We Have in Jesus." Still wet, Beth sat shivering in her grandmother's lap all night long.

No, no, no, Beth thought. I don't want to remember this anymore. I don't want to think about it now. She stood up to shake the thoughts out of her head. But embedded in the ghost fibers of that memory was the image of her mother's body caught in the branches of the big oak. She'd tried to hang on to the tree, but it hadn't saved her.

God, girl. Why didn't you stay in New Orleans? Nothing will change here. On the bed in the guest room was a doll Grandma crocheted for Beth years ago. It was supposed to sit on top of a roll of toilet paper, like the ones Grandma crocheted for the St. Thomas bazaar every fall. Beth used to hide bubblegum under her doll's skirt. Its plastic head was coming unglued from the pink yarn dress. Why would she want to raise a child in such a sad place? Just because she and her mother had both grown up here didn't mean she had to impose the past on another daughter. But one's heritage was a duty, wasn't it, maybe even her birthright? The past wasn't all bad, and memories must be preserved. Not in photographs, but in blood. In tiny cells with Grandma's heartbeat and Momma's breaths.

Thunder rumbled, somewhere offshore. An October cold front coming down, meeting the fog. Beth walked back to the kitchen and stared out the window. The old memories were suffocating her. There wasn't space in this house for her anymore. There wasn't room for a baby to grow.

Suddenly, a tree limb scraped up against the kitchen window. Beth jumped, and then got mad at herself for being scared. Her heart still thumping, she ran outside to her car as the first drops of rain fell. The Realtor had told her to trim the tree. She popped the trunk and got out the chainsaw. It was heavy. She dragged it over to the oak and looked up. The tree was hundreds of years old, and protected by local tree ordinances. She would be fined thousands of dollars.

She walked around the tree, carefully noting where the house and her car were, and started the chainsaw.

Robin Bridges lives in Gulfport, Mississippi with her husband, two children, and two mastiffs named Grendel and Monster.

THE FINAL BLESSING

By Carol Hightshoe

After the Gods created Man, they gave him Woman to be his friend and companion as he journeyed through life. To woman they gave a chest containing blessings for her descendants. Woman was told never to open the chest, lest these precious gifts escape. Curiosity finally led Woman to open the chest and the divine blessings were lost—all but one.

Elpis shook his silver mane as the darkness surrounded him. How long had it been since he was last called? As the firstborn of those who guarded the final blessing of the gods, he was summoned only when there seemed to be nothing left but defeat and despair. There were other guardians in the mortal realms; they were the ones who should be answering the normal calls. He stepped onto the ancient path and felt the ground pull at his hooves and the air grow heavy with the despair calling to him. When the darkness cleared, he found himself standing on a beach. He tossed his head and a golden glow from his horn surrounded him, pushing back the chill that hung like the touch of death. The stench of rotting bodies mixed with the salt spray of the ocean, creating a palpable fog. Red-tinged water swirled around his hooves as he carefully followed the call that brought him here.

He stepped around a large outcropping of rocks and saw a man sleeping next to a small fire. He stepped closer and lay down beside the man. The ornateness of the man's armor and sword, which lay under his right hand, indicated he was a person of some importance in this place and time. Elpis studied the rugged face for a moment, noting the streaks where tears had flowed during the man's dreams.

He bowed his head, and gently, as not to wake him, touched the man's forehead with his horn. With practiced ease he entered the man's thoughts and began drawing the despair from his soul.

* * *

Odysseus shook his head as he surveyed the battle area. Bodies of both Greek and Trojan warriors lay together on the blood-stained sand. In death, their differences appeared to vanish. He wondered how many would meet as companions in the Elysium Fields of the afterlife.

The leader of the Greek armies turned toward the ocean to hide the tears he felt burning a path down his face. He refused to leave the area until the last Greek soldier's body was collected and prepared for the funeral rites tonight. So many lives, he thought. And, for what? Is one woman worth such a high price? It was a question he had heard many asking each other as well as in prayer to the Gods. The Gods, of course, refused to answer. After all, men were nothing more than playthings for the Gods' amusement.

He turned and glanced back at the high walls surrounding the city of Troy. Her defenders alert in their observation of the activity on the beach. Despite the temporary cease-fire to collect the bodies, it wouldn't take much to start another deadly rain of arrows from those walls. His men had found no way into the city and by now, most of them knew that was the only way they were going to defeat the Trojans and return Helen to her husband Menelaus. There had been discussion before this last battle of quitting the field and returning home. Something Odysseus had strongly opposed, but was now beginning to accept.

Odysseus felt something bump his back and he spun around, his hand going to his sword. There was nothing and no one there. He looked down at the ground and noticed a single print—small and delicate, but similar to a horse's hoof. He stared at the print for several minutes. Could the solution be something as simple as this? And it did seem so simple. After so long on the field, with so many dead it seemed unlikely, but there was something about that single print in the sand. He glanced back at the walls of the city and nodded. The Trojans claimed Poseidon as their patron and the horse was sacred to the Sea God. Perhaps there was a way to breach those walls after all.

* * *

Elpis woke suddenly. A shrill neigh pierced the stillness of his grove, then ended abruptly. He felt his heart tighten in a grip colder than the touch of Nyx herself. The area of the call was close to where he had visited before. But this time it wasn't the defeat of a single individual that was calling him, it was stronger; it was the despair of many. He stood and reared, neighing a challenge into the wind, calling for the one who guarded the gift for the city now buried in fear and defeat. It was a call that was not returned as it should have been.

The unicorn neighed again and stepped into the darkness that now hung before him. He found himself standing in a walled city, people running in different directions, fires dancing brightly. His nostrils burned from the smoke filling the city and his ears were deafened by the screams of the dying.

A man with a brightly polished sword stepped in front of him, not seeing him. Elpis snorted and took a startled step back. It was the same man he had visited before. The one whose sense of defeat had called him to this area. To whom he had brought the gift. Elpis felt his knees buckle and he dropped to the ground. Slowly, he bowed his head and touched the blood-stained ground with his horn in silent benediction to the unicorn who had once been the guardian of this now-lost city. The most precious of the Gods' gifts, hope, had been abused and was now gone from this place.

* * *

Elpis fought against the despair that threatened to engulf him as the death scream of another unicorn echoed in his soul. The screams had been coming more frequently over the centuries and he had lost count of the number of times he had heard that shrill neigh. Each time he thought he was ready for the pain, but he never was. How can one be prepared for the pain involved with losing a part of one's self—a part of one's own soul?

This time was the worst. It felt as if the pain from all the previous deaths had been multiplied together. He tried to neigh his challenge, but fell to the ground, his legs too weak to support him. His vision blurred, and then all he could see were swirling lights. His breathing became labored and he gasped, trying to keep his lungs functioning. He felt his heart drumming erratically as if it was desperately trying to escape the confines of his chest.

He closed his eyes and forced himself to take long, deep breaths. He fought for a semblance of calm until the pain passed. He got slowly to his feet, his legs still shaking, his body trembling. Elpis shook himself and a spray of water fell from his body. He raised his head and neighed a weak challenge to the cloud of despair that hung over his grove. As the blackness thickened, Elpis once again stepped onto the ancient path.

The unicorn had to fight for every step he took on the path. The ground protested loudly as he pulled each hoof free from its grasp. The weight of the air tried to force the air from his lungs and push him to the ground with each agonizing step.

Loud explosions in the distance accompanied a sudden call of despair deeper than the one that had brought him here originally.

* * *

Elpis paused and looked around; each time he was called to the mortal realms, it seemed to have changed in significant ways. Tall buildings reached up to grasp at the sky and the hard, black surface of the ground was covered in thick dust, twisted pieces of metal, broken buildings and shattered glass. Elpis stepped carefully through the debris. He briefly touched noses with one of the search dogs who was standing with his head hung and his eyes glazed as he stared at the area. As he walked away, Elpis heard a sharp bark from the dog. He turned to see the rescue team pull a young child from the rubble. He stopped and looked up at the thick black smoke from the explosion that had wrought this destruction and felt the despair that hung over this city. His knees buckled at the weight of it pressed down on him.

The unicorn fell to the debris-strewn ground, unable to move. He was only one: the last of the ancient guardians. In a world filled with sorrow, hatred, fear, and their related emotions, he was the only bringer of hope left.

A ghostly shape appeared before him. It was a woman carrying a black box with the symbols of the most ancient Gods carved on it. She smiled sadly, her eyes downcast, as she slowly opened the box. From its depths, small globes of darkness flew out and surrounded the fallen unicorn. Elpis tried to stand, but the darkness blanketed him, and trapped him in its cold embrace.

He looked up to see the woman close the box, then reach out to grasp his horn. "I give you that which I have protected since the beginning. I give you the last gift." At her touch, the blanket of darkness sank into his body. Elpis shuddered as he fought against the pain and coldness that invaded his heart and soul. As suddenly as the despair had touched him, it vanished.

Elpis felt warmth grow in his soul and begin to swell outward. A golden glow surrounded him and burst over the area. He reared up and neighed his challenge to the despair that hung over the city.

A soft whinny caught his attention, and he turned his head slowly to see a woman pick up and embrace the girl rescued from the rubble only moments before. At the woman's side was a unicorn.

Tears filled his eyes, and through their glittering curtain, Elpis began to see more shimmering shapes as they began to take on the forms of silver-maned, golden-horned unicorns. As the unicorns began to spread out through the area, Elpis watched as people began to search again with a new sense of purpose. People turned to strangers to offer words of comfort and encouragement or just simply a place to cry.

Elpis neighed again, his voice filled with joy, not challenge. His call was joined by a multitude of other neighs that echoed through the air. Gradually, other golden glows spread over the area and the despair began loosening its stranglehold on the city. This was one city that would not be lost. From this place, hope would again find its way into the hearts of man. The greatest gift of the Gods was reborn in the world.

Carol Hightshoe's first professionally published story "Midnight Song" appeared in the Creature Fantastic Anthology and was a tale of hope and lost love rejoined, a common theme in Carol's writing. She hopes this story will be able to bring a sense of hope to the victims of Katrina. Visit Carol's homepage at www.carolhightshoe.com. She can also be reached at petaQ@msn.com.